XENOS 2

DOOM FROM BEYOND

CONTENTS

PRODUCED BY GAMES WORKSHOP IN NOTTINGHAM

With thanks to the Mournival for their additional playtesting services

Games Workshop Ltd, Willow Rd, Lenton, Nottingham, NG7 2WS

games-workshop.com

INTRODUCTION

Welcome to the second volume of *Index: Xenos*. This book is one of five mighty tomes which together contain updated rules for every unit of miniatures in Warhammer 40,000. If you have an army of Orks, T'au, Tyranids or Genestealer Cultists, this volume contains all the information you need to field your models in the new edition of the Warhammer 40,000 game.

Within these pages are detailed rules entries, known as datasheets, for every Citadel Miniature within the Orks, T'au Empire, Tyranids and Genestealer Cults ranges. When taken together with the *Warhammer 40,000* rulebook, you will have everything you need to field the armies of these deadly xenos on the battlefield. The knowledge contained in this tome will enable you to further the ideals of the Greater Good, enact the predatory will of the Hive Mind or stomp your foe into the ground whilst bellowing 'Waaagh!' at the top of your lungs.

The xenos hordes that assail the Imperium are without number. Though disparate and localised, together they claw down the edifice of the Imperium piece by piece. These hosts of hostile species are united only by their desire to end Humanity's reign over the stars – whether by bloody conquest, assimilation at the barrel of a gun, creeping infection or total consumption driven by immortal, alien hunger. The Orks live to fight, and in their endless crusades of violence they have battered down the defences of the Imperium time and time again. The T'au are ostensibly a bright and optimistic race that wishes to help the galaxy thrive under one rule, but those who do not join their cause willingly soon find themselves humbled by the advanced war-tech of their warrior caste. The Genestealer Cults are even better at hiding their true intentions, for they skulk in the shadows, multiplying like a virus before taking over their prey worlds in meticulously planned mass uprisings. The Tyranids these cultists worship are the most alien of all, a race from beyond the stars that exists only to devour every shred of biomass in the galaxy. The doom of Man is close at hand…

INSIDE YOU WILL FIND:

- **Army Lists:** The first four sections of this book present all of the datasheets that you will need in order to use your Orks, T'au, Tyranids and Genestealer Cults miniatures in games of Warhammer 40,000, along with the additional rules and psychic disciplines that make each of these factions unique.

- **Battle-forged Armies:** A guide on how to organise your miniatures into an army for matched play games, including photocopiable Army Roster sheets.

- **Appendix:** This section contains all of the profiles and rules for the wargear carried by the units covered in this book, as well as all of the points values you will need to use your army in matched play games.

DATASHEETS

1. Battlefield Role

This is typically used when making a Battle-forged army.

2. Power Rating

The higher this is, the more powerful the unit! You can determine the Power Level of your entire army by adding up the Power Ratings of all the units in your army.

3. Unit Name

Models move and fight in units, which can have one or more models. Here you'll find the name of the unit.

4. Profiles

These contain the following characteristics that tell you how mighty the models in the unit are:

Move (M): This is the speed at which a model moves across the battlefield.

Weapon Skill (WS): This tells you a model's skill at hand-to-hand fighting. If a model has a Weapon Skill of '-' it is unable to fight in melee and cannot make close combat attacks at all.

Ballistic Skill (BS): This shows how accurate a model is when shooting with ranged weapons. If a model has a Ballistic Skill of '-' it has no proficiency with ranged weapons and cannot make shooting attacks at all.

Strength (S): This indicates how strong a model is and how likely it is to inflict damage in hand-to-hand combat.

Toughness (T): This reflects the model's resilience against physical harm.

Wounds (W): Wounds show how much damage a model can sustain before it succumbs to its injuries.

Attacks (A): This tells you how many times a model can strike blows in hand-to-hand combat.

Leadership (Ld): This reveals how courageous, determined or self-controlled a model is.

Save (Sv): This indicates the protection a model's armour gives.

WARBOSS

NAME	M	WS	BS	S	T	W	A	Ld	Sv
Warboss	5"	2+	5+	6	5	6	4	8	4+

A Warboss is a single model armed with a kustom shoota, a big choppa and stikkbombs.

WEAPON	RANGE	TYPE	S	AP	D	ABILITIES
Kustom shoota	18"	Assault 4	4	0	1	-
Attack squig	Melee	Melee	4	-1	1	Each time a model with an attack squig fights, it can make 2 additional attacks with this weapon.
Big choppa	Melee	Melee	+2	-1	2	-
Stikkbomb	6"	Grenade D6	3	0	1	-

WARGEAR OPTIONS
- This model may replace its kustom shoota with one item from the *Shooty Weapons* or *Choppy Weapons* lists.
- This model may replace its big choppa with one item from the *Choppy Weapons* list.
- This model may take an attack squig.

ABILITIES
'Ere We Go, Mob Rule (pg 10)

Waaagh!: Friendly **ORK INFANTRY** units within 6" of this model at the start of the Charge phase can charge even if they Advanced this turn.

Breakin' Heads: If a <CLAN> unit fails a Morale test within 3" of a friendly <CLAN> **WARBOSS**, they can restore order with a brutal display of violence. If they do, the unit suffers D3 mortal wounds but the Morale test is then considered to have been passed.

FACTION KEYWORDS ORK, <CLAN>

KEYWORDS CHARACTER, INFANTRY, WARBOSS

---

5. Unit Composition & Wargear

This tells you what models are in the unit and covers the basic weapons and equipment the models are armed with.

6. Weapons

The weapons that a unit comes equipped with are described using a set of characteristics as follows:

Range: How far the weapon can shoot. Weapons with a range of 'Melee' can only be used in hand-to-hand combat. All other weapons are referred to as ranged weapons.

Type: These are all explained under the Shooting and Fight phases of the core rules.

Strength (S): How likely the weapon is to inflict damage. If a weapon's Strength lists 'User', it is equal to the wielder's current Strength. If a weapon lists a modifier such as '+1' or 'x2', you should modify the user's current Strength characteristic as shown to determine the weapon's Strength. For example, if a weapon's Strength was 'x2', and the user had a Strength characteristic of 6, that weapon has Strength 12.

Armour Penetration (AP): How good it is at getting through armour.

Damage (D): The amount of damage inflicted by a successful hit.

7. Wargear Options

Some units have a number of choices as to which gear they take into battle – this section describes these options. Weapons which a unit may take as an optional choice are typically described in the appendix.

8. Abilities

Many units have exciting special abilities that are not covered by the core rules; these will be described here.

9. Keywords

All datasheets have a list of keywords, sometimes separated into Faction keywords and other keywords. The former can be used as a guide to help decide which models to include in your army, but otherwise both sets of keywords are functionally the same. Sometimes a rule will say that it applies to models that have a specific keyword. For example, a rule might say that it applies to 'all **ORKS** models'. This means it would only apply to models that have the Orks keyword on their datasheet.

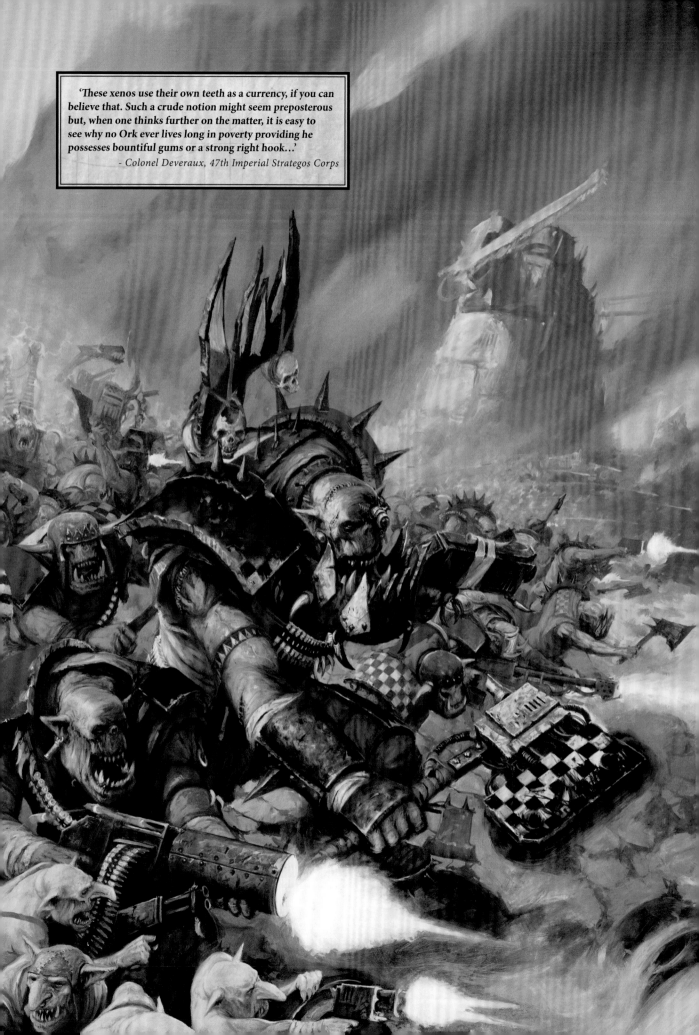

'These xenos use their own teeth as a currency, if you can believe that. Such a crude notion might seem preposterous but, when one thinks further on the matter, it is easy to see why no Ork ever lives long in poverty providing he possesses bountiful gums or a strong right hook…'

- Colonel Deveraux, 47th Imperial Strategos Corps

ORKS

The Orks are the most belligerent and resourceful race in the galaxy. Rampaging across the void in their billions, the greenskins devastate everything in their path with their ramshackle weapons and war machines, taking brutish glee in wanton destruction and revelling in warfare for its own sake.

Orks live to fight. No matter the odds, no matter the foe, they hurl themselves into battle with shootas roaring and choppas swinging. Their ramshackle war engines rumble across the battlefield, filling the air with hails of shells and corkscrewing rockets, while artillery pieces of insane and illogical design crush enemy tanks like ration-tins, or snatch aircraft from above with beams of crackling light. The Orks fill the skies with waves of thundering attack craft that rain explosives and firebombs, while at the very heart of the battle the Orks' monstrous leaders tear their enemies limb from limb. To face the Orks in battle is to stand against a tidal wave of barbarous ferocity that is as unstoppable as it is terrifying.

Though they appear crude – possibly even stupid – to the more advanced races of the galaxy, the greenskins are nonetheless a deadly threat thanks to their unremitting savagery and phenomenal resilience. In large numbers – and Orks rarely attack in anything but – they are all but fearless. Massed into charging mobs, the greenskins' momentum carries them through even the fiercest firestorms and into the heart of the enemy's ranks. If Orks give any thought to their own mortality it is in only the vaguest terms, and so they take risks and attempt gambits that other races would consider tantamount to suicide. This in itself makes the greenskins as unpredictable as they are dangerous, and has seen countless disciplined armies overrun by Orks who charged straight through supposedly untraversable minefields, surged from the toxic depths of chem-swamps to attack an undefended flank, or crash-landed their spacecraft straight into the middle of their foes with no thought whatsoever for casualties.

The Orks infest the galaxy from end to end. Their society and ecology is so robust that it can survive almost anywhere, from carnivorous jungles and airless asteroids to volcanic hellscapes and radiation-drenched death worlds. No matter how inimical the conditions, Orks don't just survive, they prosper – in their own bloody-minded fashion. Though an Ork tribe might begin with just a few dozen of the creatures, their numbers increase exponentially, and soon enough the greenskins' strange ecosystem overwhelms local flora and fauna to provide them with ideal living conditions. No scientist or scholar of any galactic race has ever been able to adequately explain how Orks proliferate so swiftly, though theories abound from spores and cellular sub-division to the notion of great green deities vomiting their numberless progeny across the galaxy with wild abandon.

Their origins are far from the only mystery surrounding the Orks. Amongst their society exist specialists known collectively as Oddboyz, who appear to spontaneously develop the knowledge required to transform their tribes from barbarous rabble into conquering hordes. Mekboyz, for example, are able to gather whatever scrap metal and junk they can find to hand, fashioning it into spectacular weapons and war engines that – while neither safe nor reliable – are horrifically lethal. Painboyz, meanwhile, know precisely how the Ork anatomy functions, and will merrily root around inside the most hideously maimed warriors, sawing, stapling and riveting away until their unfortunate 'patient' is as good as new. Such skill and wisdom is entirely instinctive for Oddboyz – the Orks themselves neither know nor care where it comes from, simply attributing such inexplicable gifts to their thuggish gods, Gork and Mork.

The strangest aspect of the Orks is the phenomenon known as the Waaagh!. This word has several, equally important meanings within Ork 'kultur'. First off, it is the favoured war cry of greenskins the galaxy over, usually bellowed with spittle-spraying gusto while burying several feet of rusty metal in some unfortunate's skull. Beyond this, the Waaagh! is both the gestalt energy of the Orkoid race that their Weirdboyz channel and vomit into the foe, and the name for their immense armies of interstellar conquest. An Ork Waaagh! is part migration, part holy war, the Orks gathering in their millions and building titanic mobile effigies, before taking to their lumbering warships and setting off into space in search of battle.

THE GREAT WAAAGH!

The mightiest Ork Warlord in the galaxy is Ghazghkull Mag Uruk Thraka, the Beast of Armageddon and prophet of the Ork gods Gork and Mork. While it is the galaxy's great misfortune to play host to Ork Warlords beyond counting, Ghazghkull is quite possibly the biggest, meanest, most violent and – crucially – the most visionary of them all.

For many years, Ghazghkull obsessed over the stalwart Imperial world of Armageddon. This planet, with its towering hive cities, sweeping jungles and vast, dusty plains, was one of the Imperium's greatest industrial powerhouses before the onset of Waaagh! Ghazghkull. It became a never-ending cauldron of war and devastation, embroiled in carnage and destruction on an apocalyptic scale. This was Ghazghkull's doing, yet it was not grand enough for him. Since suffering a crippling head injury many years before, Ghazghkull had borne witness to agonising visions that he claimed were sent by Gork and Mork, and on Armageddon he endured his worst premonition yet. Spurred on by it, Ghazghkull left the planet and declared a Great Waaagh!. The Warlord vowed to trample a warpath so grand and spectacular across the galaxy that the Ork gods themselves would be able to tear their way into reality and join the carnage. In the name of this crusade, Ghazghkull has razed dozens of planets and subjugated hundreds of Ork tribes, forging an ever larger Waaagh!. Now he leads a horde that blackens the stars, a ramshackle armada so vast that it can blanket entire star systems in devastation with but a part of its unbelievable might. Still it is not enough, for Ghazghkull will not rest until he fights alongside the greenskin gods themselves.

COMPOSITION OF A WAAAGH!

When an Ork Waaagh! begins, worlds shake with its fury. Millions upon millions of Orks mass around their towering war effigies, bellowing in animal fury as they work themselves into a rabid battle-frenzy. The air hums with strange energies, and billowing clouds of smoke and dust rise like thunderheads. Enemies of the green tide quail in fear, and rightly so, for the power of the Waaagh! is a force of primal destruction without equal.

To the untrained eye, an Ork Waaagh! resembles an endless ocean of green muscle, rusted metal, and crudely coloured glyphs and banners. Ork military formations – such as they are – are sprawling and anarchic, bleeding into one another as the greenskins surge forward in massed mobs. Boyz, Battlewagon crews, colossal Stompas and begoggled Ork Flyboyz all race toward the enemy as fast as they can, jostling, trampling, barging and ramming with all the discipline of a stampede of rabid Grox. Yet amidst the mayhem there is order, crude and resilient military structures that the Orks comprehend on an instinctive level.

TRIBES AND CLANS

First and foremost, every greenskin from the biggest and most muscle-bound Ork to the scrawniest Grot slave, belongs to a tribe. This is the closest analogue that Imperial strategists have been able to draw to any kind of formal Ork 'regiment', though the composition and sizes of Ork tribes varies wildly.

Most tribes are led by a Warboss. Inevitably this will be the biggest, loudest, meanest greenskin of the lot, a scar-covered brute who has bullied and bludgeoned his way to the top of the heap. Ork Warbosses get the best loot, the best fights, and the biggest guns, choppas and suits of armour, while every other Ork in the tribe does what

they say without question. Orks do not see such tyranny as a bad thing; to them, it is simply the natural order of things. Occasionally a tribe may be led by a Big Mek or Painboss, an Oddboy who has gotten so big and powerful that either they have taken command of the tribe by force, or else been kicked out by their Warboss as a potential threat and so started up a tribe of their own.

Directly below the leader of the tribe are his Boss Nobz. Huge brutes second only to the Warboss in size and ferocity, these tusk-mawed killers keep the Boyz in line and brawl mercilessly to prove who's the best. If there is ever a challenge to the Warboss' leadership, it will likely come from amongst his Nobz as the largest and meanest amongst them takes a swing at claiming ultimate power. The Warboss' Oddboyz also exist within this social strata, making their unique skills available to their master in exchange for his favour (or at least not being beaten to a pulp).

The rest of the tribe is made up of Ork mobs. Many of these fight on foot, gathering in great numbers beneath the boss-pole of one Nob or another and following them howling into battle. Other Orks hurtle to war in smoke-belching Trukks, Buggies and Battlewagons, or sitting astride snarling Warbikes. Others still build huge and preposterous guns with which to shred their victims from

a distance, or else charge madly into the fight spewing fire from dubious-looking flamethrowers. Squadrons of hurtling aircraft, convoys of looted tanks, clanking, saw-fisted walkers and batteries of bizarre field artillery – all of these mobs and many more can be found within most Ork tribes to one degree or another.

Entirely separate to the crude strata of Ork tribes are the six clans. In some ways, the clans are closer to spiritual groupings, while in others they resemble distinct nationalities or philosophies within Ork society. Of course, the Orks themselves see things far more simply; every Ork belongs to a clan, which means he prefers certain colours, has particular likes and dislikes, and is one hundred percent certain that his clan is the best and most important of the lot.

Within a single tribe there may well be mobs of Orks from several different clans, all fighting together despite their sometimes violent rivalries. Such diversity actually benefits the Ork tribes immensely, for each clan's Orks tend toward certain violent proclivities and specialisms that complement each other upon the field of battle.

GROTS

Smaller and scrawnier than their Ork masters, Grots form the natural underclass of Ork society. In truth, Grots are substantially cleverer and more sneaky than Orks, and it is only this natural cunning that enables the luckless creatures to survive. Orks treat Grots as their slaves – when not herding them into battle to soak up enemy fire or clear minefields the hard way, Orks rely upon Grots to do all the menial tasks, from crewing field guns and carrying ammo to crawling into the mechanical guts of stalled war engines and smacking them with wrenches until they start working again. Constantly kicked, beaten, thrust into harm's way or just plain eaten by their larger cousins, the Grots endure countless indignities in their short and brutal lives. For all this, Grots accept their lot largely without question, venting their spite upon one another, the enemy, or whatever luckless captives the Orks take in battle.

The Goff Clan has as its symbol an angry bull's head on a field of black and white checks. It typically produces the biggest, meanest greenskins around. Goff Boyz wear black, white and red, and their hides are usually criss-crossed with the scars of countless brutal close combats. The Goffs consider massed infantry charges the only true way for Orks to fight, describing anything more strategic or technological as 'muckin' about'. Goff Boyz and Nobz have a prominent place in the battle-line of many Ork tribes, and can usually be found where the fighting is thickest, running headlong through hails of fire in order to tear the enemy limb from limb.

The Evil Sunz Clan embodies the Orks' obsessive love of speed. Clad in red and orange garb, often decorated with stylized flames, Evil Sunz Boyz typically pile aboard the fastest vehicles they can so as to hurtle into battle in the vanguard of the Waaagh!. This clan is especially famed for their throngs of Warbikes and their lunatic pilots, who hurtle to war with the leering sun glyph of their clan visible to all.

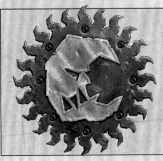

The Orks of the Bad Moons Clan are the richest of all their kind, for their teeth – the basis of all Ork currency – grow at twice the normal rate. Because of their wealth, Bad Moons favour bright yellow wargear and the shine of any sort of precious metals, while their clan glyph is a leering moon whose mouth brims with wicked fangs. The Bad Moons have all the best gear, from engine-driven saw-choppas to triple-barrelled plasma-rocket-shootas, and they're not shy in bragging about it to every other greenskin who will listen. Going into battle against such spectacularly over-equipped Orks is a terrifying prospect, for while they may not be any better a shot than their kin from other clans, the sheer destructive firepower generated by massed Bad Moons is enough to blow the leg off an Imperial Titan.

The Orks of the Deathskulls Clan are light-fingered thieves who share an almost Mekboy-like knack for tinkering with Ork technology. Their clan glyph is a horned skull, while their favoured colours are white and blue, the latter being traditionally associated by the greenskins with good luck. Though the Deathskulls enjoy a good fight as much as the next Ork, their inherent kleptomania leads them to see every battle as just another thrilling excuse to scavenge, loot or steal whatever they can get their hands on. When not blazing away with their preposterously huge deffguns, the Deathskulls are more than happy to indulge in such battlefield larceny, and will merrily club to death anyone who gets in their way.

The Blood Axe Clan is unique amongst all of Orkdom for its members' belief that battles should be fought to an actual plan. It is not that the Blood Axes are less courageous or psychotically violent than other Orks, but rather they simply possess a rudimentary comprehension of strategy, tactics and stealth. The Blood Axe Clan uses crossed choppas as its glyph, and rather than having a single, unifying clan colour, its Boyz garb themselves in luridly mangled approximations of Imperial camouflage patterns. The Blood Axes are famed for their Kommandos and, while other Orks tend to see them as untrustworthy gits who are not sufficiently 'Orky', there is no denying that their grasp of such strategic intricacies as concentration of fire, flank attacks, and not just running headlong into artillery fire have proven invaluable to many a Warboss the galaxy over.

The Orks of the Snakebites Clan wear natural, brownish hues and boast a stylised snake as their glyph. They see themselves as staunch traditionalists, and care little that the other clans mock them for their backwards ways. The Snakebites specialise in the breeding of squigs, or squiggly beasts, the strange, fungoid monsters that make up much of the Orks' bizarre ecosystem. These creatures can grow to enormous size and savagery under the husbandry of the hard-bitten Snakebites, eventually becoming the behemoth monsters known as Squiggoths. When the Snakebites take to the field in their armoured howdahs atop their bellowing Squiggoth herds, the other clans stop their sniggering pretty quickly.

ORKS ARMY LIST

This section contains all of the datasheets that you will need in order to fight battles with your Ork miniatures. Each datasheet includes the characteristics profiles of the unit it describes, as well as any wargear and special abilities it may have. Some rules are common to several Ork units, and are described on these pages and referenced on the datasheets.

KEYWORDS

Throughout this section you will come across a keyword that is within angular brackets, specifically <CLAN>. This is shorthand for a keyword of your own choosing, as described below.

<CLAN>

All Orks belong to a clan, a group of like-minded greenskins that share a propensity for a certain kind of warfare.

Some datasheets specify what clan the unit is drawn from (e.g. Ghazghkull Thraka has the GOFF keyword, so is from the Goff clan). If an ORK datasheet does not specify which clan it is drawn from, it will have the <CLAN> keyword. When you include such a unit in your army, you must nominate which clan that unit is from. You then simply replace the <CLAN> keyword in every instance on that unit's datasheet with the name of your chosen clan.

For example, if you were to include a Warboss in your army, and you decided he was from the Evil Sunz clan, his <CLAN> Faction keyword is changed to EVIL SUNZ and his Breakin' Heads ability would then say 'If an EVIL SUNZ unit fails a Morale test within 3" of a friendly EVIL SUNZ WARBOSS, they can restore order with a brutal display of violence. If they do, the unit suffers D3 mortal wounds but the Morale test is then considered to have been passed.'

ABILITIES

The following abilities are common to several Ork units:

'Ere We Go!

A unit with this ability can re-roll failed charge rolls.

Mob Rule

A unit with this ability can use the number of models in their unit as their Leadership characteristic. In addition, a unit with this ability can use the Leadership characteristic of any friendly ORK unit within 6".

POWER OF THE WAAAGH! DISCIPLINE

Before the battle, generate the psychic powers for **PSYKERS** that can use powers from the Power of the Waaagh! discipline using the table below. You can either roll a D3 to generate their powers randomly (re-roll any duplicate results), or you can select the psychic powers you wish the psyker to have.

POWER OF THE WAAAGH! DISCIPLINE

D3	PSYCHIC POWER
1	**'Eadbanger** *'Eadbanger* has a warp charge value of 6. If manifested, roll a D6 and compare it to the Toughness characteristic of the closest visible enemy model within 9" of the psyker. If the result is higher than the model's Toughness, it is slain.
2	**Warpath** *Warpath* has a warp charge value of 7. If manifested, select a friendly **ORK** unit within 6" of the psyker. Increase that unit's Attacks characteristic by 1 until your next Psychic phase.
3	**Da Jump** *Da Jump* has a warp charge value of 7. If manifested, select a friendly **ORK INFANTRY** unit within 6" of the psyker. Remove this unit from the battlefield, and then set it up anywhere on the battlefield more than 9" from any enemy models. This unit counts as having moved for the purposes of any rules (e.g. firing Heavy weapons).

WARGEAR

Many of the units you will find on the following pages reference one or more of the following wargear lists (e.g. Shooty Weapons). When this is the case, the unit may take any item from the appropriate list below. The profiles for the weapons in these lists can be found in the appendix (pg 132-133).

SHOOTY WEAPONS
- Shoota
- Kustom shoota
- Kombi-weapon with rokkit launcha
- Kombi-weapon with skorcha

SOUPED-UP WEAPONS
- Kombi-weapon with rokkit launcha
- Kustom mega-blasta
- Rokkit launcha
- Kombi-weapon with skorcha
- Kustom mega-slugga

'EAVY WEAPONS
- Big shoota
- Rokkit launcha

CHOPPY WEAPONS
- Big choppa
- Power klaw

WARBOSS

☠ | 4 POWER

NAME	M	WS	BS	S	T	W	A	Ld	Sv
Warboss	5"	2+	5+	6	5	6	4	8	4+

A Warboss is a single model armed with a kustom shoota, a big choppa and stikkbombs.

WEAPON	RANGE	TYPE	S	AP	D	ABILITIES
Kustom shoota	18"	Assault 4	4	0	1	-
Attack squig	Melee	Melee	4	-1	1	Each time a model with an attack squig fights, it can make 2 additional attacks with this weapon.
Big choppa	Melee	Melee	+2	-1	2	
Stikkbomb	6"	Grenade D6	3	0	1	-

WARGEAR OPTIONS	• This model may replace its kustom shoota with one item from the *Shooty Weapons* or *Choppy Weapons* lists. • This model may replace its big choppa with one item from the *Choppy Weapons* list. • This model may take an attack squig.
ABILITIES	'Ere We Go, Mob Rule (pg 10) Waaagh!: Friendly ORK INFANTRY units within 6" of this model at the start of the Charge phase can charge even if they Advanced this turn. Breakin' Heads: If a <CLAN> unit fails a Morale test within 3" of a friendly <CLAN> WARBOSS, they can restore order with a brutal display of violence. If they do, the unit suffers D3 mortal wounds but the Morale test is then considered to have been passed.
FACTION KEYWORDS	ORK, <CLAN>
KEYWORDS	CHARACTER, INFANTRY, WARBOSS

WARBOSS
IN MEGA ARMOUR

☠ | 7 POWER

NAME	M	WS	BS	S	T	W	A	Ld	Sv
Warboss in Mega Armour	4"	2+	5+	6	5	7	4	8	2+

A Warboss in Mega Armour is a single model armed with a kustom shoota and power klaw.

WEAPON	RANGE	TYPE	S	AP	D	ABILITIES
Kustom shoota	18"	Assault 4	4	0	1	-
Power klaw	Melee	Melee	x2	-3	D3	When attacking with this weapon, you must subtract 1 from the hit roll.

WARGEAR OPTIONS	• This model may replace its kustom shoota with one item from the *Shooty Weapons* or *Choppy Weapons* lists.
ABILITIES	'Ere We Go, Mob Rule (pg 10) Waaagh!: Friendly ORK INFANTRY units within 6" of this model at the start of the Charge phase can charge even if they Advanced this turn.	Breakin' Heads: If a <CLAN> unit fails a Morale test within 3" of a friendly <CLAN> WARBOSS, they can restore order with a brutal display of violence. If they do, the unit suffers D3 mortal wounds but the Morale test is then considered to have been passed.
FACTION KEYWORDS	ORK, <CLAN>
KEYWORDS	CHARACTER, INFANTRY, MEGA ARMOUR, WARBOSS

WARBOSS
on Warbike

NAME	M	WS	BS	S	T	W	A	Ld	Sv
Warboss on Warbike	14"	2+	5+	6	6	7	4	8	4+

A Warboss on Warbike is a single model armed with a big choppa and stikkbombs. The warbike is equipped with two dakkaguns.

WEAPON	RANGE	TYPE	S	AP	D	ABILITIES
Dakkagun	18"	Assault 3	5	0	1	-
Attack squig	Melee	Melee	4	-1	1	Each time a model with an attack squig fights, it can make 2 additional attacks with this weapon.
Big choppa	Melee	Melee	+2	-1	2	-
Stikkbomb	6"	Grenade D6	3	0	1	-

WARGEAR OPTIONS	• This model may replace its big choppa with one item from the *Choppy Weapons* list. • This model may take one item from the *Shooty Weapons* list. • This model may take an attack squig.
ABILITIES	'Ere We Go, Mob Rule (pg 10) **Waaagh!:** Friendly Ork Infantry units within 6" of this model at the start of the Charge phase can charge even if they Advanced this turn. **Breakin' Heads:** If a \<Clan\> unit fails a Morale test within 3" of a friendly \<Clan\> Warboss, they can restore order with a brutal display of violence. If they do, the unit suffers D3 mortal wounds but the Morale test is then considered to have been passed.
FACTION KEYWORDS	Ork, \<Clan\>
KEYWORDS	Biker, Character, Warboss

WEIRDBOY

NAME	M	WS	BS	S	T	W	A	Ld	Sv
Weirdboy	5"	3+	5+	5	4	4	3	6	6+

A Weirdboy is a single model armed with a Weirdboy staff.

WEAPON	RANGE	TYPE	S	AP	D	ABILITIES
Weirdboy staff	Melee	Melee	+2	-1	D3	-

ABILITIES	'Ere We Go, Mob Rule (pg 10) **Waaagh! Energy:** Add 1 to any Psychic test rolls made for this model for every 10 friendly Ork models within 10". However, if the total result of the test is 12+, this model immediately suffers Perils of the Warp exactly as if you had rolled a double 1 or a double 6.
PSYKER	This model can attempt to manifest one psychic power in each friendly Psychic phase, and attempt to deny one psychic power in each enemy Psychic phase. It knows the *Smite* psychic power and one psychic power from the Power of the Waaagh! discipline (pg 11).
FACTION KEYWORDS	Ork, \<Clan\>
KEYWORDS	Character, Infantry, Psyker, Weirdboy

BIG MEK

NAME	M	WS	BS	S	T	W	A	Ld	Sv
Big Mek	5"	3+	5+	5	4	4	3	7	4+
Grot Oiler	5"	5+	4+	2	2	1	1	4	6+

A Big Mek is a single model armed with a slugga, choppa and stikkbombs. It may be accompanied by a Grot Oiler.

WEAPON	RANGE	TYPE	S	AP	D	ABILITIES
Shokk attack gun	60"	Heavy D6	2D6	-5	D3	Before firing this weapon, roll once to determine the Strength of all its shots. If the result is 11+, do not make wound rolls – instead, each attack that hits causes D3 mortal wounds.
Slugga	12"	Pistol 1	4	0	1	-
Choppa	Melee	Melee	User	0	1	Each time the bearer fights, it can make 1 additional attack with this weapon.
Killsaw	Melee	Melee	x2	-4	2	When attacking with this weapon, you must subtract 1 from the hit roll.
Stikkbomb	6"	Grenade D6	3	0	1	-

WARGEAR OPTIONS	
	• This model may replace its slugga with one item from the *Souped-up Weapons* or *Choppy Weapons* lists, or either a kustom force field or a shokk attack gun.
	• This model may replace its choppa with one item from the *Souped-up Weapons* or *Choppy Weapons* lists, or a killsaw.

ABILITIES	
	'Ere We Go, Mob Rule (pg 10)
	Kustom Force Field: If this model is equipped with a kustom force field, friendly <Ork> units that are entirely within 9" have a 5+ invulnerable save against ranged weapons. If the Big Mek is embarked, the vehicle transporting it has a 5+ invulnerable save against ranged weapons instead.
	Big Mekaniak: At the end of your Movement phase, this model can repair a single friendly <Clan> Vehicle (other than models that can Fly) within 3". That model regains D3 wounds lost earlier in the battle. A vehicle can only be repaired once each turn.
	Grot Oiler: Once per game, a Grot Oiler can assist its master in making repairs. When it does so, the vehicle the Mek is repairing regains one additional wound.
	When rolling to wound this unit, always use the Mek's Toughness (while it is on the battlefield). The death of a Grot Oiler is ignored for the purposes of morale. The Grot Oiler is considered to have the **Character** keyword for the purposes of shooting attacks.

FACTION KEYWORDS	ORK, <CLAN>
KEYWORDS (BIG MEK)	CHARACTER, INFANTRY, BIG MEK
KEYWORDS (GROT OILER)	INFANTRY, GRETCHIN, GROT OILER

BIG MEK
IN MEGA ARMOUR

NAME	M	WS	BS	S	T	W	A	Ld	Sv
Big Mek in Mega Armour	4"	3+	5+	5	4	5	3	8	2+
Grot Oiler	5"	5+	4+	2	2	1	1	4	6+

A Big Mek in mega armour is a single model armed with a kustom mega-blasta and a power klaw. It may be accompanied by a Grot Oiler.

WEAPON	RANGE	TYPE	S	AP	D	ABILITIES
Kustom mega-blasta	24"	Assault 1	8	-3	D3	On a hit roll of 1, the bearer suffers a mortal wound.
Tellyport blasta	12"	Assault D3	8	-2	1	If a model suffers any unsaved wounds from this weapon and is not slain, roll a D6 at the end of the phase. If the result is greater than that model's Wounds characteristic, it is slain.
Killsaw	Melee	Melee	x2	-4	2	When attacking with this weapon, you must subtract 1 from the hit roll.
Power klaw	Melee	Melee	x2	-3	D3	When attacking with this weapon, you must subtract 1 from the hit roll.

WARGEAR OPTIONS	• This model may replace its kustom mega-blasta with one item from the *Shooty Weapons* list or a killsaw. • This model may take either a tellyport blasta or a kustom force field.

ABILITIES	'Ere We Go, Mob Rule (pg 10) **Kustom Force Field:** If this model is equipped with a kustom force field, friendly <Ork> units that are entirely within 9" have a 5+ invulnerable save against ranged weapons. If the Big Mek is embarked, the vehicle transporting it has a 5+ invulnerable save against ranged weapons instead. **Big Mekaniak:** At the end of your Movement phase, this model can repair a single friendly <Clan> Vehicle (other than models that can Fly) within 3". That model regains D3 wounds lost earlier in the battle. A vehicle can only be repaired once each turn.	**Grot Oiler:** Once per game, a Grot Oiler can assist its master in making repairs. When it does so, the vehicle the Mek is repairing regains one additional wound. When rolling to wound this unit, always use the Mek's Toughness (while it is on the battlefield). The death of a Grot Oiler is ignored for the purposes of morale. The Grot Oiler is considered to have the **Character** keyword for the purposes of shooting attacks.

FACTION KEYWORDS	ORK, <Clan>
KEYWORDS (BIG MEK)	CHARACTER, INFANTRY, MEGA ARMOUR, BIG MEK
KEYWORDS (GROT OILER)	INFANTRY, GRETCHIN, GROT OILER

Big Meks are masters of the ramshackle technologies that power the Ork war machine.

BIG MEK
on Warbike

6 POWER

NAME	M	WS	BS	S	T	W	A	Ld	Sv
Big Mek on Warbike	14"	3+	5+	5	5	5	3	7	4+

A Big Mek on Warbike is a single model armed with a slugga, choppa and stikkbombs. The warbike is equipped with two dakkaguns.

WEAPON	RANGE	TYPE	S	AP	D	ABILITIES
Dakkagun	18"	Assault 3	5	0	1	-
Shokk attack gun	60"	Heavy D6	2D6	-5	D3	Before firing this weapon, roll once to determine the Strength of all its shots. If the result is 11+, do not make wound rolls – instead, each attack that hits causes D3 mortal wounds.
Slugga	12"	Pistol 1	4	0	1	-
Choppa	Melee	Melee	User	0	1	Each time the bearer fights, it can make 1 additional attack with this weapon.
Killsaw	Melee	Melee	x2	-4	2	When attacking with this weapon, you must subtract 1 from the hit roll.
Stikkbomb	6"	Grenade D6	3	0	1	-

WARGEAR OPTIONS	• This model may replace its slugga with one item from the *Souped-up Weapons* or *Choppy Weapons* lists, or either a kustom force field or a shokk attack gun. • This model may replace its choppa with one item from the *Souped-up Weapons* or *Choppy Weapons* lists, or a killsaw.

ABILITIES	'Ere We Go, Mob Rule (pg 10) **Big Biker Mekaniak:** At the end of your Movement phase, if it didn't move more than 5", this model can repair a single friendly **<Clan> Vehicle** (other than models that can **Fly**) within 1". That model regains D3 wounds lost earlier in the battle. A vehicle can only be repaired once each turn.	**Kustom Force Field:** If this model is armed with a kustom force field, friendly **<Ork>** units that are entirely within 9" have a 5+ invulnerable save against ranged weapons.

FACTION KEYWORDS	Ork, <Clan>
KEYWORDS	Biker, Character, Big Mek

GHAZGHKULL THRAKA

11 POWER

NAME	M	WS	BS	S	T	W	A	Ld	Sv
Ghazghkull Thraka	5"	2+	5+	6	6	8	5	8	2+

Ghazghkull Thraka is a single model armed with a twin big shoota, kustom klaw and stikkbombs. Only one of this model can be included in your army.

WEAPON	RANGE	TYPE	S	AP	D	ABILITIES
Twin big shoota	36"	Assault 6	5	0	1	-
Kustom klaw	Melee	Melee	x2	-3	3	-
Stikkbomb	6"	Grenade D6	3	0	1	-

ABILITIES	'Ere We Go, Mob Rule (pg 10) **Great Waaagh!:** Friendly **Ork Infantry** units within 6" of Ghazghkull Thraka at the start of the Charge phase can charge even if they Advanced this turn. Furthermore, friendly **Ork Infantry** models add 1 to their Attacks characteristic if they charged this turn and Ghazghkull Thraka is within 6" of their unit when they fight.	**Prophet of Gork and Mork:** Ghazghkull Thraka has a 4+ invulnerable save. **The Boss is Watchin':** If a friendly **<Ork>** unit fails a Morale test and they are within 6" of Ghazghkull Thraka, he can restore order with a brutal display of violence. If he does, the unit suffers D3 mortal wounds but the Morale test is then considered to have been passed.

FACTION KEYWORDS	Ork, Goff
KEYWORDS	Character, Infantry, Mega Armour, Warboss, Ghazghkull Thraka

KAPTIN BADRUKK

5 POWER

NAME	M	WS	BS	S	T	W	A	Ld	Sv
Kaptin Badrukk	5"	2+	4+	5	4	6	4	8	3+
Ammo Runt	5"	5+	4+	2	2	1	1	4	6+

Kaptin Badrukk is a single model armed with a slugga, a choppa, stikkbombs and Da Rippa. He may be accompanied by up to 3 Ammo Runts. Only one of this unit can be included in your army.

WEAPON	RANGE	TYPE	S	AP	D	ABILITIES
Da Rippa	When attacking with this weapon, choose one of the profiles below.					
- Standard	24"	Heavy 3	7	-3	2	-
- Supercharge	24"	Heavy 3	8	-3	3	If you roll one or more hit rolls of 1, the bearer suffers D3 mortal wounds after all of this weapon's shots have been resolved.
Slugga	12"	Pistol 1	4	0	1	-
Choppa	Melee	Melee	User	0	1	Each time the bearer fights, it can make 1 additional attack with this weapon.
Stikkbomb	6"	Grenade D6	3	0	1	-

ABILITIES	'Ere We Go, Mob Rule (pg 10)	
	Ammo Runt: Each time Kaptin Badrukk shoots, when making hit rolls for him you can re-roll one dice for each Ammo Runt accompanying him. When rolling to wound this unit, use Badrukk's Toughness (while he is on the battlefield). The death of an Ammo Runt is ignored for the purposes of morale. The Ammo Runt is considered to have the **CHARACTER** keyword for the purposes of shooting attacks.	**Flashiest Gitz:** You can re-roll hit rolls of 1 in the Shooting phase for friendly units of Flash Gitz within 6" of Kaptin Badrukk. **Goldtoof Armour:** Kaptin Badrukk has a 5+ invulnerable save.

FACTION KEYWORDS	ORK
KEYWORDS (BADRUKK)	INFANTRY, CHARACTER, FLASH GIT, KAPTIN BADRUKK
KEYWORDS (AMMO RUNTS)	INFANTRY, GRETCHIN, AMMO RUNTS

BOSS ZAGSTRUK

5 POWER

NAME	M	WS	BS	S	T	W	A	Ld	Sv
Boss Zagstruk	12"	2+	5+	6	4	6	6	7	4+

Boss Zagstruk is a single model armed with Da Vulcha's Klaws, a slugga, a choppa and stikkbombs. Only one of this model can be included in your army.

WEAPON	RANGE	TYPE	S	AP	D	ABILITIES
Slugga	12"	Pistol 1	4	0	1	-
Choppa	Melee	Melee	User	0	1	Each time the bearer fights, it can make 1 additional attack with this weapon.
Da Vulcha's Klaws	Melee	Melee	+2	-3	D3	Each time the bearer fights, only 2 attacks can be made with this weapon.
Stikkbomb	6"	Grenade D6	3	0	1	-

ABILITIES	'Ere We Go, Mob Rule (pg 10)
	Full Throttle: Boss Zagstruk can Advance and charge in the same turn, but if he does so, roll a D6 after any Overwatch has been resolved. On a roll of 1, he suffers a mortal wound. **Cybork Body:** Each time this model loses a wound, roll a D6; on a roll of 5 or 6, that wound is not lost. You cannot make a Dok's Tools or Biker Dok's Tools roll for this model if you do so. **Drill Boss:** Friendly units of **GOFF STORMBOYZ** within 6" of Boss Zagstruk automatically pass Morale tests.

FACTION KEYWORDS	ORK, GOFF
KEYWORDS	CHARACTER, INFANTRY, STORMBOY, JUMP PACK, FLY, BOSS ZAGSTRUK

BOSS SNIKROT

4 POWER

NAME	M	WS	BS	S	T	W	A	Ld	Sv
Boss Snikrot	6"	2+	5+	6	4	6	6	7	6+

Boss Snikrot is a single model armed with Mork's Teeth and stikkbombs. Only one of this model can be included in your army.

WEAPON	RANGE	TYPE	S	AP	D	ABILITIES
Mork's Teeth	Melee	Melee	User	-1	2	-
Stikkbomb	6"	Grenade D6	3	0	1	-

ABILITIES	'Ere We Go, Mob Rule (pg 10)
	Sneakiest Git: When he is in cover, add 3 instead of 1 to saving throws for Boss Snikrot.
	Kunnin' Infiltrator: During deployment, you can set up Boss Snikrot in hiding instead of placing him on the battlefield. At the end of any of your Movement phases, Snikrot can stalk from his hiding place – set him up anywhere on the battlefield that is more than 9" away from any enemy models.
	Red Skull Kommandos: You can re-roll hit rolls of 1 in the Fight phase for friendly units of **BLOOD AXE KOMMANDOS** within 6" of Boss Snikrot.
	Terrifying Killer: Enemy units taking a Morale test within 6" of Boss Snikrot add 1 to the result.
FACTION KEYWORDS	ORK, BLOOD AXE
KEYWORDS	CHARACTER, INFANTRY, KOMMANDO, BOSS SNIKROT

MEK

3 POWER

NAME	M	WS	BS	S	T	W	A	Ld	Sv
Mek	5"	3+	5+	4	4	3	2	6	6+
Grot Oiler	5"	5+	4+	2	2	1	1	4	6+

A Mek is a single model armed with a slugga, choppa and stikkbombs. It may be accompanied by a Grot Oiler.

WEAPON	RANGE	TYPE	S	AP	D	ABILITIES
Slugga	12"	Pistol 1	4	0	1	-
Choppa	Melee	Melee	User	0	1	Each time the bearer fights, it can make 1 additional attack with this weapon.
Killsaw	Melee	Melee	x2	-4	2	When attacking with this weapon, you must subtract 1 from the hit roll.
Stikkbomb	6"	Grenade D6	3	0	1	-

WARGEAR OPTIONS	• This model may replace its choppa with a killsaw. • This model may replace its slugga with one item from the *Souped-up Weapons* list.
ABILITIES	'Ere We Go, Mob Rule (pg 10) **Mekaniak:** At the end of your Movement phase, this model can repair a single friendly **<CLAN> VEHICLE** (other than models that can **FLY**) within 1". That model regains 1 wound lost earlier in the battle. A vehicle can only be repaired once each turn.	**Grot Oiler:** Once per game, a Grot Oiler can assist its master in making repairs. When it does so, the vehicle the Mek is repairing regains one additional wound. When rolling to wound this unit, always use the Mek's Toughness (while it is on the battlefield). The death of a Grot Oiler is ignored for the purposes of morale. The Grot Oiler is considered to have the **CHARACTER** keyword for the purposes of shooting attacks.
FACTION KEYWORDS	ORK, <CLAN>
KEYWORDS (MEK)	CHARACTER, INFANTRY, MEK
KEYWORDS (GROT OILER)	INFANTRY, GRETCHIN, GROT OILER

PAINBOY

4 POWER

NAME	M	WS	BS	S	T	W	A	Ld	Sv
Painboy	5"	3+	5+	5	4	4	4	6	6+
Grot Orderly	5"	5+	4+	2	2	1	1	4	6+

A Painboy is a single model armed with an 'urty syringe and a power klaw. It may be accompanied by a Grot Orderly.

WEAPON	RANGE	TYPE	S	AP	D	ABILITIES
Killsaw	Melee	Melee	x2	-4	2	When attacking with this weapon, you must subtract 1 from the hit roll.
Power klaw	Melee	Melee	x2	-3	D3	When attacking with this weapon, you must subtract 1 from the hit roll.
'Urty syringe	Melee	Melee	User	0	1	This weapon always wounds targets (other than **Vehicles**) on a roll of 2+.

WARGEAR OPTIONS	• This model may replace its power klaw with a killsaw.

ABILITIES	'Ere We Go, Mob Rule (pg 10)	Dok's Tools: Roll a D6 each time a <Clan> Infantry or <Clan> Biker unit loses a wound whilst within 3" of any friendly <Clan> Painboyz. On a 6, that unit does not lose that wound.
	Grot Orderly: If this model is accompanied by a Grot Orderly, once per game, when the Painboy is attempting to heal a model using Dok's Tools, you may re-roll the dice, either when determining if the surgery is successful, or when calculating the number of wounds regained.	In addition, at the end of your Movement phase, a Painboy can attempt to heal a single <Clan> Infantry or <Clan> Biker model within 1". Roll a D6; on a 1, the model you were attempting to heal loses a wound, but on any other result that model regains D3 wounds lost earlier in the battle. You can only make one attempt to heal a given model with the Dok's Tools or Biker Dok's Tools ability in each turn.
	When rolling to wound this unit, use the Painboy's Toughness (while it is on the battlefield). The death of a Grot Orderly is ignored for the purposes of morale. The Grot Orderly is considered to have the **Character** keyword for the purposes of shooting attacks.	

FACTION KEYWORDS	ORK, <CLAN>
KEYWORDS (PAINBOY)	CHARACTER, INFANTRY, PAINBOY
KEYWORDS (GROT ORDERLY)	INFANTRY, GRETCHIN, GROT ORDERLY

PAINBOY
ON WARBIKE

6 POWER

NAME	M	WS	BS	S	T	W	A	Ld	Sv
Painboy on Warbike	14"	3+	5+	5	5	5	4	6	4+

A Painboy on Warbike is a single model armed with an 'urty syringe and a power klaw. It rides a warbike equipped with two dakkaguns.

WEAPON	RANGE	TYPE	S	AP	D	ABILITIES
Dakkagun	18"	Assault 3	5	0	1	-
Killsaw	Melee	Melee	x2	-4	2	When attacking with this weapon, you must subtract 1 from the hit roll.
Power klaw	Melee	Melee	x2	-3	D3	When attacking with this weapon, you must subtract 1 from the hit roll.
'Urty syringe	Melee	Melee	User	0	1	This weapon always wounds targets (other than **Vehicles**) on a roll of 2+.

WARGEAR OPTIONS	• This model may replace its power klaw with a killsaw.

ABILITIES	'Ere We Go, Mob Rule (pg 10)
	Biker Dok's Tools: Roll a D6 each time a friendly <Clan> Infantry or <Clan> Biker unit loses a wound whilst within 3" of any <Clan> Painboyz. On a 6, that unit does not lose that wound.
	In addition, at the end of your Movement phase, if it didn't move more than 5" this model can attempt to heal a single <Clan> Infantry or <Clan> Biker model within 1". Roll a D6; on a 1, the model you were attempting to heal loses a wound, but on any other result, that model regains D3 wounds lost earlier in the battle. You can only make one attempt to heal a given model with the Dok's Tools or Biker Dok's Tools ability in each turn.

FACTION KEYWORDS	ORK, <CLAN>
KEYWORDS	BIKER, CHARACTER, PAINBOY

MAD DOK GROTSNIK

7 POWER

NAME	M	WS	BS	S	T	W	A	Ld	Sv
Mad Dok Grotsnik	5"	2+	5+	5	5	4	4	8	4+

Mad Dok Grotsnik is a single model armed with a slugga, a power klaw and an 'urty syringe. Only one of this model can be included in your army.

WEAPON	RANGE	TYPE	S	AP	D	ABILITIES
Slugga	12"	Pistol 1	4	0	1	-
Power klaw	Melee	Melee	x2	-3	D3	When attacking with this weapon, you must subtract 1 from the hit roll.
'Urty syringe	Melee	Melee	User	0	1	This weapon always wounds targets (other than **Vehicles**) on a roll of 2+.

ABILITIES	'Ere We Go, Mob Rule (pg 10)

Dok's Tools: Roll a D6 each time an **Ork Infantry** or **Ork Biker** unit loses a wound whilst within 3" of Mad Dok Grotsnik. On a 6, that unit does not lose that wound. This is not cumulative with other Dok's Tools or Biker Dok's Tools.

In addition, at the end of your Movement phase, Mad Dok Grotsnik can attempt to heal a single **Ork Infantry** or **Ork Biker** model within 1". Roll a D6; on a 1, the model you were attempting to heal loses a wound, but on any other result that model regains D3 wounds lost earlier in the battle. You can only make one attempt to heal a given model with the Dok's Tools or Biker Dok's Tools ability in each turn.

Super Cybork Body: Each time this model loses a wound, roll a D6; on a roll of 5 or 6, that wound is not lost.

One Scalpel Short of a Medpack: If, at the start of the Charge phase, there are no friendly **Ork Infantry** units within 3" of Mad Dok Grotsnik, he will attempt to charge the nearest enemy unit, if there is one within 12". He will do this even if he Advanced or Fell Back this turn, but not if he is already within 1" of an enemy unit.

FACTION KEYWORDS	ORK, DEATHSKULLS
KEYWORDS	CHARACTER, INFANTRY, PAINBOY, MAD DOK GROTSNIK

BOYZ

5 POWER

NAME	M	WS	BS	S	T	W	A	Ld	Sv
Ork Boy	5"	3+	5+	4	4	1	2	6	6+
Boss Nob	5"	3+	5+	5	4	2	3	7	6+

This unit contains 10 Ork Boyz. It can include up to 10 additional Ork Boyz (**Power Rating +4**) or up to 20 additional Ork Boyz (**Power Rating +8**). Each model is armed with a slugga, choppa and stikkbombs. A Boss Nob may take the place of one Ork Boy.

WEAPON	RANGE	TYPE	S	AP	D	ABILITIES
Shoota	18"	Assault 2	4	0	1	-
Slugga	12"	Pistol 1	4	0	1	-
Choppa	Melee	Melee	User	0	1	Each time the bearer fights, it can make 1 additional attack with this weapon.
Stikkbomb	6"	Grenade D6	3	0	1	

WARGEAR OPTIONS	• Any Ork Boy may replace his choppa and slugga with a shoota. • The Boss Nob may replace his choppa with one item from the *Choppy Weapons* list. • The Boss Nob may replace his slugga with one item from the *Shooty Weapons* list. • For every 10 models in the unit, one Ork Boy may replace his choppa and slugga with one item from the *'Eavy Weapons* list.
ABILITIES	'Ere We Go, Mob Rule (pg 10) **Green Tide:** If this unit includes 20 or more models, add 1 to the Attacks characteristic of each model in the unit.
FACTION KEYWORDS	ORK, <CLAN>
KEYWORDS	INFANTRY, BOYZ

GRETCHIN

2 POWER

NAME	M	WS	BS	S	T	W	A	Ld	Sv
Gretchin	5"	5+	4+	2	2	1	1	4	6+

This unit contains 10 Gretchin. It can include up to 10 additional Gretchin (**Power Rating +1**), or up to 20 additional Gretchin (**Power Rating +2**). Each model is equipped with a grot blasta.

WEAPON	RANGE	TYPE	S	AP	D	ABILITIES
Grot blasta	12"	Pistol 1	3	0	1	-

ABILITIES	**Surprisingly Dangerous in Large Numbers:** If a unit of Gretchin includes 20 or more models, you can add 1 to their hit rolls.
FACTION KEYWORDS	ORK, <CLAN>
KEYWORDS	INFANTRY, GRETCHIN

RUNTHERD

1 POWER

NAME	M	WS	BS	S	T	W	A	Ld	Sv
Runtherd	5"	3+	5+	4	4	4	3	7	6+

A Runtherd is a single model armed with a slugga, grabba stikk and stikkbombs.

WEAPON	RANGE	TYPE	S	AP	D	ABILITIES
Slugga	12"	Pistol 1	4	0	1	-
Grabba stikk	Melee	Melee	+1	0	1	Each time the bearer fights, it can make 1 additional attack with this weapon.
Grot-prod	Melee	Melee	+2	-1	1	-
Stikkbomb	6"	Grenade D6	3	0	1	-

WARGEAR OPTIONS	• This model may replace its grabba stikk with a grot-prod. • This model may take either a grot lash or a squig hound.
ABILITIES	'Ere We Go, Mob Rule (pg 10) **Squig Hound:** If a unit comprised entirely of GRETCHIN fails a Morale test and is within 3" of any friendly Runtherds with a squig hound, ignore the result. D3 models from the unit are slain instead. **Grot Lash:** If a unit comprised entirely of GRETCHIN is within 3" of any Runtherds with a grot lash, you can re-roll hit rolls of 1 for them in the Fight phase.
FACTION KEYWORDS	ORK, <CLAN>
KEYWORDS	CHARACTER, INFANTRY, RUNTHERD

The irascible bullies known as Runtherds are responsible for corralling mobs of Gretchin and goading them towards the foe.

BURNA BOYZ

5 POWER

NAME	M	WS	BS	S	T	W	A	Ld	Sv
Burna Boy	5"	3+	5+	4	4	1	2	6	6+
Spanner	5"	3+	5+	4	4	1	2	6	6+

This unit contains 5 Burna Boyz. It can include up to 5 additional Burna Boyz (**Power Rating +4**) or up to 10 additional Burna Boyz (**Power Rating +8**). Up to 3 Spanners can each take the place of a Burna Boy.
• Each Burna Boy is armed with a burna and stikkbombs.
• Each Spanner is armed with a slugga, choppa and stikkbombs.

WEAPON	RANGE	TYPE	S	AP	D	ABILITIES
Burna (shooting)	8"	Assault D3	4	0	1	Before a unit fires its burnas, roll once for the number of attacks and use this for all burnas fired by the unit in this phase. When firing a burna, it automatically hits its target.
Slugga	12"	Pistol 1	4	0	1	-
Burna (melee)	Melee	Melee	User	-2	1	-
Choppa	Melee	Melee	User	0	1	Each time the bearer fights, it can make 1 additional attack with this weapon.
Killsaw	Melee	Melee	x2	-4	2	When attacking with this weapon, you must subtract 1 from the hit roll.
Stikkbomb	6"	Grenade D6	3	0	1	-

WARGEAR OPTIONS	• Any Spanner may replace his choppa with a killsaw. • Any Spanner may replace his slugga with one item from the *Souped-up Weapons* list.
ABILITIES	**'Ere We Go, Mob Rule** (pg 10) **Mekaniak:** At the end of your Movement phase, a Spanner can repair a single friendly <CLAN> VEHICLE (other than models that can FLY) within 1". That model regains 1 wound lost earlier in the battle. A vehicle can only be repaired once each turn. **Pyromaniaks:** If this unit destroys an enemy unit in the Shooting phase, it automatically passes Morale tests until the start of your next turn.
FACTION KEYWORDS	ORK, <CLAN>
KEYWORDS	INFANTRY, BURNA BOYZ

Burna Boyz are enthusiastic arsonists who like nothing more than wreathing their targets in gouts of flame.

TANKBUSTAS

NAME	M	WS	BS	S	T	W	A	Ld	Sv
Tankbusta	5"	3+	5+	4	4	1	2	6	6+
Boss Nob	5"	3+	5+	5	4	2	3	7	6+
Bomb Squig	5"	2+	2+	3	4	1	1	4	6+

This unit contains 5 Tankbustas. It can include up to 5 additional Tankbustas (**Power Rating +3**) or up to 10 additional Tankbustas (**Power Rating +6**). For every 5 Tankbustas or Boss Nobz in the unit, it may be accompanied by up to 2 Bomb Squigs. A Boss Nob can take the place of one Tankbusta.
- Each Tankbusta and Boss Nob is armed with a rokkit launcha, stikkbombs and tankbusta bombs.
- Each Bomb Squig carries a squig bomb.

WEAPON	RANGE	TYPE	S	AP	D	ABILITIES
Pair of rokkit pistols	12"	Pistol 2	7	-2	D3	-
Rokkit launcha	24"	Assault 1	8	-2	3	-
Squig bomb	18"	Assault 1	8	-2	D6	This weapon cannot target units that can **FLY**. Remove the bearer after making this attack.
Tankhammer	Melee	Melee	-	-	-	Make a single hit roll when attacking with this weapon. If it hits, inflict D3 mortal wounds on the target, then remove the bearer.
Stikkbomb	6"	Grenade D6	3	0	1	-
Tankbusta bomb	6"	Grenade D3	8	-2	D6	-

WARGEAR OPTIONS	• The Boss Nob may replace his rokkit launcha with one item from the *Choppy Weapons* list. • Up to two Tankbustas may replace their rokkit launcha with a tankhammer. • For every five models in the unit (not counting Bomb Squigs), one Tankbusta may replace their rokkit launcha with a pair of rokkit pistols.
ABILITIES	'Ere We Go, Mob Rule (pg 10) **Tank Hunters:** You can re-roll failed hit rolls for attacks made by this unit that target **VEHICLES**. **Bomb Squig:** The death of a Bomb Squig is ignored for the purposes of morale.
FACTION KEYWORDS	ORK, <CLAN>
KEYWORDS	INFANTRY, TANKBUSTAS

Tankbustas live for the thrill of destroying armoured vehicles, and equip themselves with all manner of high-explosive devices.

NOBZ

NAME	M	WS	BS	S	T	W	A	Ld	Sv
Nob	5"	3+	5+	5	4	2	3	6	4+
Boss Nob	5"	3+	5+	5	4	2	3	7	4+
Ammo Runt	5"	5+	4+	2	2	1	1	4	6+

This unit contains 1 Boss Nob and 4 Nobz. It can include up to 5 additional Nobz (**Power Rating +10**). Each Nob and Boss Nob is armed with a slugga, choppa and stikkbombs. Any Nob or Boss Nob may be accompanied by an Ammo Runt.

WEAPON	RANGE	TYPE	S	AP	D	ABILITIES
Slugga	12"	Pistol 1	4	0	1	-
Choppa	Melee	Melee	User	0	1	Each time the bearer fights, it can make 1 additional attack with this weapon.
Killsaw	Melee	Melee	x2	-4	2	When attacking with this weapon, you must subtract 1 from the hit roll.
Power stabba	Melee	Melee	User	-2	1	-
Stikkbomb	6"	Grenade D6	3	0	1	-

WARGEAR OPTIONS	
	• Any model may replace its slugga with one item from the *Shooty Weapons* list.
	• Any model may replace its choppa with a killsaw, power stabba or one item from the *Choppy Weapons* list.
	• For every 5 models in the unit (excluding Ammo Runts), one may have a cybork body.

ABILITIES

'Ere We Go, Mob Rule (pg 10)

Keepin' Order: Roll a D6 for each model that flees from a <CLAN> unit that is within 3" of any friendly <CLAN> unit with this ability. On a 6, that model doesn't flee.

Cybork Body: Each time a model with a cybork body loses a wound, roll a D6; on a 6, that wound is not lost. You cannot make a Dok's Tools or Biker Dok's Tools roll for this model if you do so.

Ammo Runt: Each time this unit shoots, when making hit rolls for it you can re-roll one dice for each Ammo Runt accompanying it.

When rolling to wound this unit, use the Nobz' Toughness (while they are on the battlefield). The death of an Ammo Runt is ignored for the purposes of morale.

FACTION KEYWORDS	ORK, <CLAN>
KEYWORDS (NOBZ)	INFANTRY, NOBZ
KEYWORDS (AMMO RUNTS)	INFANTRY, GRETCHIN, AMMO RUNTS

NOB
WITH WAAAGH! BANNER

NAME	M	WS	BS	S	T	W	A	Ld	Sv
Nob with Waaagh! Banner	5"	3+	5+	5	4	4	3	6	4+

A Nob with Waaagh! Banner is a single model. It is armed with a Waaagh! banner, a kustom shoota and stikkbombs.

WEAPON	RANGE	TYPE	S	AP	D	ABILITIES
Kustom shoota	18"	Assault 4	4	0	1	-
Waaagh! banner	Melee	Melee	+2	0	2	-
Stikkbomb	6"	Grenade D6	3	0	1	-

ABILITIES

'Ere We Go, Mob Rule (pg 10)

Waaagh! Banner: <CLAN> units within 6" of any friendly Waaagh! banners add 1 to their hit rolls in the Fight phase.

Keepin' Order: Roll a D6 for each model that flees from a <CLAN> unit that is within 3" of any friendly <CLAN> unit with this ability. On a 6, that model doesn't flee.

FACTION KEYWORDS	ORK, <CLAN>
KEYWORDS	CHARACTER, INFANTRY, NOB

NOBZ
ON WARBIKES

10 POWER

NAME	M	WS	BS	S	T	W	A	Ld	Sv
Nob on Warbike	14"	3+	5+	5	5	3	3	6	4+
Boss Nob on Warbike	14"	3+	5+	5	5	3	3	7	4+

This unit contains 1 Boss Nob on Warbike and 2 Nobz on Warbikes. It can include up to 3 additional Nobz on Warbikes (**Power Rating +9**), or up to 6 additional Nobz on Warbikes (**Power Rating +18**). Each model is armed with a slugga, a choppa and stikkbombs, and rides a warbike equipped with two dakkaguns.

WEAPON	RANGE	TYPE	S	AP	D	ABILITIES
Dakkagun	18"	Assault 3	5	0	1	-
Slugga	12"	Pistol 1	4	0	1	-
Choppa	Melee	Melee	User	0	1	Each time the bearer fights, it can make 1 additional attack with this weapon.
Stikkbomb	6"	Grenade D6	3	0	1	-

WARGEAR OPTIONS	• Any model may replace its slugga with one item from the *Shooty Weapons* list. • Any model may replace its choppa with one item from the *Choppy Weapons* list.
ABILITIES	'Ere We Go, Mob Rule (pg 10) **Keepin' Order:** Roll a D6 for each model that flees from a <CLAN> unit that is within 3" of any friendly <CLAN> units with this ability. On a 6, that model doesn't flee.
FACTION KEYWORDS	ORK, <CLAN>
KEYWORDS	BIKER, NOBZ

Nobz are the biggest and toughest Orks around, second only to the Warboss in status. Each is a scarred veteran of countless battles.

MEGANOBZ

10 POWER

NAME	M	WS	BS	S	T	W	A	Ld	Sv
Meganob	4"	3+	5+	5	4	3	3	6	2+
Boss Meganob	4"	3+	5+	5	4	3	3	7	2+

This unit contains 1 Boss Meganob and 2 Meganobz. It can include up to 7 additional Meganobz (**Power Rating +3 per model**). Each model is armed with a kustom shoota, a power klaw and stikkbombs.

WEAPON	RANGE	TYPE	S	AP	D	ABILITIES
Kombi-weapon with rokkit launcha	When attacking with this weapon, choose one or both of the profiles below. If you choose both, subtract 1 from all hit rolls.					
- Rokkit launcha	24"	Assault 1	8	-2	3	-
- Shoota	18"	Assault 2	4	0	1	-
Kombi-weapon with skorcha	When attacking with this weapon, choose one or both of the profiles below. If you choose both, subtract 1 from all hit rolls.					
- Shoota	18"	Assault 2	4	0	1	-
- Skorcha	8"	Assault D6	5	-1	1	This weapon automatically hits its target.
Kustom shoota	18"	Assault 4	4	0	1	
Killsaw	Melee	Melee	x2	-4	2	When attacking with this weapon, you must subtract 1 from the hit roll. If a model is equipped with two killsaws, add 1 to its Attacks characteristic.
Power klaw	Melee	Melee	x2	-3	D3	When attacking with this weapon, you must subtract 1 from the hit roll.
Stikkbomb	6"	Grenade D6	3	0	1	-

WARGEAR OPTIONS	• Any model may replace its kustom shoota and power klaw with two killsaws. • Any model may replace its kustom shoota with a kombi-weapon with skorcha or kombi-weapon with rokkit launcha.
ABILITIES	'Ere We Go, Mob Rule (pg 10) **Keepin' Order:** Roll a D6 for each model that flees from a <CLAN> unit that is within 3" of any friendly <CLAN> unit with this ability. On a 6, that model doesn't flee.
FACTION KEYWORDS	ORK, <CLAN>
KEYWORDS	INFANTRY, MEGA ARMOUR, NOBZ, MEGANOBZ

Kommandos are vicious and cunning Orks who favour sneaking up on their victims rather than charging them head-on.

KOMMANDOS

4 POWER

NAME	M	WS	BS	S	T	W	A	Ld	Sv
Kommando	6"	3+	5+	4	4	1	2	6	6+
Boss Nob	6"	3+	5+	5	4	2	3	7	6+

This unit contains 5 Kommandos. It can include up to 5 additional Kommandos (**Power Rating +2**) or up to 10 additional Kommandos (**Power Rating +4**). A Boss Nob can take the place of one Kommando. All models are armed with a slugga, a choppa and stikkbombs.

WEAPON	RANGE	TYPE	S	AP	D	ABILITIES
Big shoota	36"	Assault 3	5	0	1	-
Burna (shooting)	8"	Assault D3	4	0	1	Before a unit fires its burnas, roll once for the number of attacks and use this for all burnas fired by the unit in this phase. This weapon automatically hits its target.
Rokkit launcher	24"	Assault1	8	-2	3	-
Slugga	12"	Pistol 1	4	0	1	-
Burna (melee)	Melee	Melee	User	-2	1	-
Choppa	Melee	Melee	User	0	1	Each time the bearer fights, it can make 1 additional attack with this weapon.
Stikkbomb	6"	Grenade D6	3	0	1	-

WARGEAR OPTIONS	• Up to two Kommandos may replace their slugga with a big shoota, burna or rokkit launcha. • The Boss Nob may replace his choppa with one item from the *Choppy Weapons* list.

ABILITIES	'Ere We Go, Mob Rule (pg 10) **Sneaky Gits:** When they are in cover, add 2 instead of 1 to saving throws for models in this unit. **Kunnin' Infiltrators:** During deployment, you may set up a unit of Kommandos in hiding instead of placing them on the battlefield. At the end of any of your Movement phases, they can stalk from their hiding place – set them up anywhere on the battlefield that is more than 9" away from any enemy models.

FACTION KEYWORDS	ORK, <CLAN>
KEYWORDS	INFANTRY, KOMMANDOS

TRUKK

5 POWER

NAME	M	WS	BS	S	T	W	A	Ld	Sv
Trukk	*	5+	5+	*	6	10	*	6	4+

DAMAGE
Some of this model's characteristics change as it suffers damage, as shown below:

REMAINING W	M	S	A
6-10+	12"	6	3
3-5	8"	5	D3
1-2	6"	4	1

A Trukk is a single model equipped with a big shoota.

WEAPON	RANGE	TYPE	S	AP	D	ABILITIES
Big shoota	36"	Assault 3	5	0	1	-
Rokkit launcha	24"	Assault 1	8	-2	3	-
Wreckin' ball	Melee	Melee	+1	-1	1	The bearer can only make 3 attacks with this weapon each time it fights.

WARGEAR OPTIONS	• This model may replace its big shoota with a rokkit launcha. • This model may take a wreckin' ball.

ABILITIES	**Ramshackle:** Roll a D6 each time this model suffers damage from an attack that has a Damage characteristic of more than 1. On a roll of 6, reduce the damage caused by the attack to 1. **Open-topped:** Models embarked on this model can attack in their Shooting phase. Measure the range and draw line of sight from any point on this model. When they do so, any restrictions or modifiers that apply to this model also apply to its passengers; for example, the passengers cannot shoot if this model has Fallen Back in the same turn, cannot shoot (except with Pistols) if this model is within 1" of an enemy unit, and so on. **Explodes:** If this model is reduced to 0 wounds, roll a D6 before removing it from the battlefield and before any embarked models disembark. On a 6 it explodes, and each unit within 6" suffers D3 mortal wounds.

TRANSPORT	A Trukk can transport 12 ORK INFANTRY models. Each MEGA ARMOUR or JUMP PACK model takes the space of two other models.

FACTION KEYWORDS	ORK, <CLAN>
KEYWORDS	VEHICLE, TRANSPORT, TRUKK

STORMBOYZ

3 POWER

NAME	M	WS	BS	S	T	W	A	Ld	Sv
Stormboy	12"	3+	5+	4	4	1	2	6	6+
Boss Nob	12"	3+	5+	5	4	2	3	7	6+

This unit contains 5 Stormboyz. It can include up to 5 additional Stormboyz (**Power Rating +2**), up to 15 additional Stormboyz (**Power Rating +6**), or up to 25 additional Stormboyz (**Power Rating +10**). A Boss Nob can take the place of one Stormboy. Each model is armed with a slugga, a choppa and stikkbombs.

WEAPON	RANGE	TYPE	S	AP	D	ABILITIES
Slugga	12"	Pistol 1	4	0	1	-
Choppa	Melee	Melee	User	0	1	Each time the bearer fights, it can make 1 additional attack with this weapon.
Stikkbomb	6"	Grenade D6	3	0	1	-

WARGEAR OPTIONS	• The Boss Nob may replace his choppa with one item from the *Choppy Weapons* list.
ABILITIES	**'Ere We Go, Mob Rule** (pg 10) **Full Throttle:** This unit can Advance and charge in the same turn, but if it does so, roll a D6 for each model after any Overwatch has been resolved. For each roll of 1, the unit suffers a mortal wound.
FACTION KEYWORDS	ORK, <CLAN>
KEYWORDS	INFANTRY, JUMP PACK, FLY, STORMBOYZ

DEFFKOPTAS

5 POWER

NAME	M	WS	BS	S	T	W	A	Ld	Sv
Deffkopta	14"	3+	5+	4	5	4	2	6	4+

This unit contains 1 Deffkopta. It can include up to 2 additional Deffkoptas (**Power Rating +8**) or up to 4 additional Deffkoptas (**Power Rating +16**). Each model is equipped with spinnin' blades and kopta rokkits.

WEAPON	RANGE	TYPE	S	AP	D	ABILITIES
Kopta rokkits	24"	Assault 2	8	-2	3	-
Kustom mega-blasta	24"	Assault 1	8	-3	D3	On a hit roll of 1, the bearer suffers a mortal wound.
Twin big shoota	36"	Assault 6	5	0	1	-
Killsaw	Melee	Melee	x2	-4	2	When attacking with this weapon, you must subtract 1 from the hit roll.
Spinnin' blades	Melee	Melee	+1	0	1	Make D3 hit rolls for each attack made with this weapon, instead of 1.
Bigbomm	———— See Bigbomm, below ————					Each bigbomm can only be used once per battle.

WARGEAR OPTIONS	• Any Deffkopta may replace its kopta rokkits with a kustom mega-blasta or with a twin big shoota. • Any Deffkopta may take a bigbomm. • Any Deffkopta may take a killsaw.
ABILITIES	**'Ere We Go, Mob Rule** (pg 10) **Turbo-boost:** When this model Advances, add 6" to its Move characteristic for that Movement phase instead of rolling a dice. **Scoutin' Ahead:** During deployment, you can set up a unit of Deffkoptas behind enemy lines instead of placing it on the battlefield. At the end of any of your Movement phases, the Deffkoptas can swoop around to ambush the foe – set them up anywhere on the battlefield that is more than 9" away from any enemy models and within 14" of a battlefield edge. **Bigbomm:** A Deffkopta equipped with a bigbomm can drop it as it flies over enemy units in its Movement phase. After the Deffkopta has moved, pick one enemy unit that it flew over. Then, roll a D6 for each model in the enemy unit (up to a maximum of 5 dice). For each roll of 5+, the target unit suffers 1 mortal wound. It can only do this once per battle.
FACTION KEYWORDS	ORK, <CLAN>
KEYWORDS	VEHICLE, FLY, DEFFKOPTAS

DAKKAJET

POWER 7

NAME	M	WS	BS	S	T	W	A	Ld	Sv
Dakkajet	*	5+	*	6	6	12	*	6	4+

A Dakkajet is a single model equipped with four supa shootas.

DAMAGE

Some of this model's characteristics change as it suffers damage, as shown below:

REMAINING W	M	BS	A
7-12+	20-60"	5+	3
4-6	20-40"	6+	D3
1-3	20-25"	6+	1

WEAPON	RANGE	TYPE	S	AP	D	ABILITIES
Supa shoota	36"	Assault 3	6	-1	1	-

WARGEAR OPTIONS
• This model may take two additional supa shootas.

ABILITIES

Airborne: This model cannot charge, can only be charged by units that can **FLY**, and can only attack or be attacked in the Fight phase by units that can **FLY**.

Hard to Hit: Your opponent must subtract 1 from hit rolls for attacks that target this model in the Shooting phase.

Supersonic: Each time this model moves, first pivot it on the spot up to 90° (this does not contribute to how far the model moves), and then move the model straight forwards. Note that it cannot pivot again after the initial pivot. When this model Advances, increase its Move characteristic by 20" until the end of the phase – do not roll a dice.

Dakka Dakka Dakka: If a Dakkajet targets the same unit with all of its supa shootas, you can add 1 to all of those hit rolls.

Crash and Burn: If this model is reduced to 0 wounds, roll a D6 before removing it from the battlefield. On a 6 it crashes and explodes, and each unit within 6" suffers D3 mortal wounds.

FACTION KEYWORDS
ORK, <CLAN>

KEYWORDS
VEHICLE, FLY, DAKKAJET

BURNA-BOMMER

POWER 8

NAME	M	WS	BS	S	T	W	A	Ld	Sv
Burna-bommer	*	5+	*	6	6	12	*	6	4+

A Burna-bommer is a single model equipped with a twin big shoota, two supa shootas and two burna bombs.

DAMAGE

Some of this model's characteristics change as it suffers damage, as shown below:

REMAINING W	M	BS	A
7-12+	20-50"	5+	3
4-6	20-30"	6+	D3
1-3	20-25"	6+	1

WEAPON	RANGE	TYPE	S	AP	D	ABILITIES
Twin big shoota	36"	Assault 6	5	0	1	-
Skorcha missiles	24"	Assault D6	5	-1	1	Units attacked by this weapon do not gain any bonus to their saving throws for being in cover.
Supa shoota	36"	Assault 3	6	-1	1	-
Burna bomb	— See Burna Bomb, below —					Each burna bomb can only be used once per battle.

WARGEAR OPTIONS
• This model may take skorcha missiles.

ABILITIES

Burna Bombs: A Burna-bommer can drop one burna bomb as it flies over enemy units in its Movement phase. After the Burna-bommer has moved, pick one enemy unit that it flew over and roll a D6 for each model in that unit (up to a maximum of 10 dice). Add 1 to the dice rolls if the enemy unit is **INFANTRY**. For each roll of 5+, the unit being bombed suffers a mortal wound.

Supersonic: Each time this model moves, first pivot it on the spot up to 90° (this does not contribute to how far the model moves), and then move the model straight forwards. Note that it cannot pivot again after the initial pivot. When this model Advances, increase its Move characteristic by 20" until the end of the phase – do not roll a dice.

Explosive Demise: If this model is reduced to 0 wounds, roll a D6 before removing it from the battlefield. On a 4+ it crashes and explodes, and each unit within 6" suffers 3 mortal wounds.

Grot Gunner: When a Burna-bommer attacks with its twin big shoota, add 1 to its hit rolls.

Airborne: This model cannot charge, can only be charged by units that can **FLY**, and can only attack or be attacked in the Fight phase by units that can **FLY**.

Hard to Hit: Your opponent must subtract 1 from hit rolls for attacks that target this model in the Shooting phase.

FACTION KEYWORDS
ORK, <CLAN>

KEYWORDS
VEHICLE, FLY, BURNA-BOMMER

BLITZA-BOMMER

7 POWER

NAME	M	WS	BS	S	T	W	A	Ld	Sv
Blitza-bommer	*	5+	*	6	6	12	*	6	4+

A Blitza-bommer is a single model equipped with a big shoota, two supa shootas and two boom bombs.

DAMAGE
Some of this model's characteristics change as it suffers damage, as shown below:

REMAINING W	M	BS	A
7-12+	20-50"	5+	3
4-6	20-30"	6+	D3
1-3	20-25"	6+	1

WEAPON	RANGE	TYPE	S	AP	D	ABILITIES
Big shoota	36"	Assault 3	5	0	1	-
Supa shoota	36"	Assault 3	6	-1	1	-
Boom bomb	— See Boom Bomb, below —					Each boom bomb can only be used once per battle.

ABILITIES

Boom Bomb: A Blitza-bommer can drop one boom bomb as it flies over enemy units in its Movement phase. After the Blitza-bommer has moved, pick one enemy unit that it flew over. Then, roll a D6 for each model in the unit, up to a maximum of 10 dice (roll three dice instead for each **VEHICLE** or **MONSTER** in the unit). For each roll of 4+, the unit being bombed suffers a mortal wound.

Grot Gunner: When a Blitza-bommer attacks with its big shoota, add 1 to its hit rolls.

Crash and Burn: If this model is reduced to 0 wounds, roll a D6 before removing it from the battlefield. On a 6 it crashes and explodes, and each unit within 6" suffers D3 mortal wounds.

Airborne: This model cannot charge, can only be charged by units that can **FLY**, and can only attack or be attacked in the Fight phase by units that can **FLY**.

Hard to Hit: Your opponent must subtract 1 from hit rolls for attacks that target this model in the Shooting phase.

Supersonic: Each time this model moves, first pivot it on the spot up to 90° (this does not contribute to how far the model moves), and then move the model straight forwards. Note that it cannot pivot again after the initial pivot. When this model Advances, increase its Move characteristic by 20" until the end of the phase – do not roll a dice.

FACTION KEYWORDS	ORK, <CLAN>
KEYWORDS	VEHICLE, FLY, BLITZA-BOMMER

Blitza-bommers are piloted by thrill-seeking Orks who like to deposit their vessel's destructive payload at point-blank range.

WAZBOM BLASTAJET

DAMAGE
Some of this model's characteristics change as it suffers damage, as shown below:

REMAINING W	M	BS	A
7-12+	20-60"	5+	3
4-6	20-40"	6+	D3
1-3	20-25"	6+	1

NAME	M	WS	BS	S	T	W	A	Ld	Sv
Wazbom Blastajet	*	5+	*	6	6	12	*	6	4+

A Wazbom Blastajet is a single model equipped with two wazbom mega-kannons, a smasha gun and a stikkbomb flinga.

WEAPON	RANGE	TYPE	S	AP	D	ABILITIES
Smasha gun	36"	Heavy 1	*	-4	D6	Instead of making a wound roll for this weapon, roll 2D6. If the result is equal to or greater than the target's Toughness, the attack successfully wounds.
Stikkbomb flinga	12"	Assault 2D6	3	0	1	-
Supa shoota	36"	Assault 3	6	-1	1	-
Tellyport mega-blasta	24"	Assault D3	8	-2	1	If a model suffers any unsaved wounds from this weapon and is not slain, roll a D6 at the end of the phase. If the result is greater than that model's Wounds characteristic, it is slain.
Wazbom mega-kannon	36"	Heavy D3	8	-3	D3	If you roll one or more hit rolls of 1, the bearer suffers a mortal wound after all of this weapon's shots have been resolved.

WARGEAR OPTIONS	• This model may replace both wazbom mega-kannons with two tellyport mega-blastas. • This model may take two supa shootas. • This model may replace its stikkbomb flinga with a kustom force field.

ABILITIES

Airborne: This model cannot charge, can only be charged by units that can **FLY**, and can only attack or be attacked in the Fight phase by units that can **FLY**.

Hard to Hit: Your opponent must subtract 1 from hit rolls for attacks that target this model in the Shooting phase.

Supersonic: Each time this model moves, first pivot it on the spot up to 90° (this does not contribute to how far the model moves), and then move the model straight forwards. Note that it cannot pivot again after the initial pivot. When this model Advances, increase its Move characteristic by 20" until the end of the phase – do not roll a dice.

Mekbrain-enhanced Weapon-sights: A Wazbom Blastajet does not suffer the penalty to hit rolls for moving and firing Heavy weapons. In addition, this model can choose a single enemy unit each Shooting phase – add 1 to all hit rolls for attacks made against that unit with this model's smasha gun.

Kustom Force Field: If this model is armed with a kustom force field, any friendly <ORK> units that are entirely within 9" have a 5+ invulnerable save against ranged weapons.

Crash and Burn: If this model is reduced to 0 wounds, roll a D6 before removing it from the battlefield. On a 6 it crashes and explodes, and each unit within 6" suffers D3 mortal wounds.

FACTION KEYWORDS	ORK, <CLAN>
KEYWORDS	VEHICLE, FLY, WAZBOM BLASTAJET

WARBIKERS

NAME	M	WS	BS	S	T	W	A	Ld	Sv
Warbiker	14"	3+	5+	4	5	2	2	6	4+
Boss Nob	14"	3+	5+	5	5	3	3	7	4+

This unit contains 3 Warbikers. It can include up to 3 additional Warbikers (**Power Rating +4**), up to 6 additional Warbikers (**Power Rating +8**) or up to 9 additional Warbikers (**Power Rating +12**). A Boss Nob can take the place of one Warbiker. Each model is armed with a slugga, a choppa and stikkbombs, and rides a warbike equipped with two dakkaguns.

WEAPON	RANGE	TYPE	S	AP	D	ABILITIES
Dakkagun	18"	Assault 3	5	0	1	-
Slugga	12"	Pistol 1	4	0	1	-
Choppa	Melee	Melee	User	0	1	Each time the bearer fights, it can make 1 additional attack with this weapon.
Stikkbomb	6"	Grenade D6	3	0	1	

WARGEAR OPTIONS	• The Boss Nob may replace his choppa with one item from the *Choppy Weapons* list.
ABILITIES	'Ere We Go, Mob Rule (pg 10)
FACTION KEYWORDS	ORK, <CLAN>
KEYWORDS	BIKER, WARBIKERS

Ork Warbikers roar into battle at reckless speed, filling the air with a murderous storm of bullets from their blazing dakkaguns.

⚡ 4 POWER — WARTRAKKS

NAME	M	WS	BS	S	T	W	A	Ld	Sv
Wartrakk	12"	3+	5+	4	5	6	4	6	4+

A unit of Wartrakks consists of a single model. It can include up to 2 additional Wartrakks (**Power Rating +6**) or up to 4 additional Wartrakks (**Power Rating +12**). Each Wartrakk is equipped with a twin big shoota.

WEAPON	RANGE	TYPE	S	AP	D	ABILITIES
Twin big shoota	36"	Assault 6	5	0	1	-
Rack of rokkits	24"	Assault 2	8	-2	3	-

WARGEAR OPTIONS	• Any model may replace its twin big shoota with a rack of rokkits.
ABILITIES	'Ere We Go, Mob Rule (pg 10) **Outriders:** During deployment, you can set up a unit of Wartrakks on the army's flanks instead of placing it on the battlefield. At the end of any of your Movement phases, the Wartrakks can race in to encircle the foe – set them up so that each model is touching a battlefield edge and is more than 9" away from any enemy models.
FACTION KEYWORDS	ORK, <CLAN>
KEYWORDS	VEHICLE, WARTRAKKS

⚡ 4 POWER — SKORCHAS

NAME	M	WS	BS	S	T	W	A	Ld	Sv
Skorcha	12"	3+	5+	4	5	6	4	6	4+

A unit of Skorchas consists of a single model. It can include up to 2 additional Skorchas (**Power Rating +6**) or up to 4 additional Skorchas (**Power Rating +12**). Each Skorcha is equipped with a skorcha.

WEAPON	RANGE	TYPE	S	AP	D	ABILITIES
Skorcha	8"	Assault D6	5	-1	1	This weapon automatically hits its target.

ABILITIES	'Ere We Go, Mob Rule (pg 10) **Outriders:** During deployment, you can set up a unit of Skorchas on the army's flanks instead of placing it on the battlefield. At the end of any of your Movement phases the Skorchas can race in to encircle the foe – set them up so that each model is touching a battlefield edge and is more than 9" away from any enemy models.
FACTION KEYWORDS	ORK, <CLAN>
KEYWORDS	VEHICLE, SKORCHA

⚡ 4 POWER — WARBUGGIES

NAME	M	WS	BS	S	T	W	A	Ld	Sv
Warbuggy	14"	3+	5+	4	5	5	4	6	4+

A unit of Warbuggies consists of a single model. It can include up to 2 additional Warbuggies (**Power Rating +6**), or up to 4 additional Warbuggies (**Power Rating +12**). Each Warbuggy is equipped with a twin big shoota.

WEAPON	RANGE	TYPE	S	AP	D	ABILITIES
Twin big shoota	36"	Assault 6	5	0	1	-
Rack of rokkits	24"	Assault 2	8	-2	3	-

WARGEAR OPTIONS	• Any model may replace its twin big shoota with a rack of rokkits.
ABILITIES	'Ere We Go, Mob Rule (pg 10) **Outriders:** During deployment, you can set up a unit of Warbuggies on the army's flanks instead of placing it on the battlefield. At the end of any of your Movement phases, the Warbuggies can race in to encircle the foe – set them up so that each model is touching a battlefield edge and is more than 9" away from any enemy models.
FACTION KEYWORDS	ORK, <CLAN>
KEYWORDS	VEHICLE, WARBUGGIES

BIG GUNZ

POWER

NAME	M	WS	BS	S	T	W	A	Ld	Sv
Big Gun	3"	6+	4+	3	5	3	1	6	5+
Grot Gunner	5"	5+	4+	2	2	1	1	4	6+

This unit contains 1 Big Gun accompanied by 2 Grot Gunners. It can include up to 5 additional Big Gunz, each of which is accompanied by 2 Grot Gunners (**Power Rating +1 per Big Gun**). Each Big Gun is equipped with a kannon, a lobba or a zzap gun.

WEAPON	RANGE	TYPE	S	AP	D	ABILITIES
Kannon	When attacking with this weapon, choose one of the profiles below.					
- Frag	36"	Heavy D6	4	0	1	-
- Shell	36"	Heavy 1	8	-2	D6	-
Lobba	48"	Heavy D6	5	0	1	This weapon can target units that are not visible to the bearer.
Zzap gun	36"	Heavy 1	2D6	-3	3	Before firing this weapon, roll to determine the Strength of the shot. If the result is 11+, do not make a wound roll – instead, if the attack hits it causes 3 mortal wounds. The bearer then suffers a mortal wound.

ABILITIES	**Grot Krew:** A unit of Big Gunz and its accompanying Grot Gunners must be deployed with each model within 3" of at least one other model from their unit. From that point on, each Big Gun and each 2-model group of Grot Gunners acts as a single unit. **Take Cover:** Grot Gunners can only be targeted in the Shooting phase if they are the closest enemy unit.	**Artillery:** A Big Gun can only fire its ranged weapon if a friendly <CLAN> Grot Gunner unit is within 3". A single Grot Gunner cannot operate multiple Big Gunz in this way in a single turn. If all of the Grot Gunners within 6" of a Big Gun are slain, it immediately shuts down and is removed from play.
FACTION KEYWORDS	ORK, <CLAN>	
KEYWORDS (BIG GUNZ)	VEHICLE, ARTILLERY, BIG GUNZ	
KEYWORDS (GROT GUNNERS)	INFANTRY, GRETCHIN, GROT GUNNERS	

Mek Gunz are mobile artillery platforms that bear a variety of lethal yet unpredictable weapons.

MEK GUNZ

3 POWER

NAME	M	WS	BS	S	T	W	A	Ld	Sv
Mek Gun	3"	6+	4+	3	5	6	1	6	5+
Grot Gunner	5"	5+	4+	2	2	1	1	4	6+

This unit contains 1 Mek Gun and 5 Grot Gunners. It can include up to 5 additional Mek Gunz, each of which is accompanied by 5 Grot Gunners (**Power Rating +2 per Mek Gun**). Each Mek Gun is equipped with a bubblechukka, a kustom mega-kannon, a smasha gun or a traktor kannon.

WEAPON	RANGE	TYPE	S	AP	D	ABILITIES
Bubblechukka	36"	Heavy *	*	*	*	Roll 4 dice each time you fire this weapon, then take it in turns with your opponent (starting with you) to allocate one value at a time to its Strength, AP, Damage and number of attacks. Note that the dice assigned to AP is a negative number (e.g. a 3 is assigned to AP, so the shot is resolved at AP -3).
Kustom mega-kannon	36"	Heavy D6	8	-3	D3	If you roll one or more hit rolls of 1 for this weapon, the bearer suffers a mortal wound after all of this weapon's shots have been resolved.
Smasha gun	36"	Heavy 1	*	-4	D6	Instead of making a wound roll for this weapon, roll 2D6. If the result is equal to or greater than the target's Toughness, the attack successfully wounds.
Traktor kannon	36"	Heavy 1	8	-2	D3	This weapon's Damage increases to D6 against units that can **FLY**. If a traktor kannon destroys a **VEHICLE** that can **FLY**, the model automatically crashes and burns (or its equivalent) – do not roll a dice.

ABILITIES	
Grot Krew: A unit of Mek Gunz and its Grot Gunners must be deployed as a single group with each model within 3" of at least one other model from their unit. From that point on each Mek Gun and each 5-model group of Grot Gunners acts as a single unit.	**Artillery:** A Mek Gun can only fire its ranged weapon if a friendly **<CLAN>** Grot Gunner unit is within 3". A single Grot Gunner cannot operate multiple Mek Gunz in this way in a single turn. If all of the Grot Gunners within 6" of a Mek Gun are slain, it immediately shuts down and is removed from play.
Take Cover: Grot Gunners can only be targeted in the Shooting phase if they are the closest enemy unit.	

FACTION KEYWORDS	ORK, **<CLAN>**
KEYWORDS (MEK GUNZ)	**VEHICLE, ARTILLERY, MEK GUNZ**
KEYWORDS (GROT GUNNERS)	**INFANTRY, GRETCHIN, GROT GUNNERS**

BATTLEWAGON

DAMAGE
Some of this model's characteristics change as it suffers damage, as shown below:

REMAINING W	M	S	A
8-16+	12"	8	6
4-7	9"	6	D6
1-3	6"	4	D3

NAME	M	WS	BS	S	T	W	A	Ld	Sv
Battlewagon	*	5+	5+	*	7	16	*	7	4+

A Battlewagon is a single model.

WEAPON	RANGE	TYPE	S	AP	D	ABILITIES
Big shoota	36"	Assault 3	5	0	1	-
Kannon	When attacking with this weapon, choose one of the profiles below.					
- Frag	36"	Heavy D6	4	0	1	-
- Shell	36"	Heavy 1	8	-2	D6	-
Killkannon	24"	Heavy D6	7	-2	2	-
Lobba	48"	Heavy D6	5	0	1	This weapon can target units that are not visible to the bearer.
Rokkit launcha	24"	Assault 1	8	-2	3	-
Zzap gun	36"	Heavy 1	2D6	-3	3	Before firing this weapon, roll to determine the Strength of the shot. If the result is 11+, do not make a wound roll – instead, if the attack hits it causes 3 mortal wounds. The bearer then suffers a mortal wound.
Deff rolla	Melee	Melee	User	-2	1	Add 3 to hit rolls made for this weapon.
Grabbin' klaw	Melee	Melee	User	-3	D3	The bearer can only make a single attack with this weapon each time it fights.
Wreckin' ball	Melee	Melee	+1	-1	1	The bearer can only make 3 attacks with this weapon each time it fights.

WARGEAR OPTIONS	
	• This model may take a killkannon. • This model may take a kannon, lobba or zzap gun. • This model may take up to four big shootas and/or rokkit launchas. • This model may take a deff rolla, 'ard case, grabbin' klaw and/or a wreckin' ball.

ABILITIES	
	Explodes: If this model is reduced to 0 wounds, roll a D6 before removing it from the battlefield and before any embarked models disembark. On a 6 it explodes, and each unit within 6" suffers D6 mortal wounds. **'Ard Case:** A Battlewagon with an 'ard case has a Toughness characteristic of 8, but loses the Open-topped ability. **Mobile Fortress:** A Battlewagon ignores the penalty for moving and firing Heavy weapons. **Open-topped:** Models embarked on this model can attack in their Shooting phase. Measure the range and draw line of sight from any point on this model. When they do so, any restrictions or modifiers that apply to this model also apply to its passengers; for example, the passengers cannot shoot if this model has Fallen Back in the same turn, cannot shoot (except with Pistols) if this model is within 1" of an enemy unit, and so on.

TRANSPORT	A Battlewagon can transport 20 **Ork Infantry** models. Each **Mega Armour** or **Jump Pack** model takes the space of two other models. A Battlewagon equipped with a killkannon can only transport 12 models.
FACTION KEYWORDS	ORK, <CLAN>
KEYWORDS	VEHICLE, TRANSPORT, BATTLEWAGON

DEFF DREADS

NAME	M	WS	BS	S	T	W	A	Ld	Sv
Deff Dread	6"	3+	5+	5	7	8	2	7	3+

This unit contains one Deff Dread. It can include 1 additional Deff Dread (**Power Rating +7**), or 2 additional Deff Dreads (**Power Rating +14**). Each Deff Dread is equipped with two big shootas and two dread klaws.

WEAPON	RANGE	TYPE	S	AP	D	ABILITIES
Big shoota	36"	Assault 3	5	0	1	-
Kustom mega-blasta	24"	Assault 1	8	-3	D3	On a hit roll of 1, the bearer suffers a mortal wound.
Rokkit launcha	24"	Assault 1	8	-2	3	-
Skorcha	8"	Assault D6	5	-1	1	This weapon automatically hits its target.
Dread klaw	Melee	Melee	x2	-3	3	Each time the bearer fights, it can make 1 additional attack with each dread klaw it is equipped with.

WARGEAR OPTIONS	• Any model may replace any of its big shootas with a rokkit launcha, kustom mega-blasta, skorcha or dread klaw.
ABILITIES	'Ere We Go (pg 10) **Dread Mob:** A unit of Deff Dreads must be deployed as a single group, with each model within 6" of at least one other model from their unit. From that point on, each Deff Dread acts as a single unit. **Explodes:** If a model in this unit is reduced to 0 wounds, roll a D6 before removing the model from the battlefield. On a 6 it explodes, and each unit within 3" suffers D3 mortal wounds.
FACTION KEYWORDS	ORK, \<CLAN\>
KEYWORDS	VEHICLE, DEFF DREADS

KILLA KANS

NAME	M	WS	BS	S	T	W	A	Ld	Sv
Killa Kans	6"	5+	4+	5	5	5	3	6	3+

This unit contains 1 Killa Kan. It can include up to 2 additional Killa Kans (**Power Rating +6**), or up to 5 additional Killa Kans (**Power Rating +15**). Each Killa Kan is equipped with a big shoota and a kan klaw.

WEAPON	RANGE	TYPE	S	AP	D	ABILITIES
Big shoota	36"	Assault 3	5	0	1	-
Grotzooka	18"	Heavy 2D3	6	0	1	-
Kustom mega-blasta	24"	Assault 1	8	-3	D3	On a hit roll of 1, the bearer suffers a mortal wound.
Rokkit launcha	24"	Assault 1	8	-2	3	-
Skorcha	8"	Assault D6	5	-1	1	This weapon automatically hits its target.
Kan klaw	Melee	Melee	+3	-3	3	-

WARGEAR OPTIONS	• Any model may replace its big shoota with a rokkit launcha, kustom mega-blasta, skorcha or grotzooka.
ABILITIES	**Explodes:** If a model in this unit is reduced to 0 wounds, roll a D6 before removing the model from the battlefield. On a 6 it explodes, and each unit within 3" suffers 1 mortal wound. **Scrag 'Em:** While a unit of Killa Kans contains 3 or more models, add 1 to their Attacks characteristic.
FACTION KEYWORDS	ORK, \<CLAN\>
KEYWORDS	VEHICLE, KILLA KANS

MORKANAUT

18 POWER

DAMAGE

Some of this model's characteristics change as it suffers damage, as shown below:

REMAINING W	M	WS	A
10-18+	8"	3+	4
5-9	6"	4+	3
1-4	4"	5+	2

NAME	M	WS	BS	S	T	W	A	Ld	Sv
Morkanaut	*	*	5+	8	8	18	*	7	3+

A Morkanaut is a single model equipped with a kustom mega-blasta, two twin big shootas, two rokkit launchas, a kustom mega-kannon and a klaw of Mork (or possibly Gork).

WEAPON	RANGE	TYPE	S	AP	D	ABILITIES
Kustom mega-blasta	24"	Assault 1	8	-3	D3	On a hit roll of 1, the bearer suffers a mortal wound.
Kustom mega-kannon	36"	Heavy D6	8	-3	D3	If you roll one or more hit rolls of 1, the bearer suffers a mortal wound after all of this weapon's shots have been resolved.
Rokkit launcha	24"	Assault 1	8	-2	3	-
Twin big shoota	36"	Assault 6	5	0	1	-
Klaw of Gork (or possibly Mork)		When attacking with this weapon, choose one of the profiles below.				
- Crush	Melee	Melee	x2	-4	D6	-
- Smash	Melee	Melee	User	-2	2	Make 3 hit rolls for each attack made with this weapon, instead of 1.

WARGEAR	• This model may take a kustom force field.

ABILITIES

'Ere We Go (pg 10)

Explodes: If this model is reduced to 0 wounds, roll a D6 before removing it from the battlefield and before any embarked models disembark. On a 6 it explodes, and each unit within 9" suffers D6 mortal wounds.

Kustom Force Field: If this model is equipped with a kustom force field, friendly <ORK> units that are entirely within 9" have a 5+ invulnerable save against ranged weapons.

Big 'n' Stompy: This model can Fall Back in your Movement phase and still shoot and/or charge during its turn. In addition, it can move and fire Heavy weapons without suffering the penalty to its hit rolls.

This model only gains a bonus to its saving throws for being in cover if at least half of the model is obscured from the firer.

TRANSPORT	This model can transport six ORK INFANTRY models. Each MEGA ARMOUR or JUMP PACK model takes the space of two other models.
FACTION KEYWORDS	ORK, <CLAN>
KEYWORDS	VEHICLE, TRANSPORT, MORKANAUT

Gorkanauts are colossal Ork-shaped war machines that bristle with shootas and rokkit launchas.

38

GORKANAUT

19 POWER

NAME	M	WS	BS	S	T	W	A	Ld	Sv
Gorkanaut	✱	✱	5+	8	8	18	✱	7	3+

DAMAGE

Some of this model's characteristics change as it suffers damage, as shown below:

REMAINING W	M	WS	A
10-18+	8"	3+	6
5-9	6"	4+	5
1-4	4"	5+	4

A Gorkanaut is a single model equipped with a deffstorm mega-shoota, two twin big shootas, two rokkit launchas, a skorcha and a klaw of Gork (or possibly Mork).

WEAPON	RANGE	TYPE	S	AP	D	ABILITIES
Deffstorm mega-shoota	36"	Heavy 3D6	6	-1	1	-
Rokkit launcha	24"	Assault 1	8	-2	3	-
Skorcha	8"	Assault D6	5	-1	1	This weapon automatically hits its target.
Twin big shoota	36"	Assault 6	5	0	1	-
Klaw of Gork (or possibly Mork)		When attacking with this weapon, choose one of the profiles below.				
- Crush	Melee	Melee	x2	-4	D6	-
- Smash	Melee	Melee	User	-2	2	Make 3 hit rolls for each attack made with this weapon, instead of 1.

ABILITIES	**'Ere We Go** (pg 10) **Explodes:** If a Gorkanaut is reduced to 0 wounds, roll a D6 before removing the model from the battlefield and before any embarked models disembark. On a 6 it explodes, and each unit within 9" suffers D6 mortal wounds.	**Big 'n' Stompy:** This model can Fall Back in the Movement phase and still shoot and/or charge that turn, and does not suffer the penalty for moving and firing Heavy weapons. This model only gains a bonus to its saving throws for being in cover if at least half of the model is obscured from the firer.
TRANSPORT	A Gorkanaut can transport six **Ork Infantry** models. Each **Mega Armour** or **Jump Pack** model takes the space of two other models.	
FACTION KEYWORDS	**Ork, <Clan>**	
KEYWORDS	**Vehicle, Transport, Gorkanaut**	

LOOTAS

8 POWER

NAME	M	WS	BS	S	T	W	A	Ld	Sv
Loota	5"	3+	5+	4	4	1	2	6	6+
Spanner	5"	3+	5+	4	4	1	2	6	6+

This unit contains 5 Lootas. It can include up to 5 additional Lootas (**Power Rating +4**) or up to 10 additional Lootas (**Power Rating +8**). Up to 3 Spanners can each take the place of a Loota.
- Each Loota is armed with a deffgun and stikkbombs.
- Each Spanner is armed with a slugga, choppa and stikkbombs.

WEAPON	RANGE	TYPE	S	AP	D	ABILITIES
Deffgun	48"	Heavy D3	7	-1	2	When a unit fires its deffguns, roll once for the number of attacks and use this for all deffguns fired by the unit in this phase.
Slugga	12"	Pistol 1	4	0	1	-
Choppa	Melee	Melee	User	0	1	Each time the bearer fights, it can make 1 additional attack with this weapon.
Killsaw	Melee	Melee	x2	-4	2	When attacking with this weapon, you must subtract 1 from the hit roll.
Stikkbomb	6"	Grenade D6	3	0	1	-

WARGEAR OPTIONS	• Any Spanner may replace his choppa with a killsaw. • Any Spanner may replace his slugga with one item from the *Souped-up Weapons* list.
ABILITIES	**'Ere We Go, Mob Rule** (pg 10) **Mekaniak:** At the end of your Movement phase, a Spanner can repair a single friendly **<Clan> Vehicle** (other than models that can **Fly**) within 1". That model regains 1 wound lost earlier in the battle. A vehicle can only be repaired once each turn.
FACTION KEYWORDS	**Ork, <Clan>**
KEYWORDS	**Infantry, Lootas**

FLASH GITZ

NAME	M	WS	BS	S	T	W	A	Ld	Sv
Flash Git	5"	3+	4+	5	4	2	3	6	6+
Kaptin	5"	3+	4+	5	4	2	3	6	6+
Ammo Runt	5"	5+	4+	2	2	1	1	4	6+

This unit contains 4 Flash Gitz and 1 Kaptin. It can include up to 5 additional Flash Gitz (**Power Rating +6**). Any Flash Git or Kaptin may be accompanied by an Ammo Runt.
• Each Flash Git and the Kaptin is armed with a snazzgun and stikkbombs.

WEAPON	RANGE	TYPE	S	AP	D	ABILITIES
Slugga	12"	Pistol 1	4	0	1	-
Snazzgun	24"	Heavy 3	5	-2	1	-
Choppa	Melee	Melee	User	0	1	Each time the bearer fights, it can make 1 additional attack with this weapon.
Stikkbomb	6"	Grenade D3	3	0	1	-

WARGEAR OPTIONS	• The Kaptin may take a choppa or a slugga.

ABILITIES

'Ere We Go, Mob Rule (pg 10)

Ammo Runt: Each time this unit shoots, when making hit rolls for it you can re-roll one dice for each Ammo Runt accompanying them.

When rolling to wound this unit, use the Flash Gitz' Toughness (while they are on the battlefield). The death of an Ammo Runt is ignored for the purposes of morale.

Gun-crazy Showoffs: After this unit has shot in the Shooting phase, roll a D6. On a 6, all models in the unit must immediately shoot again, but can only target the nearest enemy unit.

FACTION KEYWORDS	ORK
KEYWORDS (FLASH GITZ)	INFANTRY, FLASH GITZ
KEYWORDS (AMMO RUNTS)	INFANTRY, GRETCHIN, AMMO RUNTS

Flash Gitz are rich, arrogant Ork mercenaries who delight in blasting enemies to glowing embers with their custom-built snazzguns.

STOMPA

DAMAGE

Some of this model's characteristics change as it suffers damage, as shown below:

REMAINING W	M	WS	S
31-40+	12"	3+	10
21-30	9"	4+	9
11-20	6"	5+	8
1-10	4"	6+	7

NAME	M	WS	BS	S	T	W	A	Ld	Sv
Stompa	*	*	5+	*	8	40	4	8	3+

A Stompa is a single model equipped with a deffkannon, a supa-gatler, three big shootas, a twin big shoota, three supa-rokkits, a skorcha and a mega-choppa.

WEAPON	RANGE	TYPE	S	AP	D	ABILITIES
Big shoota	36"	Assault 3	5	0	1	-
Deffkannon	72"	Heavy D6	10	-4	D6	When attacking a unit with 10 or more models, this weapon's Type changes to Heavy 2D6.
Skorcha	8"	Assault D6	5	-1	1	This weapon automatically hits its target.
Supa-gatler	48"	Heavy 2D6	7	-2	1	See Psycho-Dakka-Blasta!, below
Supa-rokkit	100"	Heavy D3	8	-2	D6	Only one supa-rokkit can be fired by the bearer a turn, and each can only be fired once per battle.
Twin big shoota	36"	Assault 6	5	0	1	-
Mega-choppa	When attacking with this weapon, choose one of the profiles below.					
- Smash	Melee	Melee	x2	-5	6	-
- Slash	Melee	Melee	User	-2	D3	Make 3 hit rolls for each attack made with this weapon, instead of 1.

WARGEAR OPTIONS	• This model may take up to two additional super-rokkits.

ABILITIES	'Ere We Go (pg 10) **Explodes:** If this model is reduced to 0 wounds, roll a D6 before removing it from the battlefield and before any embarked models disembark. On a 6 it explodes, and each unit within 2D6" suffers D6 mortal wounds. **Bigger 'n' Stompier:** This model can Fall Back in the Movement phase and still shoot and/or charge that turn. When a Stompa Falls Backs, it can move over enemy **INFANTRY** models, though at the end of its move it must be more than 1" from any enemy models. A Stompa does not suffer the penalty for moving and firing Heavy weapons. This model only gains a bonus to its saving throws for being in cover if at least half of the model is obscured from the firer.	**Psycho-Dakka-Blasta!:** A Stompa can fire its supa-gatler more than once in your Shooting phase. To fire the supa-gatler a second time, roll a D6; on a 2+, you can make the attack. On a 1, the weapon's ammo has been expended and it can no longer be used for the rest of the battle. To fire the supa-gatler a third time in your Shooting phase, roll a D6; on a 5+, you can make the attack. On a 4 or less, the weapon's ammo has been expended, and it can no longer be used for the rest of the battle. **Effigy:** **ORK** units within 6" of a friendly Stompa can re-roll failed Morale tests.

TRANSPORT	A Stompa can transport 20 **ORK INFANTRY** models. Each **MEGA ARMOUR** or **JUMP PACK** model takes the space of 2 other models.

FACTION KEYWORDS	ORK, <CLAN>

KEYWORDS	VEHICLE, TRANSPORT, TITANIC, STOMPA

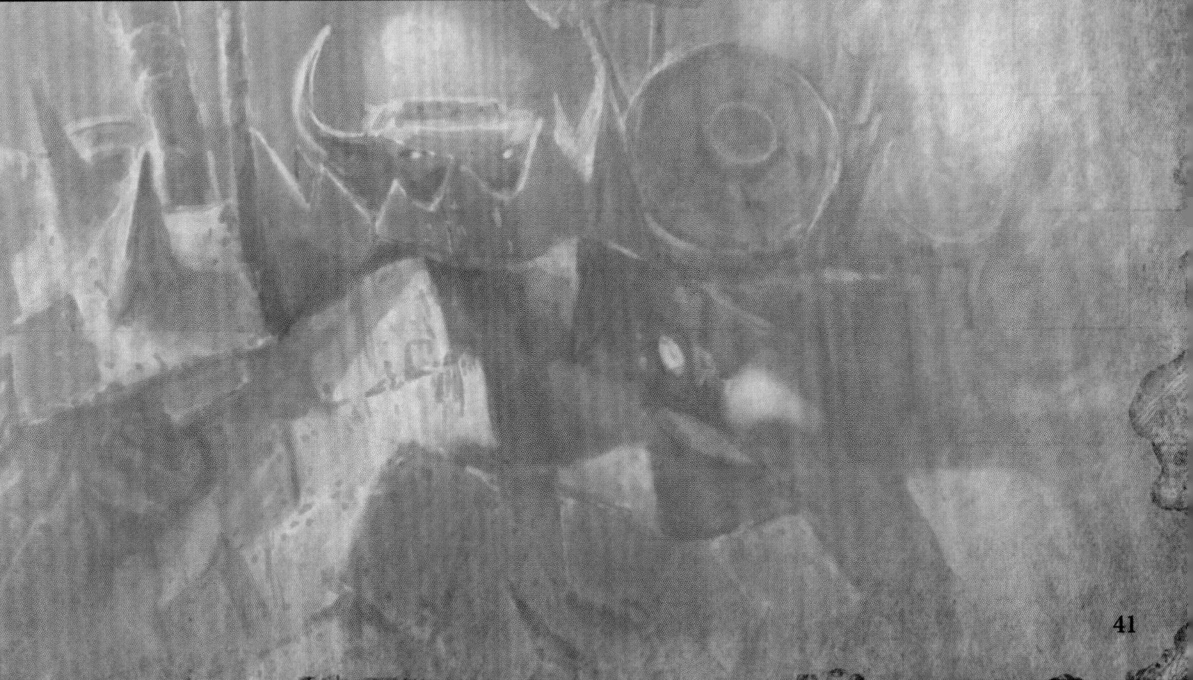

T'AU EMPIRE

The T'au Empire is a dynamic rising force in the galaxy, as yet unburdened by the bloody failures of a long history. United by their shared vision of the Greater Good, the T'au strive to bring enlightenment to other races, even if they must do so at the barrel of a gun.

With blistering speed, the T'au offensive carves deep into enemy ranks. Their sleek aircraft dominate the skies, launching volleys of missiles and pinpoint bomb strikes that cripple key defences with unerring precision. Pathfinder Teams emerge from cover, designating high-profile targets with markerlights and coordinating the ground assault with an artist's finesse. Under the cover of artillery barrages from Broadside Battlesuits and towering walkers, ranks of Fire Warriors advance, laying down a fusillade of punishing pulse fire that burns through armour plating with contemptuous ease. Standing tall upon their hover drone, a hallowed Ethereal extols their warriors to ever greater acts of heroism, their passionate oratory ringing clear across the clamour of battle. Hearts singing with the righteous creed of the Greater Good, the T'au sweep aside all before them with the power of their superior technology.

The T'au have always been scientific innovators, but in the earliest days of their civilisation, this ingenuity was not tempered with caution or wisdom. The naive and short-tempered race almost wiped itself out in a brutal civil war, and were saved only by the arrival of the Ethereals. These mysterious beings united the T'au, giving them a glimpse of the true enlightenment that would follow if they put aside their petty differences and joined as one. Ever since that day, the Ethereals have held positions of absolute power amongst their species; none know the secrets of their unquestioned authority, but the presence of a single such figure inspires a reverence in the hearts of T'au that can turn the tide of a war.

In the centuries since the Ethereals' emergence, the T'au have undergone a shockingly rapid advancement. Simmering resentments and prejudices were put aside as the entire race was divided into a rigid social structure of castes, each with their own strictly defined role. The Fire caste would be trained from birth in the art of combat, and tasked with the subjugation of those who resisted the Greater Good. The bleeding-edge technology that would be utilised by these warriors, not to mention the food and resources required to fuel the expansion of the T'au Empire, would be provided by the Earth caste, while the soldiers of the Air caste would be responsible for transporting their land-bound kin across the skies and stars. All the while, the politicians, bureaucrats and diplomats of the Water caste would ensure that the civic structure of the T'au Empire ran smoothly, handling the intricacies of trade and government while at the same time negotiating the integration of defeated alien cultures. Regardless of their given duty, these castes strove together for the Greater Good – the core philosophical concept of galactic unity that defines the T'au's every action.

Under the guidance of the Ethereal caste, the T'au began the millennia-long First Sphere Expansion, sowing the seeds of a nascent yet powerful empire. World after world was claimed, and though hostile lifeforms were encountered often, none could stand in the face of their ingenious and implacable conquerors. These newly annexed regions of space were designated as *septs*, and took their names from the great sept worlds that were established as the cultural and military capitals of each sector. During these heady days of expansion, many uncultured alien races were brought into the light of reason. The insectoid Vespid and savage, cannibalistic Kroot were two such races encountered and assimilated into the T'au's unstoppable war machine. While the noble warriors of the Fire and Air castes fought and bled for each new conquest, the scientists and builders of the Earth caste invented ever more ingenious weapons of war for them to utilise in battle.

The Second and Third Sphere Expansions followed, and the territories of the T'au Empire grew at an exponential rate with each fresh campaign. All who would deny the truth of the Greater Good were smashed aside by the T'au way of war. The key tenets of this military doctrine, which had been refined over many centuries of rigorous training and brutal experience, are manoeuvrability and the precision strike. Stealth Battlesuits and Pathfinder Teams advance ahead of the main force, identifying key targets as they map out terrain and fortifications. Only when a battle plan has been thoroughly studied and ratified are the T'au forces unleashed. Sun Shark and Razorshark fighters dominate the skies, dismantling the enemy's air response before turning their guns on ground targets. Fire Warriors seize key positions in a blaze of pulse fire. Crisis Battlesuits and their larger Riptide and Ghostkeel cousins provide the deathblow, their weapon arrays pouring streams of cannon fire or barrages of micro-missiles into the enemy as they are borne to advantageous positions by repulsor jets.

For every possible enemy response, the Earth caste has created a technological counter. Battlesuits of all description employ a dizzying variety of long-range and short-range munitions, and even the T'au's defensive emplacements can be moved at a moment's notice; no sooner does the ebb and flow of battle rearrange the front line than a Tidewall Gunrig's engines fire up, lifting the railgun platform across the battlefield to redeploy in a key tactical location. It is precisely this adaptability and cunning that has enabled the T'au to conquer a vast swathe of the galaxy.

With each leap forward, the Empire encounters new and ever deadlier threats. The belligerent Orks are always ready for war, and the bio-ships of the Tyranids drift forth from the depths of space, ravening for new worlds to devour. Around the war-torn Damocles Gulf, the stubborn Imperium of Man continues to hurl their seemingly numberless regiments and fleets into battle, uncaring of the horrific losses their vengeful crusades have wrought. And in the darkness of space there are even greater horrors, beings of infinite malice whose hungry eyes fall upon the shining sept worlds of the T'au. Despite the galaxy's many perils, the warriors of the Empire fight on, emboldened by the knowledge that they alone hold the key to unity and peace amongst the stars. All must allow the light of that truth into their hearts, or else be cleansed in the fires of war.

'Let none doubt that the T'au Empire will bring unity to all – let none doubt that now is our time. Forward, for the Greater Good!'

- Aun'Va, Ethereal Supreme, addressing the Fire caste cadres from atop the ruins of the Agrellan Hive

THE FIRE CASTE

Driven to self-improvement and mastery of form, warriors of the Fire caste spend their entire lives either preparing for battle or fighting in the field. Theirs would be a thankless existence were it not for their utter belief in the Greater Good, and the unbreakable bonds of comradeship that exist within the cadres.

The warriors of the Fire caste form the backbone of the T'au's expansion armies. Descended from the savage tribes that once dominated the plains and grasslands of blessed T'au, they were the strongest and hardiest of their race even before the Ethereals set them upon their militaristic course. Over many centuries, eugenics programmes have pruned the weakest gene-strains from amongst their number, leaving only the fiercest and most strong-willed soldiers.

Whether encased in cutting-edge battlesuits or standing side by side in a pulse rifle gun-line, those of the Fire caste face the myriad threats and horrors of the galaxy with great bravery, trusting in the beneficence and wisdom of their spiritual leaders and the deadly power of their advanced weaponry. All are guided by the Code of Fire, a combat doctrine that extols the virtues of martial training and loyalty, and defines the T'au concept of total war fought with wisdom and ruthless precision. These traits are embodied by the heroic Commanders that lead the T'au contingents into battle. Armed with the latest weapons systems and battlesuits, T'au war leaders have earned their prestige through decades of battlefield experience. None amongst their ranks are privileged nobles who have earned their commission through wealth or fortunate bloodline. Every single Commander in the T'au Empire – even names as legendary as Puretide, Shadowsun and Farsight – started their military service in the ranks of the Fire Warriors.

The Fire Warriors are the most numerous amongst their caste, dutiful soldiers trained from birth in the military arts and guided by the Code of Fire. Honour, self-sacrifice and obedience – these are the traits by which the Fire Warriors define themselves. These soldiers would not hesitate to throw themselves into the jaws of death if such an act would benefit the Greater Good. Armed with devastating pulse weaponry that packs enough punch to pierce the ceramite plate of a Space Marine, and encased in suits of nanocrystalline armour with integrated comms and diagnostics, the Fire Warriors are amongst the best-equipped line infantry in the galaxy. Strike Teams pour beams of blue-white fire into the enemy ranks with expert precision, while the close-assault Breacher Teams repel heavily armoured foes with flesh-atomising volleys from their pulse blasters. The veteran warriors designated as Cadre Fireblades guide these devastating fusillades, directing and optimising fire patterns, and inspiring the ranks to new heights of heroism with their mere presence.

Fire Warriors are often deployed to key positions by lightning-fast TY7 Devilfish transports, which glide gracefully across the battlefield aloft the invisible energies of their repulsor engines. Swift and sure, these ubiquitous transports are beloved of the Fire caste, and their daring pilots are highly respected. Smaller TX4 Piranha skimmers support the advance of the Devilfish. Speeding through hails of enemy fire, too fast to draw a bead on, these versatile craft are quick to identify and eliminate key threats. Behind them glide Hammerhead Gunships, armed with heavy ion and rail cannons. These elegant and deadly craft, whose armaments can tear through inches-thick plate armour as if it were parchment, are the T'au's response to the massed tank formations favoured by the Imperium. Sky Ray Gunships lurk at the rear of the advance, their ordnance arrays ready to deliver precise bombardments on targets lit up by markerlight beams.

The T'au military's extensive use of drone technology provides further versatility and protection to its fire teams. The Earth caste has designed countless variations of these unmanned aerial vehicles, from simple gun platforms to Grav-inhibitor Drones that slow charging enemies to a crawl, rendering them easy targets for a pinpoint fusillade of pulse energy. While Drones can operate alone, they typically accompany squads of Fire Warriors into the field, providing indispensable tactical flexibility and fire support.

The T'au way of war calls for precise coordination between every single component of an army. The might of a Battlesuit assault is of no use if it is not supported by infantry and air elements, and even the most intricate plan may fall apart upon contact with the foe. It is the task of the Pathfinders to ensure this does not happen. These light infantry units operate ahead of the main T'au advance, laying down the foundations for the fire storm that will follow. Their task is not to engage the enemy head-on, but instead to optimise firing solutions and lay down drop-beacons and markerlights that will allow their comrades to fight at maximum efficiency. That is not to say that these honoured scouts are unable to take the fight to the enemy themselves; supported by the latest drone technology and armed with lightweight pulse carbines and precision rifles, the Pathfinders can strike vulnerable targets with deadly force.

Battlesuits are the pinnacle of T'au military technology. These devastating bipedal weapon platforms are piloted by fearless members of the Fire caste who leap into the fiercest firefights with guns blazing. In mere moments, their foes are obliterated in a hail of micro-missiles and plasma fire. The front-line XV8 Crisis Battlesuit is the most recognisable of these technological marvels, but the scientists of the Earth caste have created countless variations that provide the adaptability so vital to the T'au way of war. XV25 Stealth Battlesuits operate on the fringes of the battle, appearing as if out of nowhere as they cut their adaptive camo-fields before blasting the enemy apart with point-blank salvoes. From optimised firing positions, XV88 Broadsides lay down punishing barrages of artillery fire, and towering Riptide and Ghostkeel Battlesuits possess the firepower to wipe out entire squads of Space Marine Terminators or hordes of Tyranid bio-forms. Most fearful of all is the mighty KV128 Stormsurge, a titanic walking tank whose chassis carries a truly horrifying armament of rockets, missiles, flamers and pulse cannons. Rooting itself to the ground with powerful stabilising anchors, the Stormsurge unleashes a cataclysmic barrage of white-hot death that vaporises super-heavy tanks and colossal Titans alike.

THE FARSIGHT REBELLION

The legendary O'Shovah was once the favoured son of the T'au Empire. Known as Commander Farsight for his uncanny prescience upon the battlefield, O'Shovah was a peerless warrior and bold strategist whose mastery of the Mont'ka – the most aggressive form of T'au warfare – had earned his people many glorious victories. When the T'au's frontier holdings taken in the Second Sphere Expansion came under assault from the belligerent Imperium of Man, it was to O'Shovah that the Ethereal caste turned. His campaign across the Damocles Gulf was predictably successful. Yet, despite his many victories, Farsight was left troubled by the Ethereals' callous disregard for his soldiers' lives. Doubts entered his mind. The T'au'va taught that all life had value, and yet in this war against the Imperium, so many brave heroes had been thrown under the tracks of Imperial tanks, or forced to commit unspeakable acts in the name of the Greater Good. Worse was to come when he was forced to divert his forces to counter an imminent Ork assault

that would have undone all the gains his campaign had achieved. He cornered his foe on the world of Arthas Moloch, only to come under attack from strange creatures that poured into existence from breaches in the fabric of reality. The Ethereals accompanying Farsight on his expedition were slain in the ensuing carnage. Tradition dictated that O'Shovah return to the Empire in light of such an event, but for reasons that remain unknown to all but the enigmatic commander, he instead led his forces into exile. It was many years before the Ethereals discovered that, far from dying on Arthas Moloch, Farsight had instead founded his own splinter empire. To this day he rules over the Farsight Enclaves, his life extended by some unknown process. The Ethereal caste has since expunged all records of his manifold achievements, and assigned the revered Commander Shadowsun, O'Shovah's old comrade, the task of hunting the errant leader down.

T'AU EMPIRE ARMY LIST

This section contains all of the datasheets that you will need in order to fight battles with your T'au miniatures. Each datasheet includes the characteristics profiles of the unit it describes, as well as any wargear and special abilities it may have. Some rules are common to several T'au units, and are described on these pages and referenced on the datasheets.

KEYWORDS

Throughout this section you will come across a keyword that is within angular brackets, specifically <SEPT>. This is shorthand for a keyword of your own choosing, as described below.

<SEPTS>

All T'au belong to a sept world, or hail from the breakaway Farsight Enclaves.

Some datasheets specify what sept the unit is drawn from (e.g. Commander Shadowsun has the T'AU SEPT keyword, so is from the T'au sept, while Commander Farsight has the FARSIGHT ENCLAVES keyword, so is from the Farsight Enclaves). If a T'AU EMPIRE datasheet does not specify which sept it is drawn from, it will have the <SEPT> keyword. When you include such a unit in your army, you must nominate which sept that unit is from (or nominate that unit to be from the Farsight Enclaves). You then simply replace the <SEPT> keyword on that unit's datasheet with the name of your chosen sept, or the words 'Farsight Enclaves'. You can use any of the septs that you have read about, or make up your own.

For example, if you were to include a Cadre Fireblade in your army, and you decided they were from the Vior'la sept, their <SEPT> Faction keyword is changed to VIOR'LA SEPT and their 'Volley Fire' ability would then say 'Models in VIOR'LA SEPT units within 6" of any friendly VIOR'LA SEPT Cadre Fireblades may fire an extra shot with pulse pistols, pulse carbines and pulse rifles when shooting at a target within half the weapon's range.'

ABILITIES

The following ability is common to several T'au Empire units:

For the Greater Good

When an enemy unit declares a charge, a unit with this ability that is within 6" of one of the charging unit's targets may fire Overwatch as if they were also targeted. A unit that does so cannot fire Overwatch again in this turn.

MARKERLIGHTS

If a model (other than a VEHICLE) fires a markerlight, it cannot fire any other weapons in that phase. When a unit is hit by a markerlight, place a counter next to it for the remainder of the phase. The table below describes the benefits T'AU EMPIRE models have when shooting at a unit that has markerlight counters. All benefits are cumulative.

MARKERLIGHT TABLE	
MARKERLIGHTS	BENEFIT
1	You can re-roll hit rolls of 1 for T'AU EMPIRE models attacking this unit.
2	Destroyer and seeker missiles fired at this unit use the firing model's Ballistic Skill (and any modifiers) rather than only hitting on a 6.
3	T'AU EMPIRE models attacking this unit do not suffer the penalty for moving and firing Heavy weapons or Advancing and firing Assault weapons.
4	The target unit does not gain any bonus to its saving throws for being in cover.
5 or more	Add 1 to hit rolls for T'AU EMPIRE models attacking this unit.

WARGEAR

Many of the units you will find on the following pages reference one or both of the following wargear lists (e.g. Ranged Weapons). When this is the case, the unit may take any item from the appropriate list below. The rules for the items in these lists can be found in the appendix (pg 136-137).

RANGED WEAPONS

- Airbursting fragmentation projector
- Burst cannon
- Cyclic ion blaster
- Flamer
- Fusion blaster
- Missile pod
- Plasma rifle

SUPPORT SYSTEMS

- Advanced targeting system
- Counterfire defence system
- Drone controller
- Early warning override
- Multi-tracker
- Shield generator
- Stimulant injector
- Target lock
- Velocity tracker

COMMANDER

6 POWER

NAME	M	WS	BS	S	T	W	A	Ld	Sv
Commander	8"	3+	2+	5	5	6	4	9	3+

A Commander is a single model equipped with a burst cannon and a missile pod. It may be accompanied by up to 2 Tactical Drones (pg 69) **(Power Rating +1)**.

WEAPON	RANGE	TYPE	S	AP	D	ABILITIES
Burst cannon	18"	Assault 4	5	0	1	-
Missile pod	36"	Assault 2	7	-1	D3	-

WARGEAR OPTIONS	• This model may replace its burst cannon and missile pod with two items from the *Ranged Weapons* and/or *Support Systems* lists. • This model may also take two additional items from the *Ranged Weapons* and/or *Support Systems* lists.
ABILITIES	**For the Greater Good** (pg 48) **Master of War:** Once per battle, at the beginning of your turn, a single friendly **COMMANDER** can declare either Kauyon or Mont'ka. • **Kauyon:** Until the end of the turn, you can re-roll failed hit rolls for friendly <SEPT> units within 6", but these units cannot move for any reason. • **Mont'ka:** Friendly <SEPT> units within 6" can both Advance and shoot as if they hadn't moved this turn. **Manta Strike:** During deployment, you may set up a Commander in a Manta hold instead of placing them on the battlefield. At the end of any of your Movement phases, they can use a Manta strike to enter the fray – set them up anywhere on the battlefield that is more than 9" from any enemy models.
FACTION KEYWORDS	T'AU EMPIRE, <SEPT>
KEYWORDS	BATTLESUIT, CHARACTER, JET PACK, FLY, COMMANDER

COMMANDER
IN XV86 COLDSTAR BATTLESUIT

7 POWER

NAME	M	WS	BS	S	T	W	A	Ld	Sv
Commander in XV86 Coldstar Battlesuit	20"	3+	2+	5	5	6	4	9	3+

A Commander in XV86 Coldstar Battlesuit is a single model equipped with a high-output burst cannon and a missile pod. It may be accompanied by up to 2 Tactical Drones (pg 69) **(Power Rating +1)**.

WEAPON	RANGE	TYPE	S	AP	D	ABILITIES
High-output burst cannon	18"	Assault 8	5	0	1	-
Missile pod	36"	Assault 2	7	-1	D3	-

WARGEAR OPTIONS	• This model may take up to two items from the *Support Systems* list.
ABILITIES	**For the Greater Good** (pg 48) **Master of War:** Once per battle, at the beginning of your turn, a single friendly **COMMANDER** can declare either Kauyon or Mont'ka. • **Kauyon:** Until the end of the turn, you can re-roll failed hit rolls for friendly <SEPT> units within 6", but these units cannot move for any reason. • **Mont'ka:** Friendly <SEPT> units within 6" can both Advance and shoot as if they hadn't moved this turn. **Coldstar:** When this model Advances, add 20" to its Move characteristic for that Movement phase instead of rolling a D6. **Manta Strike:** During deployment, you may set up a Commander in XV86 Coldstar Battlesuit in a Manta hold instead of placing them on the battlefield. At the end of any of your Movement phases, they can use a Manta strike to enter the fray – set them up anywhere on the battlefield that is more than 9" from any enemy models.
FACTION KEYWORDS	T'AU EMPIRE, <SEPT>
KEYWORDS	BATTLESUIT, CHARACTER, JET PACK, FLY, COMMANDER

☠ 2 POWER — ETHEREAL

NAME	M	WS	BS	S	T	W	A	Ld	Sv
Ethereal	6"	3+	4+	3	3	4	3	9	5+

An Ethereal is a single model armed with an honour blade. It may be accompanied by up to 2 Tactical Drones (pg 69) (**Power Rating +1**).

WEAPON	RANGE	TYPE	S	AP	D	ABILITIES
Equalizers	Melee	Melee	User	-1	1	A model armed with equalizers increases its Attacks characteristic by 1.
Honour blade	Melee	Melee	+2	0	1	-

WARGEAR OPTIONS
- This model may replace its honour blade with equalizers.
- This model may take a hover drone, increasing its Move characteristic to 8" and giving it the **JET PACK** and **FLY** keywords (**Power Rating +1**).

ABILITIES

Failure Is Not An Option: Friendly T'AU EMPIRE units within 6" of an ETHEREAL may use the Ethereal's Leadership characteristic instead of their own when taking Morale tests.

Invocation of the Elements: In your Movement phase, an ETHEREAL may invoke one of the elemental powers below. All friendly T'AU EMPIRE INFANTRY and BATTLESUIT units within 6" of any ETHEREAL invoking an elemental power gain that power's benefit until the start of your next turn.

- **Calm of Tides:** Subtract 1 from any Morale tests made for affected units.
- **Storm of Fire:** You may re-roll hit rolls of 1 in the Shooting phase for affected units that remain stationary in the Movement phase.
- **Sense of Stone:** Whenever an affected unit suffers an unsaved wound, roll a D6. On a 6, that wound is ignored.
- **Zephyr's Grace:** You can re-roll the dice for affected units when they Advance.

FACTION KEYWORDS — T'AU EMPIRE, \<SEPT\>

KEYWORDS — CHARACTER, INFANTRY, ETHEREAL

☠ 2 POWER — CADRE FIREBLADE

NAME	M	WS	BS	S	T	W	A	Ld	Sv
Cadre Fireblade	6"	3+	2+	3	3	5	3	8	4+

A Cadre Fireblade is a single model armed with a markerlight, pulse rifle and photon grenades. It may be accompanied by up to 2 Tactical Drones (pg 69) (**Power Rating +1**).

WEAPON	RANGE	TYPE	S	AP	D	ABILITIES
Markerlight	36"	Heavy 1	-	-	-	*See Markerlights (pg 48)*
Pulse rifle	30"	Rapid Fire 1	5	0	1	-
Photon grenade	12"	Grenade D6	-	-	-	This weapon does not inflict any damage. Your opponent must subtract 1 from any hit rolls made for INFANTRY units that have suffered any hits from photon grenades until the end of the turn.

ABILITIES

For the Greater Good (pg 48)

Volley Fire: Models in \<SEPT\> units within 6" of any friendly \<SEPT\> Cadre Fireblades may fire an extra shot with pulse pistols, pulse carbines and pulse rifles when shooting at a target within half the weapon's range.

FACTION KEYWORDS — T'AU EMPIRE, \<SEPT\>

KEYWORDS — CHARACTER, INFANTRY, CADRE FIREBLADE

COMMANDER FARSIGHT

NAME	M	WS	BS	S	T	W	A	Ld	Sv
Commander Farsight	8"	2+	2+	5	5	6	4	9	3+

Commander Farsight is a single model equipped with a plasma rifle and the Dawn Blade. Only one of this model can be included in your army.

WEAPON	RANGE	TYPE	S	AP	D	ABILITIES
Plasma rifle	24"	Rapid Fire 1	6	-3	1	-
Dawn Blade	Melee	Melee	User	-4	D3	-

ABILITIES	
For the Greater Good (pg 48) **Master of War:** Once per battle, at the beginning of your turn, a single friendly **COMMANDER** can declare either Kauyon or Mont'ka. • **Kauyon:** Until the end of the turn, you can re-roll failed hit rolls for friendly **FARSIGHT ENCLAVES** units within 6", but these units cannot move for any reason. • **Mont'ka:** Friendly **FARSIGHT ENCLAVES** units within 6" can both Advance and shoot as if they hadn't moved this turn. **Genius of Mont'ka:** Once per battle, Commander Farsight can declare Mont'ka even if Kauyon or Mont'ka has already been declared. Mont'ka and Kauyon cannot both be declared in the same turn.	**Way of the Short Blade:** You can re-roll hit rolls of 1 for friendly **FARSIGHT ENCLAVES** units within 6" of Commander Farsight in the Fight phase (or any phase if the target is an **ORK** unit). **Shield Generator:** Commander Farsight has a 4+ invulnerable save. **Manta Strike:** During deployment, you may set up Commander Farsight in a Manta hold instead of placing him on the battlefield. At the end of any of your Movement phases, he may use a Manta strike to enter the fray – set him up anywhere on the battlefield that is more than 9" from any enemy models.

FACTION KEYWORDS	T'AU EMPIRE, FARSIGHT ENCLAVES
KEYWORDS	**BATTLESUIT, CHARACTER, COMMANDER, JET PACK, FLY, FARSIGHT**

A student of the legendary Puretide, Commander Farsight is a master of the war art known as Mont'ka – the Killing Blow.

COMMANDER SHADOWSUN

9 POWER

NAME	M	WS	BS	S	T	W	A	Ld	Sv
Commander Shadowsun	8"	3+	2+	4	4	5	4	9	3+
MV52 Shield Drone	8"	5+	5+	3	4	1	1	6	4+
MV62 Command-link Drone	8"	5+	5+	3	4	1	1	6	4+

Commander Shadowsun is a single model equipped with two fusion blasters. She is accompanied by up to 3 Command Drones: 1 MV62 Command-link Drone and up to 2 MV52 Shield Drones. Only one of this unit can be included in your army.

WEAPON	RANGE	TYPE	S	AP	D	ABILITIES
Fusion blaster	18"	Assault 1	8	-4	D6	If the target is within half range of this weapon, roll two dice when inflicting damage with it and discard the lowest result.

ABILITIES		
	For the Greater Good (pg 48)	**Defender of the Greater Good:** Roll a D6 each time Shadowsun loses a wound whilst she is within 3" of a unit of friendly XV25 Stealth Battlesuits. On a 2+, a model from that unit can intercept that hit – Shadowsun does not lose a wound but that unit suffers a mortal wound.
	Master of War: Once per battle, at the beginning of your turn, a single friendly **COMMANDER** can declare either Kauyon or Mont'ka.	
	• **Kauyon:** Until the end of the turn, you can re-roll failed hit rolls for friendly **T'AU EMPIRE** units within 6", but these units cannot move for any reason.	**Drone Support:** When Commander Shadowsun is set up on the battlefield, her accompanying Drones are set up in unit coherency with her. From that point onwards, the Drones are treated as a separate unit.
	• **Mont'ka:** Friendly **T'AU EMPIRE** units within 6" can both Advance and shoot as if they hadn't moved this turn.	**Saviour Protocols:** If a **DRONES** unit is within 3" of a friendly **T'AU EMPIRE INFANTRY** or **BATTLESUIT** unit, you can choose to allocate any wounds to the Drones instead of the target unit.
	Genius of Kauyon: Once per battle, Commander Shadowsun can declare Kauyon even if Kauyon or Mont'ka has already been declared. Mont'ka and Kauyon cannot both be declared in the same turn.	**MV52 Shield Generator:** MV52 Shield Drones have a 3+ invulnerable save.
	Camouflage Fields: Your opponent must subtract 1 from all hit rolls that target Commander Shadowsun or her Command Drones.	**Command-link:** If a friendly Command-link Drone is within 3" of Commander Shadowsun at the start of any of your Shooting phases, nominate a single **T'AU EMPIRE** unit within 12" of the Drone. You can re-roll hit rolls of 1 for that unit until the end of the phase.
	Infiltrator: During deployment, Commander Shadowsun can be set up anywhere on the battlefield that is not within your opponent's deployment zone and is more than 12" from any enemy unit.	
	XV22 Stealth Battlesuit: Commander Shadowsun has a 5+ invulnerable save.	

FACTION KEYWORDS	T'AU EMPIRE, T'AU SEPT
KEYWORDS (SHADOWSUN)	INFANTRY, BATTLESUIT, CHARACTER, COMMANDER, JET PACK, FLY, SHADOWSUN
KEYWORDS (COMMAND DRONES)	DRONE, FLY, COMMAND DRONES

AUN'SHI

4 POWER

NAME	M	WS	BS	S	T	W	A	Ld	Sv
Aun'Shi	6"	2+	4+	3	3	5	5	9	-

Aun'Shi is a single model armed with an honour blade. Only one of this model can be included in your army.

WEAPON	RANGE	TYPE	S	AP	D	ABILITIES
Honour blade	Melee	Melee	+2	0	1	-

ABILITIES

Failure Is Not An Option: Friendly T'au Empire units within 6" of an Ethereal may use the Ethereal's Leadership characteristic instead of their own when taking Morale tests.

Shield Generator: Aun'Shi has a 4+ invulnerable save.

Blademaster: At the beginning of each Fight phase, choose one of the following effects to last until the end of the phase:
- Aun'Shi's close combat attacks have AP -2.
- You may re-roll failed invulnerable saves for Aun'Shi.

Invocation of the Elements: In your Movement phase, Aun'Shi may invoke one of the elemental powers below. All T'au Empire Infantry and Battlesuit units within 6" of any Ethereal invoking an elemental power gain the relevant benefit until the start of your next turn.
- **Calm of Tides:** Subtract 1 from any Morale tests made for affected units.
- **Storm of Fire:** You may re-roll hit rolls of 1 in the Shooting phase for affected units that remain stationary in the Movement phase.
- **Sense of Stone:** Whenever an affected unit suffers an unsaved wound, roll a D6. On a 6, that wound is ignored.
- **Zephyr's Grace:** You can re-roll the dice for affected units when they Advance.

FACTION KEYWORDS	T'au Empire, Vior'la Sept

KEYWORDS	Character, Infantry, Ethereal, Aun'Shi

AUN'VA

4 POWER

NAME	M	WS	BS	S	T	W	A	Ld	Sv
Aun'Va	6"	6+	4+	2	3	6	1	9	5+
Ethereal Guard	6"	3+	3+	3	3	2	3	9	5+

This unit contains Aun'Va and two Ethereal Guards. The Ethereal Guards are each armed with an honour blade. Only one of this unit can be included in your army.

WEAPON	RANGE	TYPE	S	AP	D	ABILITIES
Honour blade	Melee	Melee	+2	0	1	-

ABILITIES

Failure Is Not An Option: Friendly T'au Empire units within 6" of an Ethereal may use the Ethereal's Leadership characteristic instead of their own when taking Morale tests.

Paradox of Duality: When this unit is attacked during the Shooting phase, it may add, rather than subtract, the AP of the attack to its Save characteristic (e.g. an AP -1 attack would provide a +1 bonus to its saves).

Supreme Loyalty: Whilst Aun'Va is on the battlefield, you may re-roll Morale tests for all friendly T'au Empire units.

Grand Invocation of the Elements: In your Movement phase, Aun'Va may invoke up to two elemental powers. All T'au Empire Infantry and Battlesuit units within 6" of any Ethereal invoking an elemental power gain the relevant benefit until the start of your next turn.
- **Calm of Tides:** Subtract 1 from any Morale tests made for affected units.
- **Storm of Fire:** You may re-roll hit rolls of 1 in the Shooting phase for affected units that remain stationary in the Movement phase.
- **Sense of Stone:** Whenever an affected unit suffers an unsaved wound, roll a D6. On a 6, that wound is ignored.
- **Zephyr's Grace:** You can re-roll the dice for affected units when they Advance.

FACTION KEYWORDS	T'au Empire, T'au Sept

KEYWORDS (AUN'VA)	Character, Infantry, Ethereal, Aun'Va

KEYWORDS (ETHEREAL GUARD)	Character, Infantry, Ethereal Guard

DARKSTRIDER

NAME	M	WS	BS	S	T	W	A	Ld	Sv
Darkstrider	7"	3+	2+	3	3	5	3	8	5+

Darkstrider is a single model armed with a markerlight, pulse carbine and photon grenades. Only one of this model may be included in your army.

WEAPON	RANGE	TYPE	S	AP	D	ABILITIES
Markerlight	36"	Heavy 1	-	-	-	*See Markerlights (pg 48)*
Pulse carbine	18"	Assault 2	5	0	1	-
Photon grenade	12"	Grenade D6	-	-	-	This weapon does not inflict any damage. Your opponent must subtract 1 from any hit rolls made for **INFANTRY** units that have suffered any hits from photon grenades until the end of the turn.

ABILITIES	**For the Greater Good** (pg 48)
	Vanguard: At the start of the first battle round but before the first turn begins, you can move Darkstrider up to 7". He cannot end this move within 9" of any enemy models. If both players have units that can do this, the player who is taking the first turn moves their units first.
	Structural Analyser: In your Shooting phase, choose a friendly **T'AU SEPT INFANTRY** unit within 6" and an enemy unit visible to Darkstrider. The enemy unit's Toughness is considered to be 1 point lower when that **T'AU SEPT INFANTRY** unit targets them with a shooting attack. This ability cannot be used when firing Overwatch.
	Fighting Retreat: Friendly **T'AU SEPT INFANTRY** units within 6" of Darkstrider in the Shooting phase may attack with ranged weapons even if they Fell Back this turn.
FACTION KEYWORDS	**T'AU EMPIRE, T'AU SEPT**
KEYWORDS	**CHARACTER, INFANTRY, DARKSTRIDER**

Aun'Va is the Ethereal Supreme, a beloved leader who emboldens trillions of T'au hearts with his inspirational rhetoric.

STRIKE TEAM

NAME	M	WS	BS	S	T	W	A	Ld	Sv
Fire Warrior	6"	5+	4+	3	3	1	1	6	4+
Fire Warrior Shas'ui	6"	5+	4+	3	3	1	2	7	4+
DS8 Tactical Support Turret	-	-	4+	3	3	1	0	4	4+
MV36 Guardian Drone	8"	5+	5+	3	4	1	1	6	4+

This unit contains 5 Fire Warriors. It can include up to 5 additional Fire Warriors (**Power Rating +2**), or up to 7 additional Fire Warriors (**Power Rating +3**). A Fire Warrior Shas'ui can take the place of one Fire Warrior. Each Fire Warrior and Fire Warrior Shas'ui is armed with a pulse rifle and photon grenades. This unit may be accompanied by 2 Tactical Drones (pg 69) or 1 Tactical Drone and 1 MV36 Guardian Drone (**Power Rating +1**).

WEAPON	RANGE	TYPE	S	AP	D	ABILITIES
Markerlight	36"	Heavy 1	-	-	-	*See Markerlights (pg 48)*
Missile pod	36"	Assault 2	7	-1	D3	-
Pulse carbine	18"	Assault 2	5	0	1	-
Pulse pistol	12"	Pistol 1	5	0	1	-
Pulse rifle	30"	Rapid Fire 1	5	0	1	-
Smart missile system	30"	Heavy 4	5	0	1	Smart missile systems can be fired at units that are not visible to the bearer. In addition, units attacked by this weapon do not gain any bonus to their saving throws for being in cover.
Photon grenade	12"	Grenade D6	-	-	-	This weapon does not inflict any damage. Your opponent must subtract 1 from any hit rolls made for **INFANTRY** units that have suffered any hits from photon grenades until the end of the turn.

WARGEAR OPTIONS	
	• Any Fire Warrior or Fire Warrior Shas'ui may replace their pulse rifle with a pulse carbine.
	• The Fire Warrior Shas'ui may take a markerlight and/or pulse pistol.
	• The unit may take a DS8 Tactical Support Turret equipped with either a missile pod or smart missile system.

ABILITIES		
	For the Greater Good (pg 48)	**Guardian Field:** Guardian Drones have a 5+ invulnerable save. Strike Teams within 3" of any friendly Guardian Drones have a 6+ invulnerable save.
	Bonding Knife Ritual: If you roll a 6 when taking a Morale test for this unit, the test is automatically passed.	
	Drone Support: When a Strike Team is set up on the battlefield, any accompanying Drones are set up in unit coherency with it. From that point onwards, the Drones are treated as a separate unit.	**DS8 Tactical Support Turret:** Tactical Support Turrets are not set up when their unit is set up. Instead, once per game, at the end of any of your Movement phases, you may set up the Tactical Support Turret within coherency of its unit and more than 2" away from any enemy models. The turret cannot move for any reason, and is destroyed if the Strike Team moves out of unit coherency with it.
	Saviour Protocols: If a **DRONES** unit is within 3" of a friendly **T'AU EMPIRE INFANTRY** or **BATTLESUIT** unit, you may choose to allocate any wounds to the Drones instead of the target unit.	
		The destruction of a Tactical Support Turret is ignored for the purposes of Morale tests.

FACTION KEYWORDS	T'AU EMPIRE, \<SEPT\>
KEYWORDS (STRIKE TEAM)	INFANTRY, STRIKE TEAM
KEYWORDS (GUARDIAN DRONE)	DRONE, FLY, GUARDIAN DRONE

▶ ③ POWER — BREACHER TEAM

NAME	M	WS	BS	S	T	W	A	Ld	Sv
Fire Warrior	6"	5+	4+	3	3	1	1	6	4+
Fire Warrior Shas'ui	6"	5+	4+	3	3	1	2	7	4+
DS8 Tactical Support Turret	-	-	4+	3	3	1	0	4	4+
MV36 Guardian Drone	8"	5+	5+	3	4	1	1	6	4+

This unit contains 5 Fire Warriors. It can include up to 5 additional Fire Warriors (**Power Rating +2**). A Fire Warrior Shas'ui can take the place of one Fire Warrior. Each Fire Warrior and Fire Warrior Shas'ui is armed with a pulse blaster and photon grenades. This unit may be accompanied by 2 Tactical Drones (pg 69) or 1 Tactical Drone and 1 MV36 Guardian Drone (**Power Rating +1**).

WEAPON	RANGE	TYPE	S	AP	D	ABILITIES
Markerlight	36"	Heavy 1	-	-	-	*See Markerlights (pg 48)*
Missile pod	36"	Assault 2	7	-1	D3	-
Pulse blaster	When attacking with this weapon, choose one of the profiles below.					
- Close range	5"	Assault 2	6	-2	1	-
- Medium range	10"	Assault 2	5	-1	1	-
- Long range	15"	Assault 2	4	0	1	-
Pulse pistol	12"	Pistol 1	5	0	1	-
Smart missile system	30"	Heavy 4	5	0	1	Smart missile systems can be fired at units that are not visible to the bearer. In addition, units attacked by this weapon do not gain any bonus to their saving throws for being in cover.
Photon grenade	12"	Grenade D6	-	-	-	This weapon does not inflict any damage. Your opponent must subtract 1 from any hit rolls made for **INFANTRY** units that have suffered any hits from photon grenades until the end of the turn.

WARGEAR OPTIONS	• The Fire Warrior Shas'ui may take a markerlight and/or pulse pistol. • The unit may take a DS8 Tactical Support Turret equipped with either a missile pod or smart missile system.

ABILITIES

For the Greater Good (pg 48)

Bonding Knife Ritual: If you roll a 6 when taking a Morale test for this unit, the test is automatically passed.

Drone Support: When a Breacher Team is set up on the battlefield, any accompanying Drones are set up in unit coherency with it. From that point onwards, the Drones are treated as a separate unit.

Saviour Protocols: If a **DRONES** unit is within 3" of a friendly T'AU EMPIRE INFANTRY or BATTLESUIT unit, you can choose to allocate any wounds to the Drones instead of the target unit.

Guardian Field: Guardian Drones have a 5+ invulnerable save. Breacher Teams within 3" of a friendly Guardian Drone have a 5+ invulnerable save.

DS8 Tactical Support Turret: Tactical Support Turrets are not set up when their unit is set up. Instead, once per game, at the end of any of your Movement phases, you may set up the Tactical Support Turret within coherency of its unit and more than 2" away from any enemy models. The turret cannot move for any reason, and is destroyed if the Breacher Team moves out of unit coherency with it.

The destruction of a Tactical Support Turret is ignored for the purposes of Morale tests.

FACTION KEYWORDS	T'AU EMPIRE, <SEPT>
KEYWORDS (BREACHER TEAM)	INFANTRY, BREACHER TEAM
KEYWORDS (GUARDIAN DRONE)	DRONE, FLY, GUARDIAN DRONE

KROOT CARNIVORES

POWER 3

NAME	M	WS	BS	S	T	W	A	Ld	Sv
Kroot	7"	3+	4+	3	3	1	1	6	6+

This unit contains 10 Kroot. It can include up to 10 additional Kroot (**Power Rating +3**). Each model is armed with a Kroot rifle.

WEAPON	RANGE	TYPE	S	AP	D	ABILITIES
Kroot rifle (shooting)	24"	Rapid Fire 1	4	0	1	-
Kroot rifle (melee)	Melee	Melee	+1	0	1	-

ABILITIES	**Stealthy Hunters:** At the start of the first battle round but before the first turn begins, you can move this unit up to 7". It cannot end this move within 9" of any enemy models. If both players have units that can do this, the player who is taking the first turn moves their units first.
FACTION KEYWORDS	**T'AU EMPIRE, KROOT**
KEYWORDS	**INFANTRY, KROOT CARNIVORES**

KROOTOX RIDERS

POWER 2

NAME	M	WS	BS	S	T	W	A	Ld	Sv
Krootox Rider	7"	3+	4+	6	5	3	2	6	6+

This unit contains 1 Krootox Rider. It can include 1 additional Krootox Rider (**Power Rating +2**) or 2 additional Krootox Riders (**Power Rating +4**). Each rider fires a Kroot gun and each Krootox attacks with its fists.

WEAPON	RANGE	TYPE	S	AP	D	ABILITIES
Kroot gun	48"	Rapid Fire 1	7	-1	D3	-
Krootox fists	Melee	Melee	User	0	2	-

ABILITIES	**Agile Brute:** When this unit Advances, add 6" to its Move for that Movement phase instead of rolling a D6.
FACTION KEYWORDS	**T'AU EMPIRE, KROOT**
KEYWORDS	**CAVALRY, KROOTOX RIDER**

KROOT HOUNDS

POWER 1

NAME	M	WS	BS	S	T	W	A	Ld	Sv
Kroot Hound	12"	3+	-	3	3	1	2	5	6+

This unit contains 4 Kroot Hounds. It can include up to 4 additional Kroot Hounds (**Power Rating +1**) or up to 8 additional Kroot Hounds (**Power Rating +2**). Each model attacks with its ripping fangs.

WEAPON	RANGE	TYPE	S	AP	D	ABILITIES
Ripping fangs	Melee	Melee	User	-1	1	-

ABILITIES	**Voracious Predators:** You may re-roll failed charge rolls for this unit when targeting a unit that has suffered any unsaved wounds this turn.
FACTION KEYWORDS	**T'AU EMPIRE, KROOT**
KEYWORDS	**BEASTS, KROOT HOUNDS**

KROOT SHAPER

NAME	M	WS	BS	S	T	W	A	Ld	Sv
Kroot Shaper	7"	3+	4+	3	3	5	3	7	6+

A Kroot Shaper is a single model armed with a Kroot rifle and a ritual blade.

WEAPON	RANGE	TYPE	S	AP	D	ABILITIES
Kroot rifle (shooting)	24"	Rapid Fire 1	4	0	1	-
Pulse carbine	18"	Assault 2	5	0	1	-
Pulse rifle	30"	Rapid Fire 1	5	0	1	-
Kroot rifle (melee)	Melee	Melee	+1	0	1	-
Ritual blade	Melee	Melee	User	0	1	If any models are destroyed by this weapon, friendly **KROOT** units within 6" of the bearer do not have to take Morale tests at the end of the turn.

WARGEAR OPTIONS	• This model may replace its Kroot rifle with a pulse rifle or pulse carbine.
ABILITIES	**The Shaper Commands:** You may re-roll wound rolls of 1 made for friendly **KROOT** units within 6" of this model.
	Wisest of Their Kind: KROOT units within 6" of a friendly Kroot Shaper may use the Shaper's Leadership characteristic instead of their own when taking Morale tests.
FACTION KEYWORDS	T'AU EMPIRE, KROOT
KEYWORDS	CHARACTER, INFANTRY, KROOT SHAPER

The Kroot are a race of savage hunters whose skill at ambush tactics make them the perfect vanguard troops for the T'au Empire.

6 POWER — XV25 STEALTH BATTLESUITS

NAME	M	WS	BS	S	T	W	A	Ld	Sv
Stealth Shas'ui	8"	5+	4+	4	4	2	2	7	3+
Stealth Shas'vre	8"	5+	4+	4	4	2	3	8	3+

This unit contains 3 Stealth Shas'ui. It can include up to 3 additional Stealth Shas'ui (**Power Rating +6**). A Stealth Shas'vre can take the place of one Stealth Shas'ui. Each Stealth Shas'ui and Stealth Shas'vre is equipped with a burst cannon. This unit may be accompanied by up to 2 Tactical Drones (pg 69) (**Power Rating +1**).

WEAPON	RANGE	TYPE	S	AP	D	ABILITIES
Burst cannon	18"	Assault 4	5	0	1	-
Fusion blaster	18"	Assault 1	8	-4	D6	If the target is within half range of this weapon, roll two dice when inflicting damage with it and discard the lowest result.

WARGEAR OPTIONS	• Any Stealth Shas'ui or Stealth Shas'vre may take a single item from the *Support Systems* list. • One Stealth Shas'ui or Stealth Shas'vre may replace their burst cannon with a fusion blaster. If the unit numbers six models, one additional Stealth Shas'ui may do this. • The Shas'vre may take a markerlight and target lock. • The unit may take a homing beacon.

ABILITIES	**For the Greater Good** (pg 48) **Bonding Knife Ritual:** If you roll a 6 when taking a Morale test for this unit, the test is automatically passed. **Infiltrators:** During deployment, this unit can be set up anywhere on the battlefield that is not within your opponent's deployment zone and is more than 12" from any enemy unit. **Target Lock:** A model with a target lock does not suffer the penalty to their hit rolls for moving and firing Heavy weapons, or for Advancing and firing Assault weapons. This model can also Advance and fire Rapid Fire weapons, but you must subtract 1 from its hit rolls when it does so.	**Camouflage Fields:** Your opponent must subtract 1 from all hit rolls for attacks that target this unit. **Homing Beacon:** A homing beacon may be used during your Movement phase by placing it within 1" of its unit. If there are any friendly homing beacons on the battlefield at the end of your Movement phase, one of your <SEPT> units that has been set up in a Manta hold can perform a low-altitude drop instead of a Manta strike. Set up the unit wholly within 6" of the homing beacon. The homing beacon then shorts out and is removed from the battlefield. Homing beacons are deactivated and removed from the battlefield if an enemy model ends a move within 9" of it.

FACTION KEYWORDS	T'AU EMPIRE, <SEPT>
KEYWORDS	BATTLESUIT, INFANTRY, JET PACK, FLY, XV25 STEALTH BATTLESUITS

XV25 Stealth Battlesuits materialise behind enemy positions in utter silence, before eliminating them with merciless precision.

XV8 CRISIS BATTLESUITS

POWER 11

NAME	M	WS	BS	S	T	W	A	Ld	Sv
Crisis Shas'ui	8"	5+	4+	5	5	3	2	7	3+
Crisis Shas'vre	8"	5+	4+	5	5	3	3	8	3+

This unit contains 3 Crisis Shas'ui. It can include up to 3 additional Crisis Shas'ui (**Power Rating +11**) or up to 6 additional Crisis Shas'ui (**Power Rating +22**). A Crisis Shas'vre can take the place of one Crisis Shas'ui. Each Crisis Battlesuit is equipped with a burst cannon, and may be accompanied by up to 2 Tactical Drones (pg 69) (**Power Rating +1**).

WEAPON	RANGE	TYPE	S	AP	D	ABILITIES
Burst cannon	18"	Assault 4	5	0	1	-

WARGEAR OPTIONS	• Any Crisis Shas'ui or Crisis Shas'vre may replace their burst cannon with up to three items from the *Ranged Weapons* and/or *Support Systems* list.

ABILITIES	**For the Greater Good** (pg 48) **Bonding Knife Ritual:** If you roll a 6 when taking a Morale test for this unit, the test is automatically passed. **Manta Strike:** During deployment, you may set up Crisis Battlesuits in a Manta hold instead of placing them on the battlefield. At the end of any of your Movement phases, they can use a Manta strike to enter the fray – set them up anywhere on the battlefield that is more than 9" from any enemy models.
FACTION KEYWORDS	T'AU EMPIRE, <SEPT>
KEYWORDS	BATTLESUIT, JET PACK, FLY, XV8 CRISIS BATTLESUITS

XV8 CRISIS BODYGUARDS

POWER 12

NAME	M	WS	BS	S	T	W	A	Ld	Sv
Crisis Bodyguard	8"	5+	4+	5	5	3	3	8	3+

This unit contains 3 Crisis Bodyguards. It can include up to 3 additional Crisis Bodyguards (**Power Rating +12**) or up to 6 additional Crisis Bodyguards (**Power Rating +24**). Each Crisis Bodyguard is equipped with a burst cannon, and may be accompanied by up to 2 Tactical Drones (pg 69) (**Power Rating +1**).

WEAPON	RANGE	TYPE	S	AP	D	ABILITIES
Burst cannon	18"	Assault 4	5	0	1	-

WARGEAR OPTIONS	• Any Crisis Bodyguard may replace their burst cannon with up to three items from the *Ranged Weapons* and/or *Support Systems* list.

ABILITIES	**For the Greater Good** (pg 48) **Bonding Knife Ritual:** If you roll a 6 when taking a Morale test for this unit, the test is automatically passed. **Sworn Protectors:** Roll a D6 each time a friendly <SEPT> CHARACTER loses a wound whilst they are within 3" of this unit. On a 2+, a model from this unit can intercept that hit – the CHARACTER does not lose a wound but this unit suffers a mortal wound. **Manta Strike:** During deployment, you may set up Crisis Bodyguards in a Manta hold instead of placing them on the battlefield. At the end of any of your Movement phases, they can use a Manta strike to enter the fray – set them up anywhere on the battlefield that is more than 9" from any enemy models.
FACTION KEYWORDS	T'AU EMPIRE, <SEPT>
KEYWORDS	BATTLESUIT, JET PACK, FLY, XV8 CRISIS BODYGUARDS

XV95 GHOSTKEEL BATTLESUIT

NAME	M	WS	BS	S	T	W	A	Ld	Sv
Ghostkeel Shas'vre	*	5+	*	6	6	10	*	8	3+
MV5 Stealth Drones	12"	5+	5+	4	4	1	1	6	4+

POWER 10

DAMAGE

Some of this model's characteristics change as it suffers damage, as shown below:

REMAINING W	M	BS	A
6-10+	12"	4+	3
3-5	8"	5+	2
1-2	4"	5+	1

Each XV95 Ghostkeel Battlesuit consists of 1 Ghostkeel Shas'vre accompanied by 2 MV5 Stealth Drones. The Ghostkeel Shas'vre is equipped with a fusion collider and two flamers.

WEAPON	RANGE	TYPE	S	AP	D	ABILITIES
Burst cannon	18"	Assault 4	5	0	1	-
Cyclic ion raker	When attacking with this weapon, choose one of the profiles below.					
- Standard	24"	Heavy 6	7	-1	1	-
- Overcharge	24"	Heavy D6	8	-1	D3	If you make one or more hit rolls of 1, the bearer suffers a mortal wound after all of this weapon's shots have been resolved.
Flamer	8"	Assault D6	4	0	1	This weapon automatically hits its target.
Fusion blaster	18"	Assault 1	8	-4	D6	If the target is within half range of this weapon, roll two dice when inflicting damage with it and discard the lowest result.
Fusion collider	18"	Heavy D3	8	-4	D6	If the target is within half range of this weapon, roll two dice when inflicting damage with it and discard the lowest result.

WARGEAR OPTIONS	
	• A Ghostkeel Shas'vre may replace its fusion collider with a cyclic ion raker.
	• A Ghostkeel Shas'vre may replace both its flamers with two burst cannons or two fusion blasters.
	• A Ghostkeel Shas'vre may take up to two items from the *Support Systems* list.

ABILITIES		
	For the Greater Good (pg 48)	**Saviour Protocols:** If a **DRONES** unit is within 3" of a friendly **T'AU EMPIRE INFANTRY** or **BATTLESUIT** unit, you can choose to allocate any wounds to the Drones instead of the target unit.
	Infiltrator: During deployment, this unit may be set up anywhere on the battlefield that is not within your opponent's deployment zone and is more than 12" from any enemy unit.	**Stealth Field:** Models shooting at a Stealth Drone or any Ghostkeel Battlesuit within 3" of a friendly Stealth Drone subtract 1 from their hit rolls. (This is cumulative with the Ghostkeel Electrowarfare Suite ability.)
	Ghostkeel Electrowarfare Suite: Your opponent must subtract 1 from hit rolls for models attacking a Ghostkeel Shas'vre from more than 12" away.	**Drone Support:** When a Ghostkeel Battlesuit is set up on the battlefield, any accompanying Drones are set up in unit coherency with it. From that point onwards, the Drones are treated as a separate unit.

FACTION KEYWORDS	T'AU EMPIRE, <SEPT>
KEYWORDS (GHOSTKEEL)	BATTLESUIT, MONSTER, JET PACK, FLY, XV95 GHOSTKEEL BATTLESUIT
KEYWORDS (STEALTH DRONE)	DRONE, FLY, MV5 STEALTH DRONES

XV104 RIPTIDE BATTLESUIT

DAMAGE
Some of this model's characteristics change as it suffers damage, as shown below:

REMAINING W	M	BS	A
7-14+	12"	4+	4
4-6	8"	5+	3
1-3	4"	5+	2

NAME	M	WS	BS	S	T	W	A	Ld	Sv
Riptide Shas'vre	*	5+	*	6	7	14	*	8	2+
MV84 Shielded Missile Drone	12"	5+	5+	4	4	1	1	6	4+

A Riptide Shas'vre is a single model equipped with a heavy burst cannon and two smart missile systems. It may be accompanied by up to 2 MV84 Shielded Missile Drones (**Power Rating +2**), each equipped with a missile pod.

WEAPON	RANGE	TYPE	S	AP	D	ABILITIES
Fusion blaster	18"	Assault 1	8	-4	D6	If the target is within half range of this weapon, roll two dice when inflicting damage with it and discard the lowest result.
Heavy burst cannon		When attacking with this weapon, choose one of the profiles below. You may only use the nova-charge setting in accordance with the Riptide Shas'vre's Nova Reactor ability (see below).				
- Standard	36"	Heavy 8	6	-1	1	-
- Nova-charge	36"	Heavy 12	6	-2	1	-
Ion accelerator		When attacking with this weapon, choose one of the profiles below. You may only use the nova-charge setting in accordance with the Riptide Shas'vre's Nova Reactor ability (see below).				
- Standard	72"	Heavy 3	7	-3	1	-
- Overcharge	72"	Heavy D6	8	-3	D3	If you roll one or more hit rolls of 1, the bearer suffers a mortal wound after all of this weapon's shots have been resolved.
- Nova-charge	72"	Heavy D6	9	-3	3	-
Missile pod	36"	Assault 2	7	-1	D3	-
Plasma rifle	24"	Rapid Fire 1	6	-3	1	
Smart missile system	30"	Heavy 4	5	0	1	Smart missile systems can be fired at units that are not visible to the bearer. In addition, units attacked by this weapon do not gain any bonus to their saving throws for being in cover.

WARGEAR OPTIONS	• A Riptide Shas'vre may replace both its smart missile systems with two plasma rifles or two fusion blasters. • A Riptide Shas'vre may replace its heavy burst cannon with an ion accelerator. • A Riptide Shas'vre may take up to two items from the *Support Systems* list.

ABILITIES	For the Greater Good (pg 48) **Riptide Shield Generator:** A Riptide Shas'vre has a 5+ invulnerable save. **Saviour Protocols:** If a **DRONES** unit is within 3" of a friendly **T'AU EMPIRE INFANTRY** or **BATTLESUIT** unit, you can choose to allocate any wounds to the Drones instead of the target unit. **Shield Generator:** Shielded Missile Drones have a 4+ invulnerable save. **Drone Support:** When a Riptide Battlesuit is set up on the battlefield, any accompanying Drones are set up in unit coherency with it. From that point onwards, the Drones are treated as a separate unit.	**Nova Reactor:** In your Movement phase you can choose to use a Riptide Shas'vre's Nova Reactor. If you do, the Riptide Shas'vre suffers a mortal wound. Choose one of the following effects to last until the beginning of your next turn: • **Nova Shield:** The Riptide Shas'vre has a 3+ invulnerable save. • **Boost:** The Riptide Shas'vre can move 2D6" in your charge phase (even if it doesn't declare a charge). • **Nova-charge:** The Riptide Shas'vre's ion accelerator or heavy burst cannon can fire using its nova-charge profile.

FACTION KEYWORDS	T'AU EMPIRE, <SEPT>

KEYWORDS (RIPTIDE)	BATTLESUIT, MONSTER, JET PACK, FLY, XV104 RIPTIDE BATTLESUIT

KEYWORDS (SHIELDED MISSILE DRONES)	DRONE, FLY, MV84 SHIELDED MISSILE DRONES

PATHFINDER TEAM

3 POWER

NAME	M	WS	BS	S	T	W	A	Ld	Sv
Pathfinder	7"	5+	4+	3	3	1	1	6	5+
Pathfinder Shas'ui	7"	5+	4+	3	3	1	2	7	5+
MV31 Pulse Accelerator Drone	8"	5+	5+	3	4	1	1	6	4+
MV33 Grav-inhibitor Drone	8"	5+	5+	3	4	1	1	6	4+
MB3 Recon Drone	8"	5+	5+	4	4	2	1	6	4+

This unit contains 5 Pathfinders. It can include up to 5 additional Pathfinders (**Power Rating +3**). A Pathfinder Shas'ui can take the place of one Pathfinder. Each Pathfinder and Pathfinder Shas'ui is armed with a markerlight, pulse carbine and photon grenades. This unit may be accompanied by up to 2 Tactical Drones (pg 69) (**Power Rating +1**) and/or an MB3 Recon Drone equipped with a burst cannon and up to 2 Support Drones: 1 MV31 Pulse Accelerator Drone and/or 1 MV33 Grav-inhibitor Drone (**Power Rating +1**).

WEAPON	RANGE	TYPE	S	AP	D	ABILITIES
Ion rifle	When attacking with this weapon, choose one of the profiles below.					
- Standard	30"	Rapid Fire 1	7	-1	1	-
- Overcharge	30"	Heavy D3	8	-1	1	If you roll one or more hit rolls of 1, the bearer suffers a mortal wound after all of this weapon's shots have been resolved.
Markerlight	36"	Heavy 1	-	-	-	*See Markerlights (pg 48)*
Pulse carbine	18"	Assault 2	5	0	1	-
Pulse pistol	12"	Pistol 1	5	0	1	-
Rail rifle	30"	Rapid Fire 1	6	-4	D3	For each wound roll of 6+ made for this weapon, the target unit suffers a mortal wound in addition to the normal damage.
Photon grenade	12"	Grenade D6	-	-	-	This weapon does not inflict any damage. Your opponent must subtract 1 from any hit rolls made for **INFANTRY** units that have suffered any hits from photon grenades until the end of the turn.

WARGEAR OPTIONS	
	• Up to three Pathfinders may replace their markerlight and pulse carbine with an ion rifle or a rail rifle.
	• The Pathfinder Shas'ui may take a pulse pistol.

ABILITIES	
	For the Greater Good (pg 48)

Drone Support: When a Pathfinder Team is set up on the battlefield, any accompanying Drones are set up in unit coherency with it. From that point onwards, the Drones are treated as a separate unit.

Saviour Protocols: If a **DRONES** unit is within 3" of a friendly **T'AU EMPIRE INFANTRY** or **BATTLESUIT** unit, you can choose to allocate any wounds to the Drones instead of the target unit.

Vanguard: At the start of the first battle round but before the first turn begins, you can move this unit up to 7". It cannot end this move within 9" of any enemy models. If both players have units that can do this, the player who is taking the first turn moves their units first.

Recon Suite: Units making saves against attacks made by a Pathfinder Team that is within 3" of a friendly Recon Drone do not gain any bonus to their saving throws for being in cover.

Pulse Accelerator: **T'AU EMPIRE INFANTRY** units within 3" of a friendly Pulse Accelerator Drone have the range of their pulse pistols, pulse carbines and pulse rifles increased by 6".

Bonding Knife Ritual: If you roll a 6 when taking a Morale test for this unit, the test is automatically passed.

Gravity Wave Projector: Enemy units beginning a charge move within 12" of a Grav-inhibitor Drone reduce their charge distance by D3".

FACTION KEYWORDS	T'AU EMPIRE, <SEPT>
KEYWORDS (PATHFINDERS)	**INFANTRY, PATHFINDER TEAM**
KEYWORDS (SUPPORT DRONES)	**DRONE, FLY, SUPPORT DRONES**
KEYWORDS (RECON DRONE)	**DRONE, FLY, RECON DRONE**

TX4 PIRANHAS

NAME	M	WS	BS	S	T	W	A	Ld	Sv
TX4 Piranha	16"	6+	4+	4	5	6	2	6	4+
MV1 Gun Drone	8"	5+	5+	3	4	1	1	6	4+

This unit contains 1 TX4 Piranha accompanied by 2 MV1 Gun Drones. It can include up to 4 additional TX4 Piranhas, each of which is accompanied by 2 MV1 Gun Drones (**Power Rating +4 per TX4 Piranha**). Each TX4 Piranha is equipped with a burst cannon, and each MV1 Gun Drone is equipped with two pulse carbines.

WEAPON	RANGE	TYPE	S	AP	D	ABILITIES
Burst cannon	18"	Assault 4	5	0	1	-
Fusion blaster	18"	Assault 1	8	-4	D6	If the target is within half range of this weapon, roll two dice when inflicting damage with it and discard the lowest result.
Pulse carbine	18"	Assault 2	5	0	1	-
Seeker missile	72"	Heavy 1	-	-	-	A unit hit by this weapon suffers a mortal wound. Each seeker missile can only be used once per battle. This weapon only hits on a roll of 6, regardless of the firing model's Ballistic Skill or any modifiers.

WARGEAR OPTIONS	• Any TX4 Piranha may replace its burst cannon with a fusion blaster and may take up to two seeker missiles.

ABILITIES	**Explodes:** If a Piranha is reduced to 0 wounds, roll a D6 before removing it from the battlefield and before any embarked models disembark. On a 6 it explodes, and each unit within 3" suffers a mortal wound. **Saviour Protocols:** If a **DRONES** unit is within 3" of a friendly **T'AU EMPIRE INFANTRY** or **BATTLESUIT** unit, you can choose to allocate any wounds to the Drones instead of the target unit. **Threat Identification Protocols:** In the Shooting phase, Gun Drones can only target the nearest visible enemy unit. If two units are equally close, you may choose which is targeted.	**Attached Drones:** When a Piranha is set up, its accompanying Gun Drones are attached, and are treated as being embarked. Whilst the Gun Drones remain attached, the Piranha is considered to be equipped with the Drones' weapons in addition to its own. Both Drones can detach at the start of any of your Movement phases by disembarking. From that point onwards, the Drones are treated as a separate unit. They cannot reattach during the battle.

FACTION KEYWORDS	T'AU EMPIRE, <SEPT>
KEYWORDS (PIRANHA)	VEHICLE, FLY, TX4 PIRANHAS
KEYWORDS (GUN DRONES)	DRONE, FLY, GUN DRONES

The TX4 Piranha is a swift and versatile skimmer, capable of mowing down infantry or destroying enemy vehicles many times its size.

TY7 DEVILFISH

NAME	M	WS	BS	S	T	W	A	Ld	Sv
TY7 Devilfish	*	6+	*	6	7	12	*	8	3+
MV1 Gun Drone	8"	5+	5+	3	4	1	1	6	4+

DAMAGE

Some of this model's characteristics change as it suffers damage, as shown below:

REMAINING W	M	BS	A
7-12+	12"	4+	3
4-6	6"	5+	D3
1-3	3"	6+	1

A TY7 Devilfish is a single model armed with a burst cannon. It is accompanied by 2 MV1 Gun Drones, each equipped with two pulse carbines.

WEAPON	RANGE	TYPE	S	AP	D	ABILITIES
Burst cannon	18"	Assault 4	5	0	1	-
Pulse carbine	18"	Assault 2	5	0	1	-
Seeker missile	72"	Heavy 1	-	-	-	A unit hit by this weapon suffers a mortal wound. Each seeker missile can only be used once per battle. This weapon only hits on a roll of 6, regardless of the firing model's Ballistic Skill or any modifiers.
Smart missile system	30"	Heavy 4	5	0	1	Smart missile systems can be fired at units that are not visible to the bearer. In addition, units attacked by this weapon do not gain any bonus to their saving throws for being in cover.

WARGEAR OPTIONS	
	• Instead of being accompanied by two MV1 Gun Drones, this model may take two smart missile systems. • This model may take up to two seeker missiles.

ABILITIES	
	Hover Tank: Distances must be measured to and from the hull of this model rather than its base. **Explodes:** If a Devilfish is reduced to 0 wounds, roll a D6 before removing it from the battlefield and before any embarked models disembark. On a 6 it explodes, and each unit within 6" suffers D3 mortal wounds. **Turret Mounting:** Units attacked by a Devilfish with an MB3 Recon Drone embarked within it do not gain any bonus to their saving throws for being in cover. **Threat Identification Protocols:** In the Shooting phase, Gun Drones can only target the nearest visible enemy unit. If two units are equally close, you may choose which is targeted.	**Saviour Protocols:** If a DRONES unit is within 3" of a friendly T'AU EMPIRE INFANTRY or BATTLESUIT unit, you can choose to allocate any wounds to the Drones instead of the target unit. **Attached Drones:** When a Devilfish is set up, any accompanying Gun Drones are attached, and are treated as being embarked, though they do not count towards the total number of models embarked on the Devilfish. Whilst the Gun Drones remain attached, the Devilfish is considered to be equipped with the Drones' weapons in addition to its own. Both Drones can detach at the start of any of your Movement phases by disembarking. From that point onwards, the Drones are treated as a separate unit. They cannot reattach during the battle.

TRANSPORT	
	A Devilfish can transport up to 12 <SEPT> INFANTRY or DRONE models. It cannot transport BATTLESUITS. It can transport only a single MB3 Recon Drone, but it does not count towards the total number of models embarked on the Devilfish.

FACTION KEYWORDS	T'AU EMPIRE, <SEPT>

KEYWORDS (DEVILFISH)	VEHICLE, TRANSPORT, FLY, TY7 DEVILFISH

KEYWORDS (GUN DRONES)	DRONE, FLY, GUN DRONES

AX3 RAZORSHARK STRIKE FIGHTER

8 POWER

NAME	M	WS	BS	S	T	W	A	Ld	Sv
AX3 Razorshark Strike Fighter	*	6+	*	6	6	12	*	6	4+

An AX3 Razorshark Strike Fighter is a single model equipped with a burst cannon, a quad ion turret and two seeker missiles.

DAMAGE
Some of this model's characteristics change as it suffers damage, as shown below:

REMAINING W	M	BS	A
7-12+	20"-50"	4+	3
4-6	20"-30"	5+	D3
1-3	20"-25"	5+	1

WEAPON	RANGE	TYPE	S	AP	D	ABILITIES
Burst cannon	18"	Assault 4	5	0	1	-
Missile pod	36"	Assault 2	7	-1	D3	-
Quad ion turret		When attacking with this weapon, choose one of the profiles below. Add 1 to hit rolls for this weapon against targets that can't **FLY**.				
- Standard	30"	Heavy 4	7	-1	1	-
- Overcharge	30"	Heavy D6	8	-1	D3	If you make one or more hit rolls of 1, the bearer suffers a mortal wound after all of this weapon's shots have been resolved.
Seeker missile	72"	Heavy 1	-	-	-	A unit hit by this weapon suffers a mortal wound. Each seeker missile can only be used once per battle. This weapon only hits on a roll of 6, regardless of the firing model's Ballistic Skill or any modifiers.

WARGEAR OPTIONS	• This model may replace its burst cannon with a missile pod.

ABILITIES	**Airborne:** This model cannot charge, can only be charged by units that can **FLY**, and can only attack or be attacked in the Fight phase by units that can **FLY**. **Supersonic:** Each time this model moves, first pivot it on the spot up to 90° (this does not contribute to how far the model moves), and then move the model straight forwards. Note that it cannot pivot again after the initial pivot. When this model Advances, increase its Move characteristic by 20" until the end of the phase – do not roll a dice.	**Hard to Hit:** Your opponent must subtract 1 from hit rolls for attacks that target this model in the Shooting phase. **Crash and Burn:** If this model is reduced to 0 wounds, roll a D6 before removing it from the battlefield. On a 6 it explodes, and each unit within 6" suffers D3 mortal wounds.

FACTION KEYWORDS	T'AU EMPIRE, \<SEPT\>

KEYWORDS	VEHICLE, FLY, AX3 RAZORSHARK STRIKE FIGHTER

AX3 Razorshark Strike Fighters are as adept in breakneck dogfights as they are at blasting apart ground targets.

AX39 SUN SHARK BOMBER

9 POWER

NAME	M	WS	BS	S	T	W	A	Ld	Sv
AX39 Sun Shark Bomber	*	6+	*	6	6	12	*	6	4+
MV17 Interceptor Drone	20"	5+	5+	3	4	1	1	6	4+

DAMAGE

Some of this model's characteristics change as it suffers damage, as shown below:

REMAINING W	M	BS	A
7-12+	20"-50"	4+	3
4-6	20"-30"	5+	D3
1-3	20"-25"	5+	1

An AX39 Sun Shark Bomber is a single model equipped with a markerlight, a missile pod and two seeker missiles. It is accompanied by 2 MV17 Interceptor Drones, each equipped with an ion rifle.

WEAPON	RANGE	TYPE	S	AP	D	ABILITIES
Ion rifle	When attacking with this weapon, choose one of the profiles below.					
- Standard	30"	Rapid Fire 1	7	-1	1	
- Overcharge	30"	Heavy D3	8	-1	1	If you make one or more hit rolls of 1, the bearer suffers a mortal wound after all of this weapon's shots have been resolved.
Markerlight	36"	Heavy 1	-	-	-	*See Markerlights (pg 48)*
Missile pod	36"	Assault 2	7	-1	D3	-
Seeker missile	72"	Heavy 1	-	-	-	A unit hit by this weapon suffers a mortal wound. Each seeker missile can only be used once per battle. This weapon only hits on a roll of 6, regardless of the firing model's Ballistic Skill or any modifiers.

WARGEAR OPTIONS	• This model may take a second missile pod.

ABILITIES	

Airborne: This model cannot charge, can only be charged by units that can **Fly**, and can only attack or be attacked in the Fight phase by units that can **Fly**.

Supersonic: Each time this model moves, first pivot it on the spot up to 90° (this does not contribute to how far the model moves), and then move the model straight forwards. Note that it cannot pivot again after the initial pivot. When this model Advances, increase its Move characteristic by 20" until the end of the phase – do not roll a dice.

Hard to Hit: Your opponent must subtract 1 from hit rolls for attacks that target this model in the Shooting phase.

Pulse Bombs: A Sun Shark Bomber may drop one pulse bomb as it flies over enemy units in its Movement phase. To do so, after the model has moved, target one enemy unit that it flew over. Then, roll a D6 for each model in that unit (up to a maximum of 10), adding 1 to the result if the enemy unit is **Infantry**. For each roll of 5+, the target unit suffers 1 mortal wound.

Crash and Burn: If this model is reduced to 0 wounds, roll a D6 before removing it from the battlefield and before any embarked models disembark. On a 6 it explodes, and each unit within 6" suffers D3 mortal wounds.

Attached Drones: When a Sun Shark Bomber is set up, its accompanying Interceptor Drones are attached, and are treated as being embarked. Whilst the Interceptor Drones remain attached, the Sun Shark Bomber is considered to be equipped with the Drones' weapons in addition to its own. However, a hit roll of 1 when firing the ion rifle on overcharge setting results in one of the Drones being slain rather than the Sun Shark Bomber.

Both Drones can detach at the start of any of your Movement phases by disembarking. From that point onwards, the Drones are treated as a separate unit. They cannot reattach during the battle.

Saviour Protocols: If a **Drones** unit is within 3" of a friendly **T'au Empire Infantry** or **Battlesuit** unit, you can choose to allocate any wounds to the Drones instead of the target unit.

FACTION KEYWORDS	T'au Empire, <Sept>
KEYWORDS (SUN SHARK BOMBER)	Vehicle, Fly, AX39 Sun Shark Bomber
KEYWORDS (INTERCEPTOR DRONES)	Drone, Fly, Interceptor Drones

⚡ (2 POWER) TACTICAL DRONES

NAME	M	WS	BS	S	T	W	A	Ld	Sv
MV1 Gun Drone	8"	5+	5+	3	4	1	1	6	4+
MV4 Shield Drone	8"	5+	5+	3	4	1	1	6	4+
MV7 Marker Drone	8"	5+	5+	3	4	1	1	6	4+

This unit contains 4 Tactical Drones. It can include up to 4 additional Tactical Drones (**Power Rating +2**), or up to 8 additional Tactical Drones (**Power Rating +4**). Each Drone in the unit must be either an MV1 Gun Drone armed with two pulse carbines, an MV4 Shield Drone or an MV7 Marker Drone armed with a markerlight. Note that this datasheet is also used for Tactical Drones that accompany many T'au Empire units (see Drone Support, below).

WEAPON	RANGE	TYPE	S	AP	D	ABILITIES
Markerlight	36"	Heavy 1	-	-	-	*See Markerlights (pg 48)*
Pulse carbine	18"	Assault 2	5	0	1	-

ABILITIES	
For the Greater Good (pg 48) **Drone Support:** Tactical Drones often accompany other T'au Empire units. In such instances, a unit's datasheet will instruct you if, and how many, Tactical Drones may accompany it. Tactical Drones included in your army in this way have the Battlefield Role of the unit they accompany. When a unit is set up, any accompanying Drones must be placed in unit coherency with it. From that point onwards, the accompanying Drones are treated as a separate unit.	**Saviour Protocols:** If a DRONES unit is within 3" of a friendly T'AU EMPIRE INFANTRY or BATTLESUIT unit, you can choose to allocate any wounds to the Drones instead of the target unit. **Threat Identification Protocols:** In the Shooting phase, Gun Drones can only target the nearest visible enemy unit. If two units are equally close, you may choose which is targeted. **Shield Generator:** Shield Drones have a 4+ invulnerable save. **Stable Platform:** Marker Drones do not suffer the penalty for moving and firing Heavy weapons.

FACTION KEYWORDS	T'AU EMPIRE, <SEPT>
KEYWORDS	DRONE, FLY, TACTICAL DRONES

⚡ (3 POWER) VESPID STINGWINGS

NAME	M	WS	BS	S	T	W	A	Ld	Sv
Vespid Stingwing	14"	4+	4+	3	4	1	1	5	4+
Vespid Strain Leader	14"	4+	4+	3	4	1	2	8	4+

This unit contains 4 Vespid Stingwings. It can include up to 4 additional Vespid Stingwings (**Power Rating +3**), or up to 8 additional Vespid Stingwings (**Power Rating +6**). A Vespid Strain Leader can take the place of one Vespid Stingwing. Each model is equipped with a neutron blaster.

WEAPON	RANGE	TYPE	S	AP	D	ABILITIES
Neutron blaster	18"	Assault 2	5	-2	1	-

ABILITIES	
Plunge from the Sky: During deployment, you can set up a unit of Vespid Stingwings high in the sky, instead of placing them on the battlefield. If you do so, they can plunge from the sky at the end of any of your Movement phases – set them up anywhere that is more than 9" from any enemy models.	

FACTION KEYWORDS	T'AU EMPIRE, VESPID
KEYWORDS	INFANTRY, FLY, VESPID STINGWINGS

FIRESIGHT MARKSMAN

1 POWER

NAME	M	WS	BS	S	T	W	A	Ld	Sv
Firesight Marksman	5"	5+	3+	3	3	3	2	7	4+

A Firesight Marksman is a single model armed with a markerlight and pulse pistol.

WEAPON	RANGE	TYPE	S	AP	D	ABILITIES
Markerlight	36"	Heavy 1	-	-	-	*See Markerlights (pg 48)*
Pulse pistol	12"	Pistol 1	5	0	1	-

ABILITIES	For the Greater Good (pg 48)
	Drone Uplink: You can add 1 to hit rolls for **<Sept>** MV71 Sniper Drones in the Shooting phase when they attack a unit visible to a friendly **<Sept>** Firesight Marksman.
	Marksman Stealth Field: This model adds 2 rather than 1 to its saving throws when benefiting from cover.
FACTION KEYWORDS	T'au Empire, **<Sept>**
KEYWORDS	**Character, Infantry, Firesight Marksman**

MV71 SNIPER DRONES

3 POWER

NAME	M	WS	BS	S	T	W	A	Ld	Sv
MV71 Sniper Drone	8"	5+	5+	3	4	1	1	6	4+

This unit contains 3 MV71 Sniper Drones. It can include up to 3 additional MV71 Sniper Drones (**Power Rating +3**), or up to 6 additional MV71 Sniper Drones (**Power Rating +6**). Each MV71 Sniper Drone is equipped with a longshot pulse rifle.

WEAPON	RANGE	TYPE	S	AP	D	ABILITIES
Longshot pulse rifle	48"	Rapid Fire 1	5	0	1	This weapon may target a **Character** even if it is not the closest enemy unit.

ABILITIES	For the Greater Good (pg 48)
	Saviour Protocols: If a **Drones** unit is within 3" of a friendly **T'au Empire Infantry** or **Battlesuit** unit, you can choose to allocate any wounds to the Drones instead of the target unit.
	Sniper Drone Stealth Field: Your opponent must subtract 1 from hit rolls for units attacking Sniper Drones unless the Sniper Drones are the closest enemy unit.
FACTION KEYWORDS	T'au Empire, **<Sept>**
KEYWORDS	**Drone, Fly, MV71 Sniper Drones**

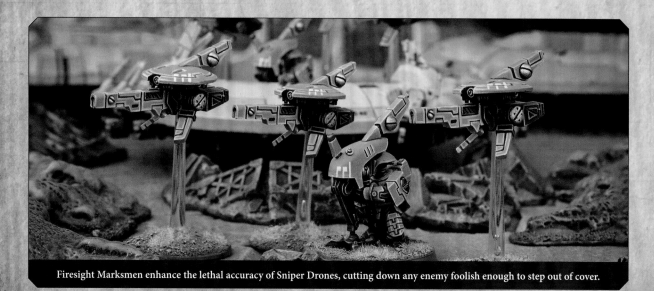

Firesight Marksmen enhance the lethal accuracy of Sniper Drones, cutting down any enemy foolish enough to step out of cover.

TX78 Sky Ray Gunship

DAMAGE
Some of this model's characteristics change as it suffers damage, as shown below:

NAME	M	WS	BS	S	T	W	A	Ld	Sv
TX78 Sky Ray Gunship	*	6+	*	6	7	13	*	8	3+
MV1 Gun Drone	8"	5+	5+	3	4	1	1	6	4+

REMAINING W	M	BS	A
7-13+	12"	3+	3
4-6	6"	4+	D3
1-3	3"	5+	1

A TX78 Sky Ray Gunship is a single model equipped with two markerlights and six seeker missiles.
It is accompanied by 2 MV1 Gun Drones, each equipped with two pulse carbines.

WEAPON	RANGE	TYPE	S	AP	D	ABILITIES
Burst cannon	18"	Assault 4	5	0	1	-
Markerlight	36"	Heavy 1	-	-	-	*See Markerlights (pg 48)*
Pulse carbine	18"	Assault 2	5	0	1	-
Seeker missile	72"	Heavy 1	-	-	-	A unit hit by this weapon suffers a mortal wound. Each seeker missile can only be used once per battle. This weapon only hits on a roll of 6, regardless of the firing model's Ballistic Skill or any modifiers.
Smart missile system	30"	Heavy 4	5	0	1	Smart missile systems can be fired at units that are not visible to the bearer. In addition, units attacked by this weapon do not gain any bonus to their saving throws for being in cover.

WARGEAR OPTIONS	
	• Instead of being accompanied by two MV1 Gun Drones, this model may take two burst cannons or two smart missile systems.

ABILITIES	
	Hover Tank: Distances must be measured to and from the hull of this model rather than its base. **Explodes:** If this model is reduced to 0 wounds, roll a D6 before removing it from the battlefield and before any embarked models disembark. On a 6 it explodes, and each unit within 6" suffers D3 mortal wounds. **Saviour Protocols:** If a **Drones** unit is within 3" of a friendly **T'au Empire Infantry** or **Battlesuit** unit, you can choose to allocate any wounds to the Drones instead of the target unit.	**Threat Identification Protocols:** In the Shooting phase, Gun Drones can only target the nearest visible enemy unit. If two units are equally close, you may choose which is targeted. **Attached Drones:** When a Sky Ray is set up, any accompanying Gun Drones are attached, and are treated as being embarked. Whilst the Gun Drones remain attached, the Sky Ray is considered to be equipped with the Drones' weapons in addition to its own. Both Drones can detach at the start of any of your Movement phases by disembarking. From that point onwards, the Drones are treated as a separate unit. They cannot reattach during the battle.

FACTION KEYWORDS	T'au Empire, <Sept>
KEYWORDS (SKY RAY)	**Vehicle, Fly, TX78 Sky Ray Gunship**
KEYWORDS (GUN DRONES)	**Drone, Fly, Gun Drones**

LONGSTRIKE

DAMAGE
Some of this model's characteristics change as it suffers damage, as shown below:

REMAINING W	M	BS	A
7-13+	12"	2+	3
4-6	6"	3+	D3
1-3	3"	4+	1

NAME	M	WS	BS	S	T	W	A	Ld	Sv
Longstrike's Gunship	*	6+	*	6	7	13	*	8	3+
MV1 Gun Drone	8"	5+	5+	3	4	1	1	6	4+

Longstrike's Gunship is a single model equipped with a railgun. It is accompanied by 2 MV1 Gun Drones, each equipped with two pulse carbines. Only one of this unit can be included in your army.

WEAPON	RANGE	TYPE	S	AP	D	ABILITIES
Burst cannon	18"	Assault 4	5	0	1	-
Ion cannon	When attacking with this weapon, choose one of the profiles below.					
- Standard	60"	Heavy 3	7	-2	2	-
- Overcharge	60"	Heavy D3	8	-2	3	Change the type to Heavy D6 against units containing 10 or more models. If you roll one or more hit rolls of 1, the bearer suffers a mortal wound after all of this weapon's shots have been resolved.
Pulse carbine	18"	Assault 2	5	0	1	-
Railgun	When attacking with this weapon, choose one of the profiles below.					
- Solid shot	72"	Heavy 1	10	-4	D6	Each time you make a wound roll of 6+ for this weapon, the target unit suffers D3 mortal wounds in addition to the normal damage.
- Submunitions	72"	Heavy D6	6	-1	1	
Seeker missile	72"	Heavy 1	-	-	-	A unit hit by this weapon suffers a mortal wound. Each seeker missile can only be used once per battle. This weapon only hits on a roll of 6, regardless of the firing model's Ballistic Skill or any modifiers.
Smart missile system	30"	Heavy 4	5	0	1	Smart missile systems can be fired at units that are not visible to the bearer. In addition, units attacked by this weapon do not gain any bonus to their saving throws for being in cover.

WARGEAR OPTIONS	• This model may replace its railgun with an ion cannon. • This model may take up to two seeker missiles. • Instead of being accompanied by two MV1 Gun Drones, this model may take two burst cannons or two smart missile systems.

ABILITIES	**For the Greater Good** (pg 48) **Hover Tank:** Distances must be measured to and from the hull of this model rather than its base. **Explodes:** If this model is reduced to 0 wounds, roll a D6 before removing it from the battlefield and before any embarked models disembark. On a 6 it explodes, and each unit within 6" suffers D3 mortal wounds. **Tank Ace:** You can add 1 to wound rolls for Longstrike's Gunship when it shoots at a **Vehicle** or **Monster**. **Fire Caste Exemplar:** You can add 1 to hit rolls in the Shooting phase for other friendly **T'au Sept** TX7 Hammerhead Gunships within 6". **Threat Identification Protocols:** In the Shooting phase, Gun Drones can only target the nearest visible enemy unit. If two units are equally close, you may choose which is targeted.	**Saviour Protocols:** If a **Drones** unit is within 3" of a friendly **T'au Empire Infantry** or **Battlesuit** unit, you can choose to allocate any wounds to the Drones instead of the target unit. **Attached Drones:** When Longstrike's Gunship is set up, any accompanying Gun Drones are attached, and are treated as being embarked. Whilst the Gun Drones remain attached, Longstrike's Gunship is considered to be equipped with the Drones' weapons in addition to its own. Both Drones can detach at the start of any of your Movement phases by disembarking. From that point onwards, the Drones are treated as a separate unit. They cannot reattach during the battle.

FACTION KEYWORDS	T'au Empire, T'au Sept
KEYWORDS (LONGSTRIKE'S GUNSHIP)	CHARACTER, VEHICLE, TX7 HAMMERHEAD GUNSHIP, FLY, LONGSTRIKE
KEYWORDS (GUN DRONES)	DRONE, FLY, GUN DRONES

TX7 HAMMERHEAD GUNSHIP

10 POWER

NAME	M	WS	BS	S	T	W	A	Ld	Sv
TX7 Hammerhead Gunship	*	6+	*	6	7	13	*	8	3+
MV1 Gun Drone	8"	5+	5+	3	4	1	1	6	4+

DAMAGE

Some of this model's characteristics change as it suffers damage, as shown below:

REMAINING W	M	BS	A
7-13+	12"	3+	3
4-6	6"	4+	D3
1-3	3"	5+	1

A TX7 Hammerhead Gunship is a single model equipped with a railgun. It is accompanied by 2 MV1 Gun Drones, each equipped with two pulse carbines.

WEAPON	RANGE	TYPE	S	AP	D	ABILITIES
Burst cannon	18"	Assault 4	5	0	1	-
Ion cannon	When attacking with this weapon, choose one of the profiles below.					
- Standard	60"	Heavy 3	7	-2	2	-
- Overcharge	60"	Heavy D3	8	-2	3	Change the type to Heavy D6 against units containing 10 or more models. If you roll one or more hit rolls of 1, the bearer suffers a mortal wound after all of this weapon's shots have been resolved.
Pulse carbine	18"	Assault 2	5	0	1	-
Railgun	When attacking with this weapon, choose one of the profiles below.					
- Solid shot	72"	Heavy 1	10	-4	D6	Each time you make a wound roll of 6+ for this weapon, the target unit suffers D3 mortal wounds in addition to the normal damage.
- Submunitions	72"	Heavy D6	6	-1	1	-
Seeker missile	72"	Heavy 1	-	-	-	A unit hit by this weapon suffers a mortal wound. Each seeker missile can only be used once per battle. This weapon only hits on a roll of 6, regardless of the firing model's Ballistic Skill or any modifiers.
Smart missile system	30"	Heavy 4	5	0	1	Smart missile systems can be fired at units that are not visible to the bearer. In addition, units attacked by this weapon do not gain any bonus to their saving throws for being in cover.

WARGEAR OPTIONS
- This model may replace its railgun with an ion cannon.
- This model may take up to two seeker missiles.
- Instead of being accompanied by two MV1 Gun Drones, this model may take two burst cannons or two smart missile systems.

ABILITIES

Hover Tank: Distances must be measured to and from the hull of this model rather than its base.

Explodes: If this model is reduced to 0 wounds, roll a D6 before removing it from the battlefield and before any embarked models disembark. On a 6 it explodes, and each unit within 6" suffers D3 mortal wounds.

Saviour Protocols: If a DRONES unit is within 3" of a friendly T'AU EMPIRE INFANTRY or BATTLESUIT unit, you can choose to allocate any wounds to the Drones instead of the target unit.

Threat Identification Protocols: In the Shooting phase, Gun Drones can only target the nearest visible enemy unit. If two units are equally close, you may choose which is targeted.

Attached Drones: When a Hammerhead Gunship is set up, any accompanying Gun Drones are attached, and are treated as being embarked. Whilst the Gun Drones remain attached, the Hammerhead Gunship is considered to be equipped with the Drones' weapons in addition to its own.

Both Drones can detach at the start of any of your Movement phases by disembarking. From that point onwards, the Drones are treated as a separate unit. They cannot reattach during the battle.

FACTION KEYWORDS	T'AU EMPIRE, <SEPT>
KEYWORDS (HAMMERHEAD)	VEHICLE, FLY, TX7 HAMMERHEAD GUNSHIP
KEYWORDS (GUN DRONES)	DRONE, FLY, GUN DRONES

73

XV88 BROADSIDE BATTLESUITS

NAME	M	WS	BS	S	T	W	A	Ld	Sv
Broadside Shas'ui	5"	5+	4+	5	5	6	2	7	2+
Broadside Shas'vre	5"	5+	4+	5	5	6	3	8	2+
MV8 Missile Drone	8"	5+	5+	3	4	1	1	6	4+

This unit contains 1 Broadside Shas'ui. It can include 1 additional Broadside Shas'ui (**Power Rating +9**) or 2 additional Broadside Shas'ui (**Power Rating +18**). A Broadside Shas'vre can take the place of one Broadside Shas'ui. Each Broadside Battlesuit is equipped with a heavy rail rifle and two smart missile systems. The unit may be accompanied by up to 2 MV8 Missile Drones, each equipped with a missile pod (**Power Rating +2**), or up to 2 Tactical Drones (pg 69) (**Power Rating +1**).

WEAPON	RANGE	TYPE	S	AP	D	ABILITIES
Heavy rail rifle	60"	Heavy 2	8	-4	D6	Each time you make a wound roll of 6+ for this weapon, the target unit suffers a mortal wound in addition to the normal damage.
High-yield missile pod	36"	Heavy 4	7	-1	D3	-
Missile pod	36"	Assault 2	7	-1	D3	-
Plasma rifle	24"	Rapid Fire 1	6	-3	1	-
Seeker missile	72"	Heavy 1	-	-	-	A unit hit by this weapon suffers a mortal wound. Each seeker missile can only be used once per battle. This weapon only hits on a roll of 6, regardless of the firing model's Ballistic Skill or any modifiers.
Smart missile system	30"	Heavy 4	5	0	1	Smart missile systems can be fired at units that are not visible to the bearer. In addition, units attacked by this weapon do not gain any bonus to their saving throws for being in cover.

WARGEAR OPTIONS	• Any Broadside Shas'ui or Shas'vre may replace their heavy rail rifle with two high-yield missile pods. • Any Broadside Shas'ui or Shas'vre may replace both smart missile systems with two plasma rifles. • Any Broadside Shas'ui or Shas'vre may take a seeker missile. • Any Broadside Shas'ui or Shas'vre may take one item from the *Support Systems* list.
ABILITIES	**For the Greater Good** (pg 48) **Bonding Knife Ritual:** If you roll a 6 when taking a Morale test for this unit, the test is automatically passed. **Drone Support:** When a unit of Broadside Battlesuits is set up on the battlefield, any accompanying Drones are set up in unit coherency with it. From that point onwards, the Drones are treated as a separate unit. **Saviour Protocols:** If a **Drones** unit is within 3" of a friendly **T'au Empire Infantry** or **Battlesuit** unit, you can choose to allocate any wounds to the Drones instead of the target unit.
FACTION KEYWORDS	T'au Empire, <Sept>
KEYWORDS (BROADSIDES)	BATTLESUIT, XV88 BROADSIDE BATTLESUITS
KEYWORDS (MV8 MISSILE DRONES)	DRONE, FLY, MV8 MISSILE DRONES

KV128 STORMSURGE

DAMAGE
Some of this model's characteristics change as it suffers damage, as shown below:

REMAINING W	BS	S	A
11-20+	4+	8	3
6-10	5+	7	D3
1-5	6+	6	1

NAME	M	WS	BS	S	T	W	A	Ld	Sv
KV128 Stormsurge	6"	5+	*	*	7	20	*	8	3+

A KV128 Stormsurge is a single model equipped with a cluster rocket system, four destroyer missiles, two flamers, a pulse blastcannon and two smart missile systems.

WEAPON	RANGE	TYPE	S	AP	D	ABILITIES
Airbursting fragmentation projector	18"	Assault D6	4	0	1	This weapon can be fired at units that are not visible to the bearer.
Burst cannon	18"	Assault 4	5	0	1	-
Cluster rocket system	48"	Heavy 4D6	5	0	1	-
Destroyer missile	60"	Heavy 1	-	-	-	A unit hit by this weapon suffers D3 mortal wounds. Each destroyer missile can only be used once per battle. This weapon only hits on a roll of 6, regardless of the firing model's Ballistic Skill or any modifiers.
Flamer	8"	Assault D6	4	0	1	This weapon automatically hits its target.
Pulse blastcannon	When attacking with this weapon, choose one of the profiles below.					
- Close range	10"	Heavy 2	14	-4	6	-
- Medium range	20"	Heavy 4	12	-2	3	-
- Long range	30"	Heavy 6	10	0	1	-
Pulse driver cannon	72"	Heavy D3	10	-3	D6	When attacking a unit with 10 or more models, this weapon's Type changes to Heavy D6.
Smart missile system	30"	Heavy 4	5	0	1	Smart missile systems can be fired at units that are not visible to the bearer. In addition, units attacked by this weapon do not gain any bonus to their saving throws for being in cover.

WARGEAR OPTIONS	• This model may replace both its flamers with two burst cannons or two airbursting fragmentation projectors. • This model may replace its pulse blastcannon with a pulse driver cannon. • This model may be equipped with up to three items from the *Support Systems* list.
ABILITIES	**Explodes:** If this model is reduced to 0 wounds, roll a D6 before removing it from the battlefield. On a 6 it explodes, and each unit within 6" suffers D6 mortal wounds. **Stabilising Anchors:** A Stormsurge may deploy its anchors at the end of your Shooting phase. While its anchors are deployed it may not move for any reason and it cannot pile in and attack in the Fight phase, but you can add 1 to its hit rolls. The Stormsurge can retract its anchors at the beginning of any of your Movement phases, and can then move, shoot and fight normally.	**Walking Battleship:** This model can Fall Back in the Movement phase and still shoot and/or charge that turn, and does not suffer the penalty for moving and firing Heavy weapons. This model can only benefit from cover when making saves if at least half of it is obscured from the firer.
FACTION KEYWORDS	T'AU EMPIRE, <SEPT>
KEYWORDS	VEHICLE, TITANIC, KV128 STORMSURGE

TIDEWALL DRONEPORT

5 POWER

NAME	M	WS	BS	S	T	W	A	Ld	Sv
Tidewall Droneport	6"	-	-	-	7	10	-	-	4+

A Tidewall Droneport is a single model. It is fitted with up to 4 Tactical Drones (see below).

ABILITIES	**Fortification:** A Tidewall Droneport cannot move independently (see below), nor can it fight in the Fight phase. Enemy models automatically hit this model in the Fight phase – do not make hit rolls. However, friendly units can still target enemy units that are within 1" of this model. **Drone Control Systems:** When you set up a Tidewall Droneport, you can also set up a unit of up to 4 Tactical Drones in the slots in the Droneport. These Drones begin the battle fully automated – they automatically shoot in each of your Shooting phases. If there is a friendly T'AU EMPIRE INFANTRY unit embarked on the Droneport at the beginning of your Movement phase, you can take control of the Drones, which then detach from the Droneport and act as a separate unit that is part of your army. In addition, while a friendly T'AU EMPIRE INFANTRY unit is embarked on the Droneport, the Tactical Drones activated in this way can use that unit's Ballistic Skill instead of their own when making shooting attacks. If the Droneport is destroyed before the Drones are activated, they are destroyed as well.
	Mobile Defence Platform: If a friendly T'AU EMPIRE INFANTRY unit is embarked on a Tidewall Droneport at the beginning of your Movement phase, you may move it in the Movement phase. A Tidewall Droneport cannot Advance or charge.
	Open-topped: Models embarked on this model can attack in their Shooting phase. Measure the range and draw line of sight from any point on this model. When they do so, any restrictions or modifiers that apply to this model also apply to its passengers; for example, the passengers cannot shoot if this model has Fallen Back in the same turn, the passengers cannot shoot (except with Pistols) if this model is within 1" of an enemy unit, and so on. **Explodes:** If a Tidewall Droneport is reduced to 0 wounds, roll a dice before removing the model from the battlefield and before any embarked models disembark; on a 6 it explodes, and each unit within 6" suffers D3 mortal wounds.
BUILDING	This model can transport any number of T'AU EMPIRE INFANTRY CHARACTERS and one other T'AU EMPIRE INFANTRY unit, but no more than 10 models in total.
FACTION KEYWORDS	T'AU EMPIRE, <SEPT>
KEYWORDS	BUILDING, VEHICLE, TRANSPORT, TIDEWALL DRONEPORT

TIDEWALL SHIELDLINE

3 POWER

NAME	M	WS	BS	S	T	W	A	Ld	Sv
Tidewall Shieldline	6"	-	-	-	6	10	-	-	4+
Tidewall Defence Platform	6"	-	-	-	7	10	-	-	4+

A Tidewall Shieldline is a single model. It can also include a Tidewall Defence Platform (**Power Rating +3**).

ABILITIES	**Fortification:** Tidewall Shieldlines and Tidewall Defences Platform cannot move independently (see below), nor can they fight in the Fight phase. Enemy models automatically hit these model in the Fight phase – do not make hit rolls. However, friendly units can still target enemy units that are within 1" of these models. **Open-topped:** Models embarked on a Tidewall Shieldline or Defence Platform can attack in their Shooting phase. Measure the range and draw line of sight from any point on the model they are embarked on. When they do so, any restrictions or modifiers that apply to this model also apply to its passengers; for example, the passengers cannot shoot if this model has Fallen Back in the same turn, the passengers cannot shoot (except with Pistols) if this model is within 1" of an enemy unit, and so on.
	Tidewall Network: When a Tidewall Shieldline that includes a Tidewall Defence Platform is set up on the battlefield, both models are placed within 1" of each other. From that point onwards, both are treated as separate units.
	Tidewall Field: A Tidewall Shieldline can reflect shots back at the enemy. For each save roll of 6+ you make in the Shooting phase for a Tidewall Shieldline, the attacking unit suffers one mortal wound after they have finished shooting.
	Mobile Defence Platform: If a friendly T'au Empire Infantry unit is embarked on a Tidewall Shieldline or a Tidewall Defence Platform at the beginning of your Movement phase, you may move it in the Movement phase. Neither a Tidewall Shieldline or a Tidewall Defence Platform can Advance or charge. **Explodes:** If a Tidewall Defence Platform is reduced to 0 wounds, roll a dice before removing the model from the battlefield and before any embarked models disembark; on a 6 it explodes, and each unit within 6" suffers D3 mortal wounds.
BUILDING	A Tidewall Shieldline and Tidewall Defence Platform can each transport any number of T'AU EMPIRE INFANTRY CHARACTERS and one other T'AU EMPIRE INFANTRY unit, but each can transport no more than 10 models in total.
FACTION KEYWORDS	T'AU EMPIRE, <SEPT>
KEYWORDS	BUILDING, VEHICLE, TRANSPORT, TIDEWALL SHIELDLINE

TIDEWALL GUNRIG

NAME	M	WS	BS	S	T	W	A	Ld	Sv
Tidewall Gunrig	6"	-	5+	-	7	10	-	-	4+

A Tidewall Gunrig is a single model equipped with a supremacy railgun.

WEAPON	RANGE	TYPE	S	AP	D	ABILITIES
Supremacy railgun	72"	Heavy 2	10	-4	D6	Each time you make a wound roll of 6+ for this weapon, the target unit suffers D3 mortal wounds in addition to the normal damage.

ABILITIES	
	Fortification: A Tidewall Gunrig cannot move independently (see below), nor can it fight in the Fight phase. Enemy models automatically hit this model in the Fight phase – do not make hit rolls. However, this model can still shoot if there are enemy models within 1" of it, and friendly units can still target enemy units that are within 1" of this model. **Open-topped:** Models embarked on this model can attack in their Shooting phase. Measure the range and draw line of sight from any point on this model. When they do so, any restrictions or modifiers that apply to this model also apply to its passengers; for example, the passengers cannot shoot if this model has Fallen Back in the same turn and so on. Note that the passengers cannot shoot (except with Pistols) if this model is within 1" of an enemy unit, even though the Tidewall Gunrig itself can.	**Mobile Defence Platform:** If a friendly T'AU EMPIRE INFANTRY unit is embarked on a Tidewall Gunrig at the beginning of your Movement phase, you may move it in the Movement phase. A Tidewall Gunrig cannot Advance or charge. **Automated Weapon:** Unless a friendly T'AU EMPIRE INFANTRY unit is embarked on this model, its supremacy railgun can only target the nearest visible enemy. If two units are equally close, you may choose which is targeted. **Explodes:** If a Tidewall Gunrig is reduced to 0 wounds, roll a dice before removing the model from the battlefield and before any embarked models disembark; on a 6 it explodes, and each unit within 6" suffers D3 mortal wounds.

BUILDING	This model can transport any number of T'AU EMPIRE INFANTRY CHARACTERS and one other T'AU EMPIRE INFANTRY unit, but no more than 10 models in total.
FACTION KEYWORDS	T'AU EMPIRE, <SEPT>
KEYWORDS	BUILDING, VEHICLE, TRANSPORT, TIDEWALL GUNRIG

The T'au are masters of mobile warfare – even their defensive emplacements are able to relocate mid-battle.

TYRANIDS

The shadow of the Tyranid race falls across the galaxy like a cloying shroud. Driven by an all-consuming imperative to feed, these horrific weaponised bioforms devour whole worlds in impossibly vast swarms, leaving them as little more than barren rocks devoid of all life.

The galaxy is a dark and terrible place, and thousands of horrors lurk amongst the stars. Yet none rival the sheer, unrelenting nightmare of the Tyranids. These ravenous aliens have no desire beyond the constant need to consume. Borne through the endless expanse of space in colossal hive fleets, the Tyranids fall upon one world after another, devouring every scrap of organic matter and leaving nothing but desolation in their wake. To see the sky darken and bruise under the fell presence of scores of Tyranid bio-ships, vomiting their locust-like swarms into the atmosphere, is to know the terror of being nothing more than prey.

None know the true origins of the Tyranids. Xenobiologists of the Imperium theorise that they hail from some incalculably distant quarter beyond the intergalactic void, and that they have been drawn to this galaxy by its proliferation of biomass much as swarming insects are drawn to fields of crops. The Tyranids' single-minded need to consume at the expense of all else is unheard of amongst any other lifeform, but it is not the only horrifying aspect unique to these monsters. The coming of a Tyranid hive fleet is preceded by a smothering shroud of psychic nothingness that envelops entire star systems. Whole worlds go silent, their astropathic communications cut off by the Shadow in the Warp. Psykers caught within this field of psychic static risk losing their minds as their connection to the empyrean is overwhelmed by the hideous chittering of the gestalt alien consciousness known as the Hive Mind. Even those who endure must use their powers sparingly and with great care, lest their psyches be torn to shreds. With astropathic communication choked off, the inhabitants of a prey world have little choice but to take up arms, fight until their last breath and hope for a miracle.

Upon encircling a world, the hive fleet disgorges wave after wave of weapon beasts into the atmosphere. Mycetic spores by the million plunge through sawing flak fire, each bloated bio-pod stuffed full of beasts ready to burst forth and slaughter all in their path. Hordes of Termagants, Hormagaunts and flying Gargoyles sweep across the planet, driven by the urging of the Hive Mind coupled with their own instinct to hunt and kill. The prey pour fire into the onrushing swarms from behind acid-scorched barricades, or else launch desperate offensives to cripple the leader-beasts that act as coordinating nodes for the Hive Mind. But for every Tyranid slain, two more take its place. Their weapons spit burrowing grubs and digestive fluids that eat through armour and flesh with horrific ease, and screaming soldiers are borne to the ground and sliced to pieces under scything claws. Where heavy resistance is encountered, hulking siege organisms such as the devastating Carnifex or the plasma-spitting Exocrine are deployed to smash enemy armour or fortifications into rubble.

When the majority of the prey-world's forces have been slaughtered, the Tyranids begin the process of hunting down the last pockets of resistance. Blade-limbed Lictors stalk the streets and underhives in search of victims, disguised by their chameleonic carapaces. Raveners burrow their way into the few remaining strongholds, falling upon the doomed occupants, hacking and slashing with their vicious talons. Soon, the stain of the Tyranid hunter-organisms has spread across the entire planet, and screaming survivors of the initial invasion wave are snatched from their hiding places and eviscerated.

With all resistance destroyed, the Tyranids begin the process of consumption. Writhing tides of feeder-organisms sweep across the planet, devouring every scrap of flesh and every drop of moisture. Nothing is left to waste, not even the ruptured remains of fallen Tyranids. This accumulated biomatter is then turned into foul-smelling gruel upon which the monstrous living ships of the hive fleet feed. Great digestion pools the size of lakes gape like cysts in the planet's surface, bubbling with virulent acids and digestive Tyranid micro-organisms. The biomass of the planet is vomited into these churning lakes by lumbering Haruspexes. This is followed by the warrior beasts of the Tyranid swarms themselves, going willingly to their own annihilation that they might be re-absorbed by the Hive Mind as raw materials for the next planetary invasion. Vile, mucus-slick capillary towers burst from the writhing crust of the planet, reaching high into the upper atmosphere where the waiting bio-ships latch on and suckle the lifeblood of the world away. When it has gorged itself fully and every shred of biomatter has been assimilated, the hive fleet finally departs, leaving nothing but a shattered planetary husk in its wake as it sets off in search of its next hunting ground.

Entire sectors of space have been scoured in this manner, as the Tyranid hive fleets drift ever closer to the galactic core. Only by the most horrendous sacrifices can this doom be held back, and even the mightiest armies in the galaxy have been forced to their knees by the Tyranids' unrelenting advance. The Ultramarines' blessed home world of Macragge was almost lost to the horror of Hive Fleet Behemoth, and were it not for the heroic defiance of the Space Marines and their Chapter Master Marneus Calgar, the tendrils of the Tyranid menace might have choked the life from Segmentum Ultima. Yet despite similar displays of bravery on a thousand worlds across the Imperium and beyond, the hive fleets will not be halted. While the galaxy's inhabitants turn their eyes to the horrors emerging from the Great Rift, the Tyranid menace continues on its implacable course, utterly focused on the consumption of all life.

> *'I was there at Asphenyx. I saw the sun darken, and the skies crawl. I saw the piles of corpses we made, and the endless tide that surged over the dead to fall upon us with razor-sharp claws and flensing teeth. I still see it every night, in my waking nightmares.'*
>
> *- Sergeant Taven Collick, 63rd Infernus Steelhides*

THE HIVE FLEETS

Drifting through the void come star-eclipsing shoals of immense creatures whose cephalopodic forms bristle with spines and feeder tendrils. Each of these living vessels is host to thousands upon thousands of dormant warrior-forms, ready to wake from their slumber when the hive fleet locates its next meal.

The Tyranids have no home world, and no domain save their swiftly ravaged planetary hunting grounds. They are a space-borne race, spreading inward from the fringes of the galaxy like a rapacious and incurable virus. They travel in hive fleets, shoals of gigantic bio-ships that also serve as their spawning grounds. The first of these hive fleets encountered by the Imperium was code-named 'Behemoth', and it struck the realm of Ultramar like a battering ram. Behemoth caused terrible destruction before it was exterminated by the combined efforts of the Ultramarines and the Imperial Navy. At that time the Imperium dared to hope that the hive fleet was an isolated phenomenon, a xenos aberration that had been dealt with and would not be seen again. That hope was dashed with the arrival of Hive Fleet Kraken, and many other hive fleets have followed since, each adapting in response to the successes and failures of those that came before.

Even when the backbone of a hive fleet is broken, the threat is not averted. Hive Fleet Kraken might have been shattered at horrific cost, but the tendrils of its splinter fleets were dispersed across the galaxy like numberless spores. Hive Fleet Leviathan, meanwhile learned still further from the failures of its predecessors; it surged into the galaxy from many ingress points simultaneously, pushing not just inwards from the fringes, but upwards from below the galactic plane. Where once the Tyranids could be considered a slow-moving and largely distant threat, now they can strike anywhere, at any time.

Understandably, given the apparent autonomy of the hive fleets, many magos biologis have classified them as sub-categories of their species, each competing for resources. The truth is far more unsettling – each fleet is but one element of a greater whole. Every warrior-beast, feeder organism and bio-ship is a single fragment of an unfathomably complex entity that stretches across the vast reaches of space. This sentience is known as the Hive Mind. It is this gestalt consciousness, still an utter mystery to the galaxy at large, that allows the Tyranids to coordinate their attacks.

Every organism, from the diminutive Rippers that devour the biological matter of conquered worlds, to colossal Tyrannofexes and Bio-Titans, is linked to the Hive Mind. Unless impelled otherwise, these creatures follow a pattern of behaviour befitting their function, though their actions are still driven by the will of the greater consciousness. Larger and more complex organisms like Tyranid Warriors and Hive Tyrants are granted far more autonomy, and possess the ability to override the natural instincts of the swarm with a synaptic form of telepathy. Thus, despite their blunt predatory desires, Tyranid forces led by such creatures operate on a far more advanced strategic level, enacting tactical manoeuvres every bit as canny as those of even the greatest generals. However, should one of these synapse creatures be slain, the link between individual organisms and the Hive Mind is severed, disrupting the cohesion of the swarm and causing each creature to revert to its instinctual state. Observant enemies quickly learn to focus their fire upon the largest and most imposing beasts within a Tyranid swarm, noting the loss of

unity that results from such kills. For this reason, Tyranid forces are often led by multiple synapse creatures that form a layered network of synaptic control, so that if one of them falls the Hive Mind's influence remains strong.

Swift adaptation to the tactics, weapons and even the physiology of their prey is the most terrifying feature of the Tyranids. The forces of the hive fleets contain creatures specialised in every conceivable aspect of warfare, and the spawning chambers of each bio-ship can actively alter and replicate these organisms to suit the needs of any battle. A tactic that works once against the Tyranids will seldom prove successful in a later campaign, or even a later battle, for the Hive Mind learns with each encounter. Where concentrated firepower wipes out its swarms, the Hive Mind floods the battlefield with too many targets for its prey to kill, girds its beasts in thick plates of chitin, or sends monsters to tunnel underneath the enemy's lines and burst up in their midst. Where the foe breaks the Tyranid swarms with armour and artillery, the Hive Mind deploys creatures whose excretions eat away at hulls and seals to poison the crews within, or else meets them with lumbering living tanks whose corrosive munitions and crushing claws make short work of vehicles. Should the prey seek to evade direct battle and orchestrate a hit-and-run war with the Tyranids, the Hive Mind sends creatures to devour and demolish the enemy's cover, despatches winged swarms to tear aerial threats from the sky, and seeds the battlefield with camouflaged murder-beasts that swiftly transform hunters to hunted.

Thus far, it seems that there is no obstacle the hive fleets cannot overcome, and the only thing that can truly stem the tide is the sacrifice of thousands upon thousands of lives, fed into the jaws of the beast in a desperate attempt to slow its progress.

LEVIATHAN'S FALL

Hive Fleet Leviathan was the greatest Tyranid threat that the Imperium of Man had ever encountered, a gathering of bio-ships so vast that even the attempts of the noble Blood Angels and all their successor Chapters could not halt its advance. Having consumed the biomass of Human, Ork and Aeldari alike during its relentless advance across the galaxy, the largest tendril of Hive Fleet Leviathan was at the very height of its power, able to form new strategies and tactical counters at an exponential rate. Upon the Blood Angels' home world of Baal, Commander Dante devised a series of formidable defensive fortifications and awaited Leviathan's arrival. When the hive fleet's shadow finally fell upon Baal and her twin moons, bloody battle was joined.

The first nineteen waves of Tyranid warrior-organisms, each larger than the last, were driven off at great loss to the Blood Angels and their successor allies. Five Chapter Masters fell in that storm of bloodshed, and inch by inch the Space Marines were forced back to their fortress monastery, where they prepared to make a defiant last stand. It was at that moment, when all seemed lost, that the Cicatrix Maledictum – the Great Rift – tore open in the fabric of reality, and a foul aetheric wind swept forth, blasting its way across the war-torn Baal System. Eventually the skies cleared and the stars shone once more, and where Hive Fleet Leviathan had once orbited Baal and its moons, now an Imperial fleet was in its place. The reawakened Primarch of the Ultramarines, Roboute Guilliman, led a vengeful assault upon the disorganised remnants of the Tyranid swarms, and Baal was quickly scoured of the xenos taint. Exactly what became of Leviathan remains a mystery, though upon the now barren and lifeless moon of Baal Prime a clue was found – millions upon millions of xenos skulls, piled high in the eight-pillared symbol of the Bloodthirster Ka'Bandha, ancient nemesis of the Blood Angels.

Leviathan's defeat came at great cost, and even then the hive fleet still has many smaller tendrils coiling through the galaxy. Worse, this defeat has merely slowed the threat posed by the Tyranids, not defeated it. With every passing year reports of new incursions arrive, as new hive fleets thrust their tendrils out of the void. Hive Fleet Hydra skirts the galactic rim, biding its time as it gathers up the scattered splinter fleets of previous invasions. Scylla and Charybdis carve parallel paths through Segmentums Pacificus and Solar, far too close to the Imperium's heartlands, while Hive Fleet Jormungandr cuts its way down from the northern edge of the galaxy. Yet the fear is that these are merely the vanguard of a far greater entity, the true form of the Hive Mind simply softening up the galaxy before it makes its presence known.

THE SWARMLORD

Amongst the numberless lifeforms linked to the Hive Mind, there exists a creature as old as the Tyranid race itself. It is a harbinger of ruin, a beast that has wrought untold carnage upon the galaxy and has preyed upon civilisations beyond count. This legendary abomination is known by many names, but to those rare few in the Imperium who have witnessed its fury and lived, it is the Swarmlord.

Originally encountered by Humanity during the First Tyrannic War, this ancient predator has appeared across the breadth of the galaxy, fighting for different hive fleets over the course of centuries. The Swarmlord is, to all intents and purposes, deathless, for its link to the Hive Mind transcends physical limitations. Should it be slain, the creature's consciousness is absorbed into the synaptic web, where it stays until its body is re-grown once more. Thus, the Swarmlord can be deployed by the Hive Mind all across the galaxy, wherever its endless reserves of cunning and tactical knowledge are most needed. So intelligent is this monster that at the Battle for Macragge it was even able to outwit the Ultramarines, long considered one of the most tactically astute forces in the galaxy. The great Marneus Calgar himself was almost slain by the four serrated bone sabres that the Swarmlord wields with a skill adapted over aeons of constant warfare.

TYRANIDS ARMY LIST

This section contains all of the datasheets that you will need in order to fight battles with your Tyranid miniatures. Each datasheet includes the characteristics profiles of the unit it describes, as well as any wargear and abilities it may have. Some rules are common to several Tyranid units – these are described below and are referenced on the datasheets.

KEYWORDS

Throughout this section you will come across a keyword that is within angular brackets, specifically <Hive Fleet>. This is shorthand for a keyword of your own choosing, as described below.

<Hive Fleet>

All Tyranids belong to a hive fleet. When you include a Tyranid unit in your army, you must nominate which hive fleet that unit is from. There are many different hive fleets to choose from; you can use any of the hive fleets described in our books, or make up your own if you prefer. You then simply replace the <Hive Fleet> keyword in every instance on that unit's datasheet, and in any psychic powers they know, with the name of your chosen hive fleet.

For example, if you were to include a Tervigon in your army, and you decided it was from the Hive Fleet Kraken, then its <Hive Fleet> keyword is changed to Kraken, and its 'Brood Progenitor' ability would say 'You can re-roll hit rolls of 1 in the Shooting phase for friendly Kraken Termagant units within 6" of this model.'

ABILITIES

The following abilities are common to several Tyranid units:

Synapse

<Hive Fleet> units automatically pass Morale tests if they are within 8" of any friendly <Hive Fleet> units with this ability.

Instinctive Behaviour

Unless a <Hive Fleet> unit with this ability is within range of the Synapse ability (see above) of any friendly <Hive Fleet> units, it can only target the nearest visible enemy unit if it shoots, and if it charges it can only declare a charge against the nearest visible enemy unit.

Shadow in the Warp

Enemy Psykers must subtract 1 from any Psychic tests they make if they are within 8" of any units with this ability. Tyranid Psykers are not affected.

HIVE MIND DISCIPLINE

Before the battle, generate the psychic powers for Psykers that can use powers from the Hive Mind Discipline using the table below. You can either roll a D3 to generate their powers randomly (re-roll any duplicate results), or you can select the psychic powers you wish the psyker to have.

HIVE MIND DISCIPLINE

D3	PSYCHIC POWER
1	**The Horror** *The Horror* has a warp charge value of 6. If manifested, select a unit within 24" that is visible to the psyker. Until the start of your next Psychic phase, that unit must subtract 1 from their hit rolls and Leadership characteristic.
2	**Catalyst** *Catalyst* has a warp charge value of 6. If manifested, select a friendly Tyranids unit within 18" of the psyker. Until the start of your next Psychic phase, each time a model from that unit suffers a wound or mortal wound, roll a D6; on a roll of 5 or 6, the model does not lose a wound.
3	**Onslaught** *Onslaught* has a warp charge value of 6. If manifested, select a friendly Tyranids unit within 18" of the psyker. That unit can Advance and shoot this turn without suffering any penalties to Ballistic Skill for moving and shooting Heavy weapons, or Advancing and shooting Assault weapons. In addition, that unit can also charge this turn.

WARGEAR

Many of the units you will find on the following pages reference one or more of the following wargear lists (e.g. Basic Bio-cannons). When this is the case, the unit may take any item from the appropriate list below. The profiles for the weapons in these lists can be found in the appendix (pg 140-141).

BASIC BIO-WEAPONS
- Scything talons
- Spinefists
- Deathspitter

BASIC BIO-CANNONS
- Barbed strangler
- Venom cannon

MELEE BIO-WEAPONS
- Rending claws
- Boneswords
- Lash whip and bonesword

MONSTROUS BIO-WEAPONS
- Monstrous rending claws
- Monstrous boneswords
- Lash whip and monstrous bonesword

MONSTROUS BIO-CANNONS
- Two deathspitters with slimer maggots
- Two devourers with brainleech worms
- Stranglethorn cannon*
- Heavy venom cannon*

*A model cannot be armed with more than one cannon.

HIVE TYRANT

DAMAGE

Some of this model's characteristics change as it suffers damage, as shown below:

REMAINING W	M	WS	BS
6-10+	9"/16"	2+	3+
3-5	7"/12"	3+	3+
1-2	5"/8"	4+	4+

NAME	M	WS	BS	S	T	W	A	Ld	Sv
Hive Tyrant	✴	✴	✴	6	6	10	5	10	3+

A Hive Tyrant is a single model armed with two pairs of monstrous scything talons and a prehensile pincer tail.

WEAPON	RANGE	TYPE	S	AP	D	ABILITIES
Monstrous scything talons	Melee	Melee	User	-3	3	You can re-roll hit rolls of 1 when attacking with this weapon. If the bearer has more than one pair of monstrous scything talons, it can make 1 additional attack with this weapon each time it fights.
Prehensile pincer tail	Melee	Melee	User	0	D3	Each time the bearer fights, one (and only one) of its attacks must be made with this weapon.

WARGEAR OPTIONS	
	• A Hive Tyrant may replace one pair of monstrous scything talons with one item from the *Monstrous Bio-cannons* or *Monstrous Bio-weapons* list.
	• A Hive Tyrant may replace both pairs of monstrous scything talons with two items from the *Monstrous Bio-cannons* or two items from the *Monstrous Bio-weapons* list, or with one item from each list.
	• This model may have wings. If it does, it uses the second set of Move characteristics in the damage table above, and it gains the **FLY** keyword.
	• This model may have toxin sacs and/or adrenal glands (pg 141).

ABILITIES	
	Shadow in the Warp, **Synapse** (pg 85) **The Will of the Hive Mind:** The range of a Hive Tyrant's Synapse and Shadow in the Warp abilities is 12" rather than 8".	**Death Throes:** If this model is reduced to 0 wounds, roll a dice before removing the model from the battlefield; on a 6, it lashes out in its death throes, and each unit within 3" suffers D3 mortal wounds. **Psychic Barrier:** A Hive Tyrant has a 5+ invulnerable save.

PSYKER	
	A Hive Tyrant can attempt to manifest two psychic powers in each friendly Psychic phase, and attempt to deny one psychic power in each enemy Psychic phase. It knows the *Smite* power and two psychic powers from the Hive Mind discipline (pg 85).

FACTION KEYWORDS	TYRANIDS, <HIVE FLEET>
KEYWORDS	CHARACTER, MONSTER, PSYKER, HIVE TYRANT

Hive Tyrants are huge and terrifying leader-beasts. They act as conduits for the ravening will of the Hive Mind.

THE SWARMLORD

(15 POWER)

NAME	M	WS	BS	S	T	W	A	Ld	Sv
The Swarmlord	*	2+	3+	*	6	12	*	10	3+

DAMAGE
Some of this model's characteristics change as it suffers damage, as shown below:

REMAINING W	M	S	A
7-12+	9"	8	7
4-6	7"	7	6
1-3	5"	6	5

The Swarmlord is a single model armed with bone sabres and a prehensile pincer tail. Only one of this model may be included on your army.

WEAPON	RANGE	TYPE	S	AP	D	ABILITIES
Bone sabres	Melee	Melee	User	-3	D6	-
Prehensile pincer tail	Melee	Melee	6	0	D3	Each time the bearer fights, one (and only one) of its attacks must be made with this weapon.

ABILITIES	Shadow in the Warp, Synapse (pg 85)	**The Will of the Hive Mind:** The range of the Swarmlord's Synapse and Shadow in the Warp abilities is 12" rather than 8".
	Psychic Barrier: The Swarmlord has a 5+ invulnerable save.	
	Blade Parry: Add 1 to the Swarmlord's invulnerable saves against wounds caused by Melee weapons.	**Death Throes:** If this model is reduced to 0 wounds, roll a dice before removing the model from the battlefield; on a 6, it lashes out in its death throes, and each unit within 3" suffers D3 mortal wounds.
	Hive Commander: In each of your Shooting phases, you can pick one friendly <Hive Fleet> unit within 6" of the Swarmlord. That unit can move (and Advance, if you wish) as if it were the Movement phase instead of shooting.	
PSYKER	The Swarmlord can attempt to manifest two psychic powers in each friendly Psychic phase, and attempt to deny two psychic powers in each enemy Psychic phase. It knows the *Smite* power and two psychic powers from the Hive Mind discipline (pg 85).	
FACTION KEYWORDS	TYRANIDS, <Hive Fleet>	
KEYWORDS	CHARACTER, MONSTER, HIVE TYRANT, PSYKER, THE SWARMLORD	

OLD ONE EYE

(7 POWER)

NAME	M	WS	BS	S	T	W	A	Ld	Sv
Old One Eye	7"	*	-	*	7	10	*	7	3+

DAMAGE
Some of this model's characteristics change as it suffers damage, as shown below:

REMAINING W	WS	S	A
6-10+	3+	7	5
3-5	3+	6	3
1-2	4+	5	D3

Old One Eye is a single model armed with monstrous crushing claws, monstrous scything talons and a thresher scythe. Only one of this model may be included in your army.

WEAPON	RANGE	TYPE	S	AP	D	ABILITIES
Monstrous crushing claws	Melee	Melee	x2	-3	3	When attacking with this weapon, you must subtract 1 from the hit roll.
Monstrous scything talons	Melee	Melee	User	-3	3	You can re-roll hit rolls of 1 when attacking with this weapon.
Thresher scythe	Melee	Melee	4	-1	1	Make D3 hit rolls for each attack made with this weapon instead of 1.

ABILITIES	Instinctive Behaviour (pg 85)	**Berserk Rampage:** Each time you make a successful hit roll for Old One Eye (except for thresher scythe attacks), you may immediately make 1 additional attack with the same weapon against the same unit. These additional attacks do not confer extra attacks.
	Immortal Battering Ram: When Old One Eye finishes a charge move, roll a dice; on a 4+ one enemy unit within 1" suffers D3 mortal wounds.	
	Alpha Leader: You can add 1 to hit rolls in the Fight phase for friendly <Hive Fleet> Carnifex units that are within 6" of this model.	**Regeneration:** At the beginning of each of your turns this model regains one wound that it has lost earlier in the battle.
FACTION KEYWORDS	TYRANIDS, <Hive Fleet>	
KEYWORDS	CHARACTER, MONSTER, CARNIFEX, OLD ONE EYE	

BROODLORD

8 POWER

NAME	M	WS	BS	S	T	W	A	Ld	Sv
Broodlord	8"	2+	-	5	5	6	6	10	4+

A Broodlord is a single model armed with monstrous rending claws.

WEAPON	RANGE	TYPE	S	AP	D	ABILITIES
Monstrous rending claws	Melee	Melee	User	-3	D3	You can re-roll failed wound rolls when attacking with this weapon. In addition, each time you make a wound roll of 6+, that hit is resolved with an AP of -6 and Damage of 3.

ABILITIES	**Synapse**, **Shadow in the Warp** (pg 85) **Lightning Reflexes:** This model has a 5+ invulnerable save. **Swift and Deadly:** This model can charge even if it Advanced during its turn. **Brood Telepathy:** You can add 1 to hit rolls in the Fight phase for <HIVE FLEET> Genestealer units within 6" of any friendly <HIVE FLEET> Broodlords.
PSYKER	A Broodlord can attempt to manifest one psychic power in each friendly Psychic phase, and attempt to deny one psychic power in each enemy Psychic phase. It knows the *Smite* psychic power and one psychic power from the Hive Mind discipline (pg 85).
FACTION KEYWORDS	**TYRANIDS, <HIVE FLEET>**
KEYWORDS	**CHARACTER, INFANTRY, GENESTEALER, PSYKER, BROODLORD**

Broodlords are huge Genestealers capable of ripping men apart with each swipe of their claws.

TYRANID PRIME

5 POWER

NAME	M	WS	BS	S	T	W	A	Ld	Sv
Tyranid Prime	6"	2+	3+	5	5	6	4	10	3+

A Tyranid Prime is a single model armed with scything talons and a devourer.

WEAPON	RANGE	TYPE	S	AP	D	ABILITIES
Devourer	18"	Assault 3	4	0	1	-
Flesh hooks	6"	Assault 2	User	0	1	This weapon can be fired within 1" of an enemy unit, and can target enemy units within 1" of friendly units.
Scything talons	Melee	Melee	User	0	1	You can re-roll hit rolls of 1 when attacking with this weapon. If the bearer has more than one pair of scything talons, it can make 1 additional attack with this weapon each time it fights.

WARGEAR OPTIONS	• This model may replace its devourer with one weapon from the *Basic Bio-weapons* list. • This model may replace its scything talons with one weapon from the *Melee Bio-weapons* list. • This model may have flesh hooks. • This model may have toxin sacs and/or adrenal glands (pg 141).
ABILITIES	**Shadow in the Warp, Synapse** (pg 85) **Alpha Warrior:** You can add 1 to hit rolls for all <Hive Fleet> Tyranid Warriors and Tyranid Shrikes that are within 6" of any friendly <Hive Fleet> Tyranid Primes.
FACTION KEYWORDS	TYRANIDS, <Hive Fleet>
KEYWORDS	CHARACTER, INFANTRY, TYRANID PRIME

TERVIGON

13 POWER

NAME	M	WS	BS	S	T	W	A	Ld	Sv
Tervigon	*	*	*	7	8	14	3	9	3+

DAMAGE
Some of this model's characteristics change as it suffers damage, as shown below:

REMAINING W	M	WS	BS
8-14+	8"	4+	4+
4-7	6"	5+	5+
1-3	4"	5+	6+

A Tervigon is a single model armed with massive scything talons. It can also fire stinger salvoes.

WEAPON	RANGE	TYPE	S	AP	D	ABILITIES
Stinger salvo	18"	Assault 4	5	-1	1	-
Massive crushing claws	Melee	Melee	x2	3	D6	When attacking with this weapon, you must subtract 1 from the hit roll.
Massive scything talons	Melee	Melee	User	-3	D6	You can re-roll hit rolls of 1 when attacking with this weapon. If the bearer has more than one pair of massive scything talons, it can make 1 additional attack with this weapon each time it fights.

WARGEAR OPTIONS	• This model may replace its massive scything talons with massive crushing claws. • This model may have toxin sacs and/or adrenal glands (pg 141).
ABILITIES	**Shadow in the Warp, Synapse** (pg 85) **Brood Progenitor:** You can re-roll hit rolls of 1 in the Shooting phase for friendly <Hive Fleet> Termagant units within 6" of this model. **Synaptic Backlash:** If a Tervigon is reduced to 0 wounds, roll a D6 before removing the model from the battlefield. Each friendly <Hive Fleet> Termagant unit within 6" of the Tervigon immediately suffers a number of mortal wounds equal to the result.	**Spawn Termagants:** At the end of your Movement phase, a Tervigon can spawn Termagants. If it does so, add a new unit of 10 Termagants to your army and set it up on the battlefield so that it is wholly within 6" of the Tervigon and more than 1" from the enemy. All of these models are armed with fleshborers. Alternatively, you can replace up to 10 models lost earlier in the battle in an existing unit of Termagants from your army that is within 6" of the Tervigon. Models placed in this way must be within 6" of the Tervigon and more than 1" from the enemy. You can only replace models armed with fleshborers. If you cannot place some of the models the excess is discarded.
PSYKER	A Tervigon can attempt to manifest one psychic power in each friendly Psychic phase, and attempt to deny one psychic power in each enemy Psychic phase. It knows the *Smite* power and one psychic power from the Hive Mind discipline (pg 85).
FACTION KEYWORDS	TYRANIDS, <Hive Fleet>
KEYWORDS	CHARACTER, MONSTER, PSYKER, TERVIGON

TYRANID WARRIORS

NAME	M	WS	BS	S	T	W	A	Ld	Sv
Tyranid Warrior	6"	3+	4+	4	4	3	3	9	4+

This unit contains 3 Tyranid Warriors. It can include up to 3 additional Tyranid Warriors (**Power Rating +5**) or up to 6 additional Tyranid Warriors (**Power Rating +10**). Each model is armed with a pair of scything talons and a devourer.

WEAPON	RANGE	TYPE	S	AP	D	ABILITIES
Devourer	18"	Assault 3	4	0	1	-
Flesh hooks	6"	Assault 2	User	0	1	This weapon can be fired within 1" of an enemy unit, and can target enemy units within 1" of friendly units.
Scything talons	Melee	Melee	User	0	1	You can re-roll hit rolls of 1 when attacking with this weapon. If the bearer has more than one pair of scything talons, it can make 1 additional attack with this weapon each time it fights.

WARGEAR OPTIONS	• Any model may replace its devourer with one weapon from the *Basic Bio-weapons* list. • Any model may replace its scything talons with one weapon from the *Melee Bio-weapons* list. • For every three models in the unit, one model may replace its devourer with one weapon from the *Basic Bio-cannons* list. • All models in the unit may have flesh hooks. • All models in the unit may have toxin sacs and/or adrenal glands (pg 141).
ABILITIES	**Synapse**, **Shadow in the Warp** (pg 85)
FACTION KEYWORDS	TYRANIDS, <HIVE FLEET>
KEYWORDS	INFANTRY, TYRANID WARRIORS

GENESTEALERS

NAME	M	WS	BS	S	T	W	A	Ld	Sv
Genestealer	8"	3+	-	4	4	1	3	9	5+

This unit contains 5 Genestealers. It can include up to 5 additional Genestealers (**Power Rating +4**), up to 10 additional Genestealers (**Power Rating +8**), or up to 15 additional Genestealers (**Power Rating +12**). Each model is armed with rending claws.

WEAPON	RANGE	TYPE	S	AP	D	ABILITIES
Rending claws	Melee	Melee	User	-1	1	Each time you make a wound roll of 6+ for this weapon, that hit is resolved with an AP of -4.
Scything talons	Melee	Melee	User	0	1	You can re-roll hit rolls of 1 when attacking with this weapon.

WARGEAR OPTIONS	• Any model may also have a pair of scything talons. • All models in the unit may have toxin sacs (pg 141).
ABILITIES	**Flurry of Claws:** Genestealers have 4 Attacks instead of 3 whilst their unit has 10 or more models. **Lightning Reflexes:** Genestealers have a 5+ invulnerable save. **Swift and Deadly:** Genestealers can charge even if they Advanced during their turn.
FACTION KEYWORDS	TYRANIDS, <HIVE FLEET>
KEYWORDS	INFANTRY, GENESTEALERS

TERMAGANTS

3 POWER

NAME	M	WS	BS	S	T	W	A	Ld	Sv
Termagant	6"	4+	4+	3	3	1	1	5	6+

This unit contains 10 Termagants. It can include up to 10 additional Termagants (**Power Rating +3**) or up to 20 additional Termagants (**Power Rating +6**). Each model is armed with a fleshborer.

WEAPON	RANGE	TYPE	S	AP	D	ABILITIES
Devourer	18"	Assault 3	4	0	1	-
Fleshborer	12"	Assault 1	4	0	1	-
Spike rifle	18"	Assault 1	3	0	1	-
Spinefists	12"	Pistol *	3	0	1	When a model fires this weapon, it makes a number of shots equal to its Attacks characteristic.
Strangleweb	8"	Assault D3	2	0	1	-

WARGEAR OPTIONS	• Any model may replace its fleshborer with a devourer, spinefists or a spike rifle. • For every ten models in the unit, one model may replace its fleshborer with a strangleweb. • All models in the unit may have toxin sacs and/or adrenal glands (pg 141).
ABILITIES	**Instinctive Behaviour** (pg 85) **Hail of Living Ammunition:** If this unit contains 20 or more models, you can re-roll wound rolls of 1 when it shoots.
FACTION KEYWORDS	TYRANIDS, <HIVE FLEET>
KEYWORDS	INFANTRY, TERMAGANTS

HORMAGAUNTS

3 POWER

NAME	M	WS	BS	S	T	W	A	Ld	Sv
Hormagaunt	8"	4+	4+	3	3	1	2	5	6+

This unit contains 10 Hormagaunts. It can include up to 10 additional Hormagaunts (**Power Rating +3**) or up to 20 additional Hormagaunts (**Power Rating +6**). Each model is armed with a pair of scything talons.

WEAPON	RANGE	TYPE	S	AP	D	ABILITIES
Scything talons	Melee	Melee	User	0	1	You can re-roll hit rolls of 1 when attacking with this weapon.

WARGEAR OPTIONS	• All models in the unit may take toxin sacs and/or adrenal glands (pg 141).
ABILITIES	**Instinctive Behaviour** (pg 85) **Bounding Leap:** Whenever this unit piles in and consolidates, it can move up to 6". **Hungering Swarm:** If this unit contains 20 or more models, you can re-roll wound rolls of 1 when it fights.
FACTION KEYWORDS	TYRANIDS, <HIVE FLEET>
KEYWORDS	INFANTRY, HORMAGAUNTS

▷ (2 POWER) RIPPER SWARM

NAME	M	WS	BS	S	T	W	A	Ld	Sv
Ripper Swarm	6"	5+	5+	3	3	3	4	4	6+

This unit contains 3 Ripper Swarms. It can include up to 3 additional Ripper Swarms (**Power Rating +2**) or up to 6 additional Ripper Swarms (**Power Rating +4**). Each model is armed with claws and teeth.

WEAPON	RANGE	TYPE	S	AP	D	ABILITIES
Spinemaw	6"	Pistol 4	2	0	1	-
Claws and teeth	Melee	Melee	User	0	1	-

WARGEAR OPTIONS	• All models in the unit may also take spinemaws.

ABILITIES	**Instinctive Behaviour** (pg 85)
	Burrowers: During deployment, you can set up a Ripper Swarm underground instead of on the battlefield. At the end of any of your Movement phases, they can tunnel up to the battlefield – set them up anywhere that is more than 9" from any enemy models.

FACTION KEYWORDS	TYRANIDS, <HIVE FLEET>
KEYWORDS:	SWARM, RIPPERS

☠ (7 POWER) TYRANT GUARD

NAME	M	WS	BS	S	T	W	A	Ld	Sv
Tyrant Guard	7"	3+	4+	5	5	3	2	6	3+

This unit contains 3 Tyrant Guard. It can include up to 3 additional Tyrant Guard (**Power Rating +7**). Each model is armed with rending claws and scything talons.

WEAPON	RANGE	TYPE	S	AP	D	ABILITIES
Crushing claws	Melee	Melee	x2	-3	D3	When attacking with this weapon, you must subtract 1 from the hit roll.
Lash whip and bonesword	Melee	Melee	User	-2	1	If the bearer is slain in the Fight phase before it has made its attacks, leave it where it is. When its unit is chosen to fight in that phase, the bearer can do so as normal before being removed from the battlefield.
Rending claws	Melee	Melee	User	-1	1	Each time you make a wound roll of 6+ for this weapon, that hit is resolved with an AP of -4.
Scything talons	Melee	Melee	User	0	1	You can re-roll hit rolls of 1 when attacking with this weapon.

WARGEAR OPTIONS	• Any model may replace its scything talons with crushing claws or a lash whip and bonesword. • All models in the unit may have toxin sacs and/or adrenal glands (pg 141).

ABILITIES	**Instinctive Behaviour** (pg 85)
	Blind Rampage: If a friendly <HIVE FLEET> HIVE TYRANT is killed within 6" of this unit, from the end of that turn each Tyrant Guard's Attacks characteristic is increased by 1 for the rest of the battle.
	Shieldwall: Roll a dice each time a friendly <HIVE FLEET> HIVE TYRANT loses a wound whilst they are within 3" of this unit; on a 2+ a model from this unit can intercept that hit – the Hive Tyrant does not lose a wound but this unit suffers a mortal wound.

FACTION KEYWORDS	TYRANIDS, <HIVE FLEET>
KEYWORDS	INFANTRY, TYRANT GUARD

HIVE GUARD

NAME	M	WS	BS	S	T	W	A	Ld	Sv
Hive Guard	5"	4+	3+	4	5	3	2	7	4+

This unit contains 3 Hive Guard. It can include up to 3 additional Hive Guard (**Power Rating +7**). Each model is armed with an impaler cannon.

WEAPON	RANGE	TYPE	S	AP	D	ABILITIES
Impaler cannon	36"	Heavy 2	8	-2	D3	This weapon can target units that are not visible to the bearer. In addition, units attacked by this weapon do not gain any bonus to their saving throws for being in cover.
Shockcannon	24"	Assault D3	7	-1	D3	If the target is a **Vehicle** and you make a wound roll of 4+, the target suffers 1 mortal wound in addition to any other damage. If you make a wound roll of 6+, inflict D3 mortal wounds instead.

WARGEAR OPTIONS	• Any model may replace its impaler cannon with a shockcannon. • All models in the unit may have toxin sacs and/or adrenal glands (pg 141).
ABILITIES	Instinctive Behaviour (pg 85)
FACTION KEYWORDS	**TYRANIDS, <HIVE FLEET>**
KEYWORDS	**INFANTRY, HIVE GUARD**

Tyranid Guards are heavily built organisms that protect the swarm's Hive Tyrant and bio-structures.

LICTOR

2 POWER

NAME	M	WS	BS	S	T	W	A	Ld	Sv
Lictor	9"	2+	4+	6	4	4	3	9	5+

A Lictor is a single model armed with flesh hooks, grasping talons and rending claws.

WEAPON	RANGE	TYPE	S	AP	D	ABILITIES
Flesh hooks	6"	Assault 2	User	0	1	This weapon can be fired within 1" of an enemy unit, and can target enemy units within 1" of friendly units.
Grasping talons	Melee	Melee	User	-1	2	-
Rending claws	Melee	Melee	User	-1	1	Each time you make a wound roll of 6+ for this weapon, that hit is resolved with an AP of -4.

ABILITIES	Instinctive Behaviour (pg 85)
	Chameleonic Skin: Your opponent must subtract 1 from their hit rolls for attacks that target this model. In addition, add 2 instead of 1 to saving throws for this model when it is in cover.
	Hidden Hunters: During deployment, you can set up a Lictor in hiding instead of placing it on the battlefield. At the end of any of your Movement phases, the Lictor can spring from its hiding place – set it up anywhere on the battlefield that is more than 9" away from any enemy models. You can re-roll the Lictor's charge distance in the turn in which it uses this ability to arrive on the battlefield.
FACTION KEYWORDS	TYRANIDS, <HIVE FLEET>
KEYWORDS	INFANTRY, LICTOR

MALECEPTOR

9 POWER

NAME	M	WS	BS	S	T	W	A	Ld	Sv
Maleceptor	7"	*	4+	*	7	12	3	9	3+

A Maleceptor is a single model armed with massive scything talons.

WEAPON	RANGE	TYPE	S	AP	D	ABILITIES
Massive scything talons	Melee	Melee	User	-3	D6	You can re-roll hit rolls of 1 when attacking with this weapon. If the bearer has more than one pair of massive scything talons, it can make 1 additional attack with this weapon each time it fights.

ABILITIES	Shadow in the Warp, Synapse (pg 85)
	Psychic Overload: Instead of manifesting any psychic powers in your Psychic phase, a Maleceptor can unleash brain-bursting psychic tendrils. If it does so, roll a dice for each enemy unit within 6", to a maximum number of units shown in the damage table above. On a 2+ the Maleceptor deals 1 mortal wound to that unit.
	Psychic Barrier: A Maleceptor has a 5+ invulnerable save.
WARGEAR OPTIONS	• This model may take adrenal glands (pg 141).
PSYKER	A Maleceptor can attempt to manifest one psychic power in each friendly Psychic phase, and attempt to deny one psychic power in each enemy Psychic phase. It knows the *Smite* psychic power and one psychic power from the Hive Mind discipline (pg 85). Whenever a Maleceptor attempts to manifest a psychic power, add 1 to its Psychic test.
FACTION KEYWORDS	TYRANIDS, <HIVE FLEET>
KEYWORDS	MONSTER, PSYKER, MALECEPTOR

DAMAGE

Some of this model's characteristics change as it suffers damage, as shown below:

REMAINING W	WS	S	PSYCHIC OVERLOAD
7-12+	4+	7	6 units
4-6	5+	6	3 units
1-3	6+	5	D3 units

ZOANTHROPES

6 POWER

NAME	M	WS	BS	S	T	W	A	Ld	Sv
Zoanthrope	5"	4+	3+	4	4	3	1	9	5+
Neurothrope	5"	4+	3+	4	4	3	1	9	5+

This unit contains 3 Zoanthropes. It can include up to 3 additional Zoanthropes (**Power Rating +6**). A Neurothrope may take the place of one Zoanthrope. Each model is armed with claws and teeth.

WEAPON	RANGE	TYPE	S	AP	D	ABILITIES
Claws and teeth	Melee	Melee	User	0	1	-

ABILITIES	**Shadow in the Warp**, **Synapse** (pg 85)
	Spirit Leech: A unit that includes a Neurothrope regains D3 wounds lost earlier in the battle whenever it slays an enemy model with the *Smite* psychic power.
	Warp Blast: When this unit manifests the *Smite* psychic power, it inflicts D3 additional mortal wounds if this unit contains 4 or more models.
	Warp Field: Models in this unit have a 3+ invulnerable save.
PSYKER	A unit of Zoanthropes can attempt to manifest one psychic power in each friendly Psychic phase, and attempt to deny one psychic power in each enemy Psychic phase. A Zoanthrope unit of 4 or more models can instead attempt to manifest two psychic powers in each friendly Psychic phase, and attempt to deny one psychic power in each enemy Psychic phase. A Zoanthrope unit knows the *Smite* psychic power and one psychic power from the Hive Mind discipline (pg 85).
	When manifesting or denying a psychic power with a Zoanthrope unit, first select a model in the unit – measure range, visibility etc. from this model. If this unit suffers Perils of the Warp, it suffers D3 mortal wounds as described in the core rules, but units within 6" will only suffer damage if the Perils of the Warp causes the last model in the Zoanthrope unit to be slain.
FACTION KEYWORDS	**TYRANIDS, <HIVE FLEET>**
KEYWORDS	**INFANTRY, FLY, PSYKER, ZOANTHROPES**

The Maleceptor sends psychic tendrils plunging into the brain of its prey, causing it to overload with the power of the Hive Mind.

VENOMTHROPES

4 POWER

NAME	M	WS	BS	S	T	W	A	Ld	Sv
Venomthrope	5"	4+	4+	4	4	3	2	5	5+

This unit contains 3 Venomthropes. It can include up to 3 additional Venomthropes (**Power Rating +4**). Each model is armed with toxic lashes.

WEAPON	RANGE	TYPE	S	AP	D	ABILITIES
Toxic lashes (shooting)	6"	Assault 2	User	0	1	This weapon can be fired within 1" of an enemy unit, and can target enemy units within 1" of friendly units. In addition, you can re-roll failed wound rolls when attacking with this weapon.
Toxic lashes (melee)	Melee	Melee	User	0	1	You can re-roll failed wound rolls when attacking with this weapon. A model armed with this weapon always fights first in the Fight phase, even if it didn't charge. If the enemy has units that have charged, or that have a similar ability, then alternate choosing units to fight with, starting with the player whose turn is taking place.

ABILITIES	Instinctive Behaviour (pg 85)
	Shrouding Spores: Your opponent must subtract 1 from hit rolls for ranged weapons that target <Hive Fleet> Infantry units within 3" of any friendly <Hive Fleet> Venomthropes.
	Toxic Miasma: At the end of the Fight phase, roll a D6 for each enemy unit within 1" of any Venomthropes. On a 5+, that unit suffers a mortal wound.
FACTION KEYWORDS	Tyranids, <Hive Fleet>
KEYWORDS	Infantry, Fly, Venomthropes

PYROVORES

2 POWER

NAME	M	WS	BS	S	T	W	A	Ld	Sv
Pyrovore	5"	4+	4+	4	4	4	2	5	4+

This unit contains 1 Pyrovore. It can include 1 additional Pyrovore (**Power Rating +2**) or 2 additional Pyrovores (**Power Rating +4**). Each model is armed with a flamespurt and acid maw.

WEAPON	RANGE	TYPE	S	AP	D	ABILITIES
Flamespurt	10"	Assault D6	5	-1	1	This weapon automatically hits its target.
Acid maw	Melee	Melee	5	-3	1	-

ABILITIES	Instinctive Behaviour (pg 85)
	Acid Blood: Each time this model loses a wound in the Fight phase, roll a dice; on a 6, the unit that inflicted the damage suffers a mortal wound after all of their attacks have been resolved.
	Volatile: When a Pyrovore is slain, roll a dice. On a 4+ it bursts in a shower of acid – the nearest enemy unit within 3" (if any) suffers a mortal wound.
FACTION KEYWORDS	Tyranids, <Hive Fleet>
KEYWORDS	Infantry, Pyrovores

HARUSPEX

12 POWER

NAME	M	WS	BS	S	T	W	A	Ld	Sv
Haruspex	7"	✷	✷	✷	8	13	4	6	3+

A Haruspex is a single model armed with a grasping tongue, a ravenous maw and shovelling claws.

DAMAGE

Some of this model's characteristics change as it suffers damage, as shown below:

REMAINING W	WS	BS	S
8-13+	4+	4+	7
4-7	4+	5+	6
1-3	5+	5+	5

WEAPON	RANGE	TYPE	S	AP	D	ABILITIES
Grasping tongue	12"	Assault 1	6	-3	D3	This weapon can be fired within 1" of an enemy unit, and can target enemy units within 1" of friendly units. In addition, when a model is slain by this weapon, the Haruspex regains 1 lost wound.
Ravenous maw	Melee	Melee	User	-1	D3	Make D3 hit rolls for each attack made with this weapon, instead of 1.
Shovelling claws	Melee	Melee	x2	-3	D6	-

ABILITIES	
	Instinctive Behaviour (pg 85)
	Acid Blood: Each time this model loses a wound in the Fight phase, roll a dice; on a 6, the unit that inflicted the damage suffers a mortal wound after all of their attacks have been resolved.
	Rapacious Hunger: Each time a Haruspex slays an enemy model with its ravenous maw, it can immediately make one extra attack with its shovelling claws. In addition, at the end of a Fight phase in which a Haruspex slew any models with its ravenous maw, it regains 1 wound lost earlier in the battle.
	Frenzied Death Throes: If a Haruspex is reduced to 0 wounds, roll a dice before removing the model from the battlefield; on a 6, it lashes out in its death throes, and each unit within 3" suffers 3 mortal wounds.

FACTION KEYWORDS	**TYRANIDS, <HIVE FLEET>**
KEYWORDS	**MONSTER, HARUSPEX**

Toxicrenes and Venomthropes emit clouds of choking, poisonous spores that dissolve the lungs of those who breathe them.

DEATHLEAPER

4 POWER

NAME	M	WS	BS	S	T	W	A	Ld	Sv
Deathleaper	9"	2+	4+	6	4	6	4	10	5+

Deathleaper is a single model armed with flesh hooks, grasping talons and rending claws. Only one of this model can be included in your army.

WEAPON	RANGE	TYPE	S	AP	D	ABILITIES
Flesh hooks	6"	Assault 2	User	0	1	This weapon can be fired within 1" of an enemy unit, and can target enemy units within 1" of friendly units.
Grasping talons	Melee	Melee	User	-1	2	-
Rending claws	Melee	Melee	User	-1	1	Each time you make a wound roll of 6+ for this weapon, that hit is resolved with an AP of -4.

ABILITIES	Instinctive Behaviour (pg 85)
	Superior Chameleonic Skin: Your opponent must subtract 2 from their hit rolls for attacks that target Deathleaper. In addition, add 2 instead of 1 to saving throws for Deathleaper when it is in cover.
	It's After Me!: During deployment, you can set up Deathleaper in hunt of a victim instead of placing it on the battlefield. If you do so, at the start of the first battle round but before the first turn begins, pick a **CHARACTER** from the opposing army. At the end of any of your Movement phases Deathleaper can pounce upon its victim – set it up anywhere on the battlefield that is within 6" of the enemy **CHARACTER** you chose, but more than 1" away from any enemy models.
FACTION KEYWORDS	**TYRANIDS, <HIVE FLEET>**
KEYWORDS	**CHARACTER, INFANTRY, LICTOR, DEATHLEAPER**

THE RED TERROR

3 POWER

NAME	M	WS	BS	S	T	W	A	Ld	Sv
The Red Terror	12"	2+	4+	5	5	6	5	7	4+

The Red Terror is a single model armed with a prehensile pincer tail and two pairs of scything talons. Only one of this model can be included in your army.

WEAPON	RANGE	TYPE	S	AP	D	ABILITIES
Prehensile pincer tail	Melee	Melee	User	0	D3	Each time the bearer fights, one (and only one) of its attacks must be made with this weapon.
Scything talons	Melee	Melee	User	0	1	You can re-roll hit rolls of 1 when attacking with this weapon. If the bearer has more than one pair of scything talons, it can make 1 additional attack with this weapon each time it fights.

ABILITIES	Instinctive Behaviour (pg 85)
	Death From Below: During deployment, you can set up the Red Terror underground instead of placing it on the battlefield. At the end of any of your Movement phases, the Red Terror can burrow to the surface – set it up anywhere on the battlefield that is more than 9" away from any enemy models.
	Feeding Frenzy: You can add 1 to hit rolls in the Fight phase for friendly **<HIVE FLEET>** Ravener units that are within 6" of this model.
	Swallow Whole: If 4 or more of the Red Terror's scything talons attacks hit, instead of causing damage normally the Red Terror can attempt to swallow a victim whole. Roll a D6, and if the result is equal to or higher than the highest Wounds characteristic of the unit, one model from that unit is slain.
FACTION KEYWORDS	**TYRANIDS, <HIVE FLEET>**
KEYWORDS	**CHARACTER, INFANTRY, THE RED TERROR**

⚡ (6 POWER) TYRANID SHRIKES

NAME	M	WS	BS	S	T	W	A	Ld	Sv
Tyranid Shrike	12"	3+	4+	4	4	3	3	9	4+

This unit contains 3 Tyranid Shrikes. It can include up to 3 additional Tyranid Shrikes (**Power Rating +6**) or up to 6 additional Tyranid Shrikes (**Power Rating +12**). Each model is armed with a devourer and scything talons.

WEAPON	RANGE	TYPE	S	AP	D	ABILITIES
Devourer	18"	Assault 3	4	0	1	-
Flesh hooks	12"	Assault 2	User	0	1	This weapon can be fired within 1" of an enemy unit, and can target enemy units within 1" of friendly units.
Scything talons	Melee	Melee	User	0	1	You can re-roll hit rolls of 1 when attacking with this weapon. If the bearer has more than one pair of scything talons, it can make 1 additional attack with this weapon each time it fights.

WARGEAR OPTIONS	• Any model may replace its devourer with one weapon from the *Basic Bio-weapons* list. • Any model may replace its scything talons with one weapon from the *Melee Bio-weapons* list. • For every three models in the unit, one model may replace its devourer with one weapon from the *Basic Bio-cannons* list. • All models in the unit may have flesh hooks. • All models in the unit may have toxin sacs and/or adrenal glands (pg 141).
ABILITIES	**Synapse, Shadow in the Warp** (pg 85)
FACTION KEYWORDS	**TYRANIDS, <HIVE FLEET>**
KEYWORDS	**INFANTRY, FLY, TYRANID SHRIKES**

⚡ (4 POWER) RAVENERS

NAME	M	WS	BS	S	T	W	A	Ld	Sv
Ravener	12"	3+	4+	4	4	3	4	5	5+

This unit contains 3 Raveners. It can include up to 3 additional Raveners (**Power Rating +4**) or up to 6 additional Raveners (**Power Rating +8**). Each model is armed with two pairs of scything talons.

WEAPON	RANGE	TYPE	S	AP	D	ABILITIES
Deathspitter	18"	Assault 3	5	-1	1	-
Devourer	18"	Assault 3	4	0	1	-
Spinefists	12"	Pistol *	3	0	1	When a model fires this weapon, it makes a number of shots equal to its Attacks characteristic.
Rending claws	Melee	Melee	User	-1	1	Each time you make a wound roll of 6+ for this weapon, that hit is resolved with an AP of -4.
Scything talons	Melee	Melee	User	0	1	You can re-roll hit rolls of 1 when attacking with this weapon. If the bearer has more than one pair of scything talons, it can make 1 additional attack with this weapon each time it fights.

WARGEAR OPTIONS	• Any model may replace one of its pairs of scything talons with rending claws. • Any model may have spinefists, a devourer or a deathspitter.
ABILITIES	**Instinctive Behaviour** (pg 85) **Death From Below:** During deployment, you can set up a Ravener unit underground instead of placing it on the battlefield. At the end of any of your Movement phases, the Raveners can burrow to the surface – set them up anywhere on the battlefield that is more than 9" away from any enemy models.
FACTION KEYWORDS	**TYRANIDS, <HIVE FLEET>**
KEYWORDS	**INFANTRY, RAVENERS**

SKY-SLASHER SWARM

2 POWER

NAME	M	WS	BS	S	T	W	A	Ld	Sv
Sky-Slasher Swarm	12"	5+	5+	3	3	3	4	4	6+

This unit contains 3 Sky-Slasher Swarms. It can include up to 3 additional Sky-Slasher Swarms (**Power Rating +2**) or up to 6 additional Sky-Slasher Swarms (**Power Rating +4**). Each model is armed with claws and teeth.

WEAPON	RANGE	TYPE	S	AP	D	ABILITIES
Spinemaw	6"	Pistol 4	2	0	1	-
Claws and teeth	Melee	Melee	User	0	1	-

WARGEAR OPTIONS	• All models in the unit may also take spinemaws.
ABILITIES	**Instinctive Behaviour** (pg 85)
FACTION KEYWORDS	TYRANIDS, <HIVE FLEET>
KEYWORDS	SWARM, FLY, SKY-SLASHERS

GARGOYLES

4 POWER

NAME	M	WS	BS	S	T	W	A	Ld	Sv
Gargoyle	12"	4+	4+	3	3	1	1	5	6+

This unit contains 10 Gargoyles. It can include up to 10 additional Gargoyles (**Power Rating + 4**) or up to 20 additional Gargoyles (**Power Rating +8**). Each model is armed with a fleshborer and blinding venom.

WEAPON	RANGE	TYPE	S	AP	D	ABILITIES
Fleshborer	12"	Assault 1	4	0	1	-
Blinding venom	Melee	Melee	3	0	1	If a unit suffers any unsaved wounds from this weapon, your opponent must subtract 1 from hit rolls for that unit until the end of the turn.

WARGEAR OPTIONS	• All models in the unit may have toxin sacs and/or adrenal glands (pg 141).
ABILITIES	**Instinctive Behaviour** (pg 85) **Hail of Living Ammunition:** If this unit contains 20 or more models, you can re-roll wound rolls of 1 when it shoots.
FACTION KEYWORDS	TYRANIDS, <HIVE FLEET>
KEYWORDS	INFANTRY, FLY, GARGOYLES

The winged Gaunts known as Gargoyles throng in the skies, sowing terror and anarchy before the main swarms attack.

⚡ 9 POWER — HARPY

NAME	M	WS	BS	S	T	W	A	Ld	Sv
Harpy	✱	✱	✱	6	6	12	3	9	4+

DAMAGE

Some of this model's characteristics change as it suffers damage, as shown below:

REMAINING W	M	WS	BS
7-12+	10-30"	4+	4+
4-6	10-20"	4+	5+
1-3	10-15"	5+	5+

A Harpy is a single model armed with two stranglethorn cannons and scything wings. It can also fire stinger salvoes.

WEAPON	RANGE	TYPE	S	AP	D	ABILITIES
Heavy venom cannon	36"	Assault D3	9	-1	D3	-
Stinger salvo	18"	Assault 4	5	-1	1	-
Stranglethorn cannon	36"	Assault D6	7	-1	2	You can add 1 to hit rolls for this weapon when attacking a unit with 10 or more models.
Scything wings	Melee	Melee	User	-2	D3	You can re-roll hit rolls of 1 when attacking with this weapon.

WARGEAR OPTIONS	• This model may replace both its stranglethorn cannons with two heavy venom cannons.

ABILITIES	**Instinctive Behaviour** (pg 85)	**Spore Mine Cysts:** A Harpy can drop Spore Mines as it flies over enemy units in its Movement phase. To do so, after the Harpy has moved, pick one enemy unit that it flew over and roll a D6 for each model in that unit, up to a maximum of 3 dice. Each time you roll a 4+ a Spore Mine has hit the target and explodes. Roll a D6 to find out how much damage is inflicted on the unit: on a 1 the Spore Mine fails to inflict any harm, on a 2-5 it inflicts 1 mortal wound, and on a 6 it inflicts D3 mortal wounds.

Death Throes: If this model is reduced to 0 wounds, roll a D6 before removing the model from the battlefield; on a 6, it lashes out in its death throes, and each unit within 3" suffers D3 mortal wounds.

Sonic Screech: When a Harpy successfully charges, until the end of the turn enemy units within 1" cannot be chosen to Fight until all other eligible units have done so.

Each time a Spore Mine misses its target, set up a single Spore Mine anywhere within 6" of the target unit and more than 3" from any enemy model (if the Spore Mine cannot be placed it is destroyed). This then follows the rules for Spore Mines (pg 103) that are part of your army, but it cannot move or charge during the turn it was set up.

FACTION KEYWORDS	TYRANIDS, <HIVE FLEET>
KEYWORDS	MONSTER, FLY, HARPY

Hive Crones and Harpies bring destruction from above, potent bio-weapons raining death upon their earthbound victims.

HIVE CRONE

8 POWER

NAME	M	WS	BS	S	T	W	A	Ld	Sv
Hive Crone	*	*	*	6	6	12	4	9	4+

DAMAGE
Some of this model's characteristics change as it suffers damage, as shown below:

REMAINING W	M	WS	BS
7-12+	10-30"	4+	4+
4-6	10-20"	4+	5+
1-3	10-15"	5+	5+

A Hive Crone is a single model armed with a drool cannon, tentaclids, scything wings and a wicked spur. It can also fire stinger salvoes.

WEAPON	RANGE	TYPE	S	AP	D	ABILITIES
Drool cannon	8"	Assault D6	6	-1	1	This weapon automatically hits its target.
Stinger salvo	18"	Assault 4	5	-1	1	-
Tentaclids	36"	Assault 2	5	0	1	You may re-roll failed hit rolls for this weapon against units that can **FLY**. In addition, if the target is a **VEHICLE** and you make a wound roll of 4+, it suffers 1 mortal wound in addition to any other damage. If you make a wound roll of 6+, inflict D3 mortal wounds instead.
Scything wings	Melee	Melee	User	-2	D3	You can re-roll hit rolls of 1 when attacking with this weapon.
Wicked spur	Melee	Melee	8	-3	D3	Each time the bearer fights, one (and only one) of its attacks must be made with this weapon.

ABILITIES	Instinctive Behaviour (pg 85)
	Death Throes: If this model is reduced to 0 wounds, roll a D6 before removing the model from the battlefield; on a 6, it lashes out in its death throes, and each unit within 3" suffers D3 mortal wounds.
FACTION KEYWORDS	TYRANIDS, <HIVE FLEET>
KEYWORDS	MONSTER, FLY, HIVE CRONE

MUCOLID SPORES

1 POWER

NAME	M	WS	BS	S	T	W	A	Ld	Sv
Mucolid Spore	3"	-	-	1	3	3	1	10	6+

This unit contains 1 Mucolid Spore. It can include 1 additional Mucolid Spore (**Power Rating +1**) or 2 additional Mucolid Spores (**Power Rating +2**).

ABILITIES	Instinctive Behaviour (pg 85)	**Living Bombs:** Mucolid Spores automatically pass Morale tests. Furthermore, Mucolid Spores are discounted for the purposes of any victory conditions – their destruction never awards victory points, they do not count towards the number of models controlling an objective, and they do not count when determining if a player has any models left on the battlefield. If you are playing a matched play game, the creation of new Mucolid Spores (e.g. from a Sporocyst's Spore Node ability) is free, and the Mucolid Spores' points cost does not come out of your pool of reinforcement points.
	Float Down: During deployment, you can set up a Mucolid Spore unit in the upper atmosphere instead of on the battlefield. At the end of any of your Movement phases, it can float down to the battlefield – set it up anywhere that is more than 12" from any enemy models.	
	Floating Death: A Mucolid Spore explodes if it is within 3" of any enemy units at the end of any Charge phase. Each time a Mucolid Spore explodes, roll a D6: on a 1 it fails to inflict any harm, on a 2-5 it inflicts D3 mortal wounds on the nearest enemy unit, and on a 6 it inflicts D6 mortal wounds on that unit. The Mucolid Spore is then destroyed.	
FACTION KEYWORDS	TYRANIDS, <HIVE FLEET>	
KEYWORDS	FLY, MUCOLID SPORES	

SPORE MINES

1 POWER

NAME	M	WS	BS	S	T	W	A	Ld	Sv
Spore Mine	3"	-	-	1	1	1	1	10	7+

This unit contains 3 Spore Mines. It can include up to 3 additional Spore Mines (**Power Rating +1**).

ABILITIES

Instinctive Behaviour (pg 85)

Float Down: During deployment, you can set up a Spore Mine unit in the upper atmosphere instead of on the battlefield. At the end of any of your Movement phases, it can float down to the battlefield – set it up anywhere that is more than 12" from any enemy models.

Floating Death: A Spore Mine explodes if it is within 3" of any enemy units at the end of any Charge phase. Each time a Spore Mine explodes, roll a D6: on a 1 it fails to inflict any harm, on a 2-5 it inflicts 1 mortal wound on the nearest enemy unit, and on a 6 it inflicts D3 mortal wounds on that unit. The Spore Mine is then destroyed.

Living Bombs: Spore Mines automatically pass Morale tests. Furthermore, Spore Mines are discounted for the purposes of any victory conditions – their destruction never awards victory points, they do not count towards the number of models controlling an objective, and they do not count when determining if a player has any models left on the battlefield. If you are playing a matched play game, the creation of new Spore Mines (e.g. from a Sporocyst's Spore Node ability) is free, and the Spore Mines' points cost does not come out of your pool of reinforcement points.

FACTION KEYWORDS | TYRANIDS, <HIVE FLEET>

KEYWORDS | FLY, SPORE MINES

TYRANNOCYTE

7 POWER

NAME	M	WS	BS	S	T	W	A	Ld	Sv
Tyrannocyte	*	5+	5+	*	6	12	*	7	4+

A Tyrannocyte is a single model armed with five deathspitters.

DAMAGE
Some of this model's characteristics change as it suffers damage, as shown below:

REMAINING W	M	S	A
7-12+	6"	5	D6
4-6	4"	4	D3
1-3	2"	3	1

WEAPON	RANGE	TYPE	S	AP	D	ABILITIES
Barbed strangler	36"	Assault D6	5	-1	1	You can add 1 to hit rolls for this weapon when attacking a unit with 10 or more models.
Deathspitter	18"	Assault 3	5	-1	1	-
Venom cannon	36"	Assault D3	8	-1	1	-

WARGEAR OPTIONS
• This model may replace all of its deathspitters with either five barbed stranglers or five venom cannons.

ABILITIES

Instinctive Behaviour (pg 85)

Invasion Organism: During deployment, you can set up a Tyrannocyte in its hive ship instead of placing it on the battlefield. If you do so, the hive ship can launch the Tyrannocyte at the end of any of your Movement phases – set it up anywhere on the battlefield that is more than 9" away from any enemy models.

Any models that are inside the Tyrannocyte (see right) must immediately disembark in the same manner as a unit disembarking from a transport, except that they must be set up more than 9" away from any enemy models. Any models that cannot be set up in this way are destroyed.

Transport Spore: When you set up a Tyrannocyte in its hive ship, you can also set up a <HIVE FLEET> INFANTRY unit of up to 20 models or a <HIVE FLEET> MONSTER with a Wounds characteristic of 14 or less inside it (this cannot be another Tyrannocyte or a Sporocyst).

Death Throes: If this model is reduced to 0 wounds, roll a dice before removing the model from the battlefield; on a 6, it lashes out in its death throes, and each unit within 3" suffers D3 mortal wounds.

FACTION KEYWORDS | TYRANIDS, <HIVE FLEET>

KEYWORDS | MONSTER, FLY, TYRANNOCYTE

CARNIFEXES

NAME	M	WS	BS	S	T	W	A	Ld	Sv
Carnifex	7"	4+	4+	6	7	8	4	6	3+

This unit contains 1 Carnifex. It can contain 1 additional Carnifex (**Power Rating +6**) or 2 additional Carnifexes (**Power Rating +12**). Each model is armed with two pairs of monstrous scything talons and a thresher scythe.

WEAPON	RANGE	TYPE	S	AP	D	ABILITIES
Bio-plasma	12"	Assault D3	7	-3	1	-
Bone mace	Melee	Melee	8	-1	D3	Each time the bearer fights, one (and only one) of its attacks must be made with this weapon.
Monstrous crushing claws	Melee	Melee	x2	-3	3	When attacking with this weapon, you must subtract 1 from the hit roll.
Monstrous scything talons	Melee	Melee	User	-3	3	You can re-roll hit rolls of 1 when attacking with this weapon. If the bearer has more than one pair of monstrous scything talons, it can make 1 additional attack with this weapon each time it fights.
Thresher scythe	Melee	Melee	4	-1	1	Make D3 hit rolls for each attack made with this weapon instead of 1.

WARGEAR OPTIONS	
	• Any model may replace one of its pairs of monstrous scything talons with an item from the *Monstrous Bio-cannons* list.
	• Any model may replace both of its pairs of monstrous scything talons with two items from the *Monstrous Bio-cannons* list.
	• Any model may replace one of its pairs of monstrous scything talons with monstrous crushing claws.
	• Any model may replace its thresher scythe with a bone mace.
	• Any model may have toxin sacs and/or adrenal glands (pg 141).
	• Any model may also be armed with bio-plasma.

ABILITIES	
	Instinctive Behaviour (pg 85)
	Living Battering Ram: When a Carnifex finishes a charge move, roll a dice; on a 4+ one enemy unit within 1" suffers a mortal wound.
	Monstrous Brood: The first time this unit is set up on the battlefield, all of its models must be placed within 6" of at least one other model in their unit. From that point onwards, each operates independently and is treated as a separate unit.

FACTION KEYWORDS	TYRANIDS, <HIVE FLEET>
KEYWORDS	MONSTER, CARNIFEXES

BIOVORES

NAME	M	WS	BS	S	T	W	A	Ld	Sv
Biovore	5"	4+	4+	4	4	4	2	5	4+

This unit contains 1 Biovore. It can include 1 additional Biovore (**Power Rating +2**) or 2 additional Biovores (**Power Rating +4**). Each model is armed with a spore mine launcher.

WEAPON	RANGE	TYPE	S	AP	D	ABILITIES
Spore mine launcher	48"	Heavy 1	-	-	-	See Spore Mine Launcher, below

ABILITIES	
Instinctive Behaviour (pg 85)	
Spore Mine Launcher: Each time a spore mine launcher hits the target, roll a D6 to find how much damage is inflicted on the target; on a 1 the Spore Mine fails to inflict any harm, on a 2-5 it inflicts 1 mortal wound, and on a 6 it inflicts D3 mortal wounds.	Each time a spore mine launcher misses its target, set up a single Spore Mine model anywhere within 6" of the target unit and more than 3" from any enemy model (if the Spore Mine cannot be placed it is destroyed). This then follows the rules for a Spore Mine (pg 103) that is part of your army, but it cannot move or charge during the turn it was set up.

FACTION KEYWORDS	TYRANIDS, <HIVE FLEET>
KEYWORDS	INFANTRY, BIOVORES

TRYGON PRIME

NAME	M	WS	BS	S	T	W	A	Ld	Sv
Trygon Prime	*	*	*	7	6	12	6	9	3+

DAMAGE

Some of this model's characteristics change as it suffers damage, as shown below:

REMAINING W	M	WS	BS
7-12+	9"	3+	4+
4-6	7"	4+	5+
1-3	5"	5+	6+

A Trygon Prime is a single model armed with a bio-electric pulse with containment spines, a biostatic rattle and three pairs of massive scything talons.

WEAPON	RANGE	TYPE	S	AP	D	ABILITIES
Bio-electric pulse with containment spines	12"	Assault 12	5	0	1	-
Biostatic rattle	Melee	Melee	User	-1	1	If a unit suffers any unsaved wounds from this weapon, add 1 to any Morale tests they take until the end of the turn.
Massive scything talons	Melee	Melee	User	-3	D6	You can re-roll hit rolls of 1 when attacking with this weapon. If the bearer has more than one pair of scything talons, it can make 1 additional attack with this weapon each time it fights.
Prehensile pincer tail	Melee	Melee	6	0	D3	Each time the bearer fights, one (and only one) of its attacks must be made with this weapon.
Toxinspike	Melee	Melee	1	0	D3	Each time the bearer fights, one (and only one) of its attacks must be made with this weapon. This weapon always wounds targets (other than **VEHICLES**) on a 2+.

WARGEAR OPTIONS	• This model may replace its biostatic rattle with a prehensile pincer tail or toxinspike. • This model may have toxin sacs and/or adrenal glands (pg 141).

ABILITIES	**Shadow in the Warp**, **Synapse** (pg 85) **Subterranean Assault:** During deployment, you can set up a Trygon Prime underground instead of placing it on the battlefield. At the same time, you can set up a <**Hive Fleet**> Troops unit in the Trygon Prime's tunnel. At the end of any of your Movement phases, set up the Trygon Prime anywhere on the battlefield that is more than 9" away from any enemy models. If there is another unit in the Trygon Prime's tunnel, set it up at the same time wholly within 3" of the Trygon Prime and more than 9" away from any enemy models. Any models that you cannot place in this way are destroyed. **Death Throes:** If this model is reduced to 0 wounds, roll a D6 before removing the model from the battlefield; on a 6, it lashes out in its death throes, and each unit within 3" suffers D3 mortal wounds.
FACTION KEYWORDS	**TYRANIDS, <HIVE FLEET>**
KEYWORDS	**MONSTER, TRYGON PRIME**

The Carnifex is a living battering ram that can smash through rockcrete walls as it barrels toward its prey.

TRYGON

8 POWER

NAME	M	WS	BS	S	T	W	A	Ld	Sv
Trygon	*	*	*	7	6	12	6	7	3+

A Trygon is a single model armed with a bio-electric pulse, three pairs of massive scything talons and a toxinspike.

WEAPON	RANGE	TYPE	S	AP	D	ABILITIES
Bio-electric pulse	12"	Assault 6	5	0	1	-
Massive scything talons	Melee	Melee	User	-3	D6	You can re-roll hit rolls of 1 when attacking with this weapon. If the bearer has more than one pair of massive scything talons, it can make 1 additional attack with this weapon each time it fights.
Prehensile pincer tail	Melee	Melee	6	0	D3	Each time the bearer fights, one (and only one) of its attacks must be made with this weapon.
Toxinspike	Melee	Melee	1	0	D3	Each time the bearer fights, one (and only one) of its attacks must be made with this weapon. This weapon always wounds targets (other than **VEHICLES**) on a 2+.

WARGEAR OPTIONS	
	• This model may replace its toxinspike with a prehensile pincer tail. • This model may have toxin sacs and/or adrenal glands (pg 141).

ABILITIES	
	Instinctive Behaviour (pg 85) **Subterranean Assault:** During deployment, you can set up a Trygon underground instead of placing it on the battlefield. At the same time, you can set up a <**HIVE FLEET**> Troops unit in the Trygon's tunnel. At the end of any of your Movement phases, set up the Trygon anywhere on the battlefield that is more than 9" away from any enemy models. If there is another unit in the Trygon's tunnel, set it up at the same time wholly within 3" of the Trygon and more than 9" away from any enemy models. Any models that you cannot place in this way are destroyed. **Death Throes:** If this model is reduced to 0 wounds, roll a D6 before removing the model from the battlefield; on a 6, it lashes out in its death throes, and each unit within 3" suffers D3 mortal wounds.

FACTION KEYWORDS	**TYRANIDS, <HIVE FLEET>**
KEYWORDS	**MONSTER, TRYGON**

Tunnelling up from beneath the battlefield come swarms of Raveners, giant Mawlocs and Trygons rearing high their midst.

MAWLOC

5 POWER

NAME	M	WS	BS	S	T	W	A	Ld	Sv
Mawloc	*	*	-	*	6	12	8	7	3+

A Mawloc is a single model armed with distensible jaws, a prehensile pincer tail and three pairs of scything talons.

DAMAGE
Some of this model's characteristics change as it suffers damage, as shown below:

REMAINING W	M	WS	S
7-12+	9"	4+	6
4-6	7"	5+	5
1-3	5"	6+	4

WEAPON	RANGE	TYPE	S	AP	D	ABILITIES
Distensible jaws	Melee	Melee	User	0	D6	Each time the bearer fights, one (and only one) of its attacks must be made with this weapon.
Prehensile pincer tail	Melee	Melee	6	0	D3	Each time the bearer fights, one (and only one) of its attacks must be made with this weapon.
Scything talons	Melee	Melee	User	0	1	You can re-roll hit rolls of 1 when attacking with this weapon. If the bearer has more than one pair of scything talons, it can make 1 additional attack with this weapon each time it fights.

ABILITIES	Instinctive Behaviour (pg 85)	Burrow: At the beginning of any of your Movement phases, any Mawloc that is not within 1" of an enemy unit can burrow. Remove it from the battlefield – it can return as described in the Terror from the Deep ability. A Mawloc may not burrow and return to the battlefield in the same turn. If the battle ends while the Mawloc is underground, it is considered to be slain.
	Terror from the Deep: During deployment, you can set up a Mawloc underground instead of placing it on the battlefield. At the end of any of your Movement phases, set up the Mawloc anywhere on the battlefield that is more than 1" away from any enemy models and more than 6" from any other Mawlocs set up this way this turn, then roll a D6 for each enemy unit within 2" of it; on a 1 the unit escapes unharmed, on a 2-3 it suffers 1 mortal wound, on a 4-5 it suffers D3 mortal wounds and on a 6 it suffers 3 mortal wounds. The Mawloc cannot charge in the same turn.	**Death Throes:** If this model is reduced to 0 wounds, roll a D6 before removing the model from the battlefield; on a 6, it lashes out in its death throes, and each unit within 3" suffers D3 mortal wounds.

FACTION KEYWORDS	TYRANIDS, <HIVE FLEET>
KEYWORDS	MONSTER, MAWLOC

EXOCRINE

11 POWER

NAME	M	WS	BS	S	T	W	A	Ld	Sv
Exocrine	6"	*	*	7	8	12	*	6	3+

An Exocrine is a single model armed with a bio-plasmic cannon and powerful limbs.

DAMAGE
Some of this model's characteristics change as it suffers damage, as shown below:

REMAINING W	WS	BS	A
7-12+	4+	4+	3
4-6	4+	5+	D3
1-3	5+	5+	1

WEAPON	RANGE	TYPE	S	AP	D	ABILITIES
Bio-plasmic cannon	36"	Heavy 6	7	-3	2	-
Powerful limbs	Melee	Melee	User	-2	2	-

ABILITIES	Instinctive Behaviour (pg 85)	Weapon Beast: If this model does not move in your Movement phase, it can shoot all of its weapons twice in your Shooting phase.
	Symbiotic Targeting: If this model does not move in its Movement phase, you can add 1 to its hit rolls in the following Shooting phase. If you do so, it cannot charge in the same turn.	**Death Throes:** If this model is reduced to 0 wounds, roll a dice before removing the model from the battlefield; on a 6, it lashes out in its death throes, and each unit within 3" suffers D3 mortal wounds.

FACTION KEYWORDS	TYRANIDS, <HIVE FLEET>
KEYWORDS	MONSTER, EXOCRINE

11 POWER TYRANNOFEX

DAMAGE
Some of this model's characteristics change as it suffers damage, as shown below:

NAME	M	WS	BS	S	T	W	A	Ld	Sv
Tyrannofex	6"	4+	*	*	8	14	*	7	3+

REMAINING W	BS	S	A
8-14+	4+	7	4
4-7	5+	6	3
1-3	5+	5	2

A Tyrannofex is a single model armed with acid spray and powerful limbs. It can also fire stinger salvoes.

WEAPON	RANGE	TYPE	S	AP	D	ABILITIES
Acid spray	18"	Heavy D6	User	-1	D3	This weapon automatically hits its target.
Fleshborer hive	18"	Heavy 20	5	0	1	-
Rupture cannon	48"	Heavy 2	10	-1	2	If both of this weapon's shots hit, the AP of the attacks is -4 and the Damage is D6.
Stinger salvo	18"	Assault 4	5	-1	1	-
Powerful limbs	Melee	Melee	User	-2	2	-

WARGEAR OPTIONS	• This model may replace its acid spray with a fleshborer hive or rupture cannon.

ABILITIES	**Instinctive Behaviour** (pg 85) **Bio-tank:** This model does not suffer the penalty to its hit rolls for moving and firing Heavy weapons. **Weapon Beast:** If this model does not move in your Movement phase, it can shoot all of its weapons twice in your Shooting phase. **Death Throes:** If a Tyrannofex is reduced to 0 wounds, roll a dice before removing the model from the battlefield; on a 6 it lashes out in its death throes, and each unit within 3" suffers D3 mortal wounds.

FACTION KEYWORDS	TYRANIDS, <HIVE FLEET>
KEYWORDS	MONSTER, TYRANNOFEX

7 POWER TOXICRENE

DAMAGE
Some of this model's characteristics change as it suffers damage, as shown below:

NAME	M	WS	BS	S	T	W	A	Ld	Sv
Toxicrene	8"	*	4+	*	7	12	*	7	3+

REMAINING W	WS	S	A
7-12+	4+	7	6
4-6	5+	6	5
1-3	6+	5	4

A Toxicrene is a single model armed with choking spores and massive toxic lashes.

WEAPON	RANGE	TYPE	S	AP	D	ABILITIES
Choking spores	12"	Assault D6	3	0	D3	You can re-roll failed wound rolls for this weapon. In addition, units attacked by this weapon do not gain any bonus to their saving throws for being in cover.
Massive toxic lashes (shooting)	8"	Assault D6	User	-1	D3	This weapon can be fired within 1" of an enemy unit, and can target enemy units within 1" of friendly units. In addition, you can re-roll failed wound rolls when attacking with this weapon.
Massive toxic lashes (melee)	Melee	Melee	User	-1	D3	You can re-roll failed wound rolls when attacking with this weapon. A model armed with this weapon always fights first in the Fight phase, even if it didn't charge. If the enemy has units that have charged, or that have a similar ability, then alternate choosing units to fight with, starting with the player whose turn is taking place.

ABILITIES	**Instinctive Behaviour** (pg 85) **Acid Blood:** Each time this model loses a wound in the Fight phase, roll a D6; on a 6, the unit that inflicted the damage suffers a mortal wound after all of their attacks have been resolved. **Hypertoxic Miasma:** At the end of the Fight phase, roll a D6 for each enemy model within 1" of any Toxicrenes. On a 6, that model's unit suffers a mortal wound.	**Frenzied Death Throes:** If this model is reduced to 0 wounds, roll a D6 before removing the model from the battlefield; on a 6, it lashes out in its death throes, and each unit within 3" suffers 3 mortal wounds.

FACTION KEYWORDS	TYRANIDS, <HIVE FLEET>
KEYWORDS	MONSTER, TOXICRENE

SPOROCYST

DAMAGE
Some of this model's characteristics change as it suffers damage, as shown below:

REMAINING W	S	A
7-12+	5	D6
4-6	4	D3
1-3	3	1

NAME	M	WS	BS	S	T	W	A	Ld	Sv
Sporocyst	-	5+	5+	✶	6	12	✶	7	4+

A Sporocyst is a single model armed with five deathspitters.

WEAPON	RANGE	TYPE	S	AP	D	ABILITIES
Barbed strangler	36"	Assault D6	5	-1	1	You can add 1 to hit rolls for this weapon when attacking a unit with 10 or more models.
Deathspitter	18"	Assault 3	5	-1	1	-
Spore node	9"	Heavy 1	-	-	-	See Spore Node, below
Venom cannon	36"	Assault D3	8	-1	1	-

WARGEAR OPTIONS	• This model may replace all of its deathspitters with either five barbed stranglers or five venom cannons.

ABILITIES	**Instinctive Behaviour** (pg 85)	**Spore Node:** Each time a spore node attack hits its target, roll a D6 to find out how much damage is inflicted on the unit; on a 1 the mines fail to inflict any harm, on a 2-5 they inflict D3 mortal wounds, and on a 6 they inflict D6 mortal wounds.

Bombardment Organism: During deployment, you can set up a Sporocyst in its hive ship instead of placing it on the battlefield. If you do so, at the beginning of the first battle round but before the first turn begins, the hive ship can launch the Sporocyst – set it up anywhere on the battlefield that is more than 9" away from any enemy models.

Bio-fortress: A Sporocyst can shoot with its weapons even if there are enemies within 1" of it.

Immobile: A Sporocyst cannot move for any reason.

Psychic Resonator: If a Sporocyst is within range of a friendly <Hive Fleet> unit's Synapse ability (pg 85), the Sporocyst has the Synapse ability.

Each time a spore node attack misses its target, set up a single Mucolid Spore or a unit of up to 3 Spore Mines, anywhere within 6" of the target unit and more than 3" from any enemy model (any models that cannot be placed are destroyed). These then follow the rules for Mucolid Spores (pg 102) or Spore Mines (pg 103) that are part of your army, but they cannot move or charge during the turn they were set up.

Death Throes: If this model is reduced to 0 wounds, roll a D6 before removing the model from the battlefield; on a 6, it lashes out in its death throes, and each unit within 3" suffers D3 mortal wounds.

FACTION KEYWORDS	TYRANIDS, <Hive Fleet>
KEYWORDS	MONSTER, SPOROCYST

The lashing tentacles of the Toxicrene are coated in hyper-toxins. Even the spilt ichor of this creature can kill in seconds.

GENESTEALER CULTS

From dark depths and shadowy streets emerge the Genestealer Cultists, malformed figures united by a sinister worship of inscrutable star-born entities. Secretive, stealthy and utterly malignant, they are the cankers growing unseen in the hidden spaces of the Imperium.

Humanity is beset on all fronts by xenos raiders and the nightmarish forces of Chaos. Billions of lives are sacrificed upon the altar of war every day to keep the enemy at bay. Yet the most insidious threat to Mankind's survival may already have seeped into the bloodstream of the Imperium. Embedded into the infrastructure of countless seemingly loyal worlds, the Genestealer Cults bide their time, spreading tendrils of corruption through the native population until they are ready to begin their bloody insurrections. Once unleashed, they rise up in a surging tide, armed with stolen Imperial weaponry and crude industrial tools turned to horrific purpose.

When the Imperium first encountered Genestealers upon the moons of Ymgarl, they thought them to be a unique species. In fact, as scientists of the Ordo Xenos discovered after a harrowing series of investigations, they are the vanguard organisms that the Tyranid hive fleets seed before them to sow chaos and fear in their path. Resilient and possessed of razor-sharp claws that can carve through battle-plate, Genestealers are used in open battle by the hive fleets as shock assault troops. When infiltrating Imperial space, however, the Genestealers instead show their capacity for stealth and cunning. Slinking and creeping, hiding and murdering in silence, solitary Genestealers stow away on spacecraft and spread along space lanes like a virus. It only takes a single Genestealer successfully slipping aboard a cargo freighter and reaching a populated world to spell the doom of an entire sector.

Once it has found a secure lair nearby a heavily populated civic area, the organism begins its dark work. In the space of a few years, hundreds of civilians will have been abducted by the creature and subjected to the Genestealer's Kiss. Thus infected with foul xenos biomass, these victims begin to see the Patriarch – as the Genestealer who instigates such a cult is known – as a messianic figure, a herald sent by benevolent saviours from another galaxy. In time, the infected give birth to new generations of tainted Acolytes. Hybrid Acolytes, those descended from the first generation of victims, are unmistakably alien, with large, domed craniums and vicious weapon-mutations. As the corruption continues to spread, subsequent generations are born who can pass alongside the human population. These abominations infiltrate every strata of the civilian and military infrastructure, and all obey the command of the Patriarch unquestioningly.

As its numbers grow, more specialised agents are created to serve the cult. A Magus, a psychically gifted individual tainted by the Patriarch's will, is blessed with unnatural charisma and tasked with converting key targets within the planet's government and military leadership. The Acolyte masses are organised and led by the Primus, a general and ambush specialist responsible for coordinating the eventual uprising. Come the fourth generation of corruption, Purestrain Genestealers and Aberrant monstrosities join the cult's ranks as heavy-hitting shock troops. Meanwhile the Patriarch, star-borne and inhuman, squats at the centre of his web of influence, expanding it with inexhaustible patience until it covers the entire world. Whether it takes a handful of months or many years, eventually the Shadow in the Warp will fall across the Patriarch's domain, signalling the approach of a Tyranid hive fleet. Only then will the creature send the synaptic order to its minions to rise up and drown the planet in blood.

THE CULT UNLEASHED

When the Patriarch's minions receive the psychic command to begin the final insurrection, the Acolytes arm themselves with purloined military gear and mining tools, and surge forth from their hidden lairs in massed tides. Guided by the cunning will of their Primus masters, they strike first at key tactical locations like communications outposts, spaceports and munition yards. Stripped of its defenses and ability to call for help, the planet is left ripe for conquest. In a frenzy of brutal violence, the cultist uprising falls upon those unsuspecting enemies who have not yet been subsumed into its ranks. Bones are shattered by ear-bursting blasts from seismic cannons, weaponised rock drills are thrust into vulnerable flesh in a horrifying eruption of gore, and mining charges are used as makeshift grenades. The banners and sigils of the cult are unveiled at last, borne aloft on wyrm-form totems by Acolyte Iconwards whose presence inspires the broodkin to new heights of savage fervour.

During the many long years of preparation for this moment, the cult has stolen and sequestered many vehicles to aid it in its murderous campaign. Rugged Goliath Trucks and Rockgrinders, a common sight in mines and manufactorums all across the Imperium, are now turned to violent purpose. Mounted with twin autocannons and heavy stubbers, Goliaths rush packs of Acolytes to the front lines, smashing their way easily through rugged terrain and releasing a chattering thunderstorm of bullets that tears through enemy infantry. Rockgrinders simply crash into the centre of enemy formations, reaping a hideous toll as their saw-toothed drilldozer blades grind screaming infantry into bloody paste. Should the threat of enemy armour emerge, the cult will respond by deploying stolen Leman Russ tanks and Sentinel walkers. These vehicles are piloted by Neophyte Hybrids who have lain hidden in the ranks of human armies for many long years. Utterly loyal to the Patriarch, they will turn their guns on their former comrades without a second thought. The psychological impact of this sudden betrayal is often enough to deal a mortal blow to the morale of the targeted regiment.

As the hive fleet vomits its swarms of warrior-organisms into the stricken world's atmosphere, the cultists sing rapturous prayers to their deliverers. Even as the Tyranids exterminate and devour every source of biomass on the planet, still the cultists hold faith in their corrupted hearts that these benevolent aliens will elevate the faithful, helping them to transcend their mortal weaknesses. Eagerly they await the blessed oneness of form and purpose they have been promised. For a while at least, the Tyranids and the Patriarch's brood fight as one, the Hive Mind's control ensuring that the cult is not preyed upon. Magus leaders hurl illusions that warp and tear at the minds of the enemy, turning them upon each other with sadistic pleasure. The Patriarch's Primus generals marshal their forces with consummate skill, spending their warriors' lives by the thousands to open a path for the Tyranid assault. In this final, exalted hour the Patriarch himself enters the fray, and his faithful are sent into a zealous frenzy as their prophet rips the unworthy apart with razored claws and shredding fangs.

As soon as the last of the enemy is overrun by the tide of chitin and scything claws, the Hive Mind subsumes the Patriarch into its greater consciousness. It becomes merely another organism in the Tyranid swarm, severing the psychic broodmind that once united its cult. In an awful moment of realisation, the cultists at last understand the truth. Those same creatures from beyond the stars once worshipped as gods now fall upon their betrayed servants in a ravening swarm, tearing and slicing them apart in a cascade of gore. Some fight back, a last gesture of defiance against the monsters that have betrayed them. Others retain their fanatical faith even now, raising their arms to the spore-choked heavens and beaming beatific smiles as they are butchered and devoured.

Alongside the bodies of the slaughtered populace, the corpses of the cultists are hurled into bubbling digestion pools that form across the surface of the conquered planet. There they are dissolved into a foul gruel that is greedily consumed by the bio-ships pressed close around the world, clustered like vast and bloated ticks upon the hide of a dying beast. Thus, the Genestealer Cult does indeed join with those it once worshipped as saviours, and having consumed its fill, the hive fleet drifts away into the inky blackness of space.

CULT OF WAR

Though secrecy and spider-like patience define the Genestealer Cults, there are times when the forces of the Patriarch must adopt a more forceful approach. Perhaps the cult has been uncovered by agents of the hated Inquisition before its plans could be properly set in place, or perhaps a xenos force threatens to unintentionally reveal its presence. If the Patriarch judges that its interests are endangered, it will not hesitate to unleash its worshippers to quash the threat. The cult's Primus war leaders are given license to select a hand-picked army from the ranks of the faithful, and this advance force will fight with maniacal determination to defend the brood. More than one Ork Waaagh! or Dark Eldar raiding party has descended upon an Imperial world, only to discover a far greater threat than they could have imagined lurking beneath the surface. Neither will the Patriarch hesitate to abandon his domain if faced with an insurmountable force. Should any foe appear close to exterminating its tainted populace, the Patriarch may order the Primus to attempt an evacuation. Should even one Purestrain Genestealer slip past the Imperials' clutches, the entire horrific process of corruption and domination can begin anew on another world.

GENESTEALER CULTS ARMY LIST

This section contains all of the datasheets that you will need in order to fight battles with your Genestealer Cults miniatures. Each datasheet includes the characteristics profiles of the unit it describes, as well as any wargear and special abilities it may have. Some abilities are common to several Genestealer Cults units, in which case they are described below and referenced on the datasheets themselves.

ABILITIES

The following abilities are common to several Genestealer Cults units:

Cult Ambush

During deployment, you can set this unit up in ambush instead of on the battlefield. At the end of any of your Movement phases, it can launch an ambush – when it does so, roll a dice and consult the table below.

If you wish, before rolling on the Cult Ambush table for a GENESTEALER CULTS CHARACTER, you can pick one friendly GENESTEALER CULTS INFANTRY unit that was also set up in ambush to arrive with them; make one roll on the Cult Ambush table and apply the same result to both units. However, each of these units must be set up within 6" of each other.

If your army is Battle-forged, a unit can only make use of this ability if every unit in its Detachment has the GENESTEALER CULTS keyword.

Unquestioning Loyalty

Each time a GENESTEALER CULTS CHARACTER loses a wound whilst they are within 3" of any friendly GENESTEALER CULTS INFANTRY units, pick one of those units and roll a dice; on a 4+ the Character does not lose a wound but one model in the unit you picked (your choice) is slain.

BROOD BROTHERS

The influence of a Genestealer Cult permeates all aspects of a society, including any Astra Militarum regiments stationed on their world. To represent the elements of such forces that have been subverted by a cult, you can include **ASTRA MILITARUM** units and **GENESTEALER CULTS** units in the same matched play army, even though these units don't have any Faction keywords in common. However, you can only include one Astra Militarum Detachment (one in which every unit has the Astra Militarum keyword) in a Battle-forged army for each Genestealer Cult Detachment (one in which every unit has the Genestealer Cults keyword) in that army. In such cases, simply ignore the Astra Militarum units when choosing your army's Faction.

CULT AMBUSH	
D6	**RESULT**
1	**Cult Reinforcements** Your opponent nominates any two battlefield edges, one after another, and then you roll a dice. On a 1-3, set the unit up wholly within 6" of the first edge; on a 4-6, set it up wholly within 6" of the other edge. The unit must be set up more than 9" from any enemy models.
2	**Encircling the Foe** You nominate any two battlefield edges, one after another, and then your opponent rolls a dice. On a 1-3, set the unit up wholly within 6" of the first edge; on a 4-6, set it up wholly within 6" of the other edge. The unit must be set up more than 9" from any enemy models.
3	**Lying in Wait** Set the unit up anywhere that is more than 12" from any enemy models. Alternatively, set it up anywhere that is more than 9" from any enemy models and not visible to any enemy models.
4	**A Perfect Ambush** Set the unit up anywhere that is more than 9" from any enemy models.
5	**A Deadly Trap** Set the unit up anywhere that is more than 9" from any enemy models. It can either move D6" or shoot with all of its ranged weapons as if it were the Shooting phase (doing so does not prevent it from shooting in the Shooting phase or charging in the Charge phase of this turn).
6	**They Came From Below** Set the unit up anywhere that is more than 9" from any enemy models. The unit can then move normally, even though it has just arrived as reinforcements.

BROODMIND DISCIPLINE

Before the battle, generate the psychic powers for **PSYKERS** that can use powers from the Broodmind Discipline using the table on the right. You can either roll a D3 to generate their powers randomly (re-roll any duplicate results), or you can select the psychic powers you wish the psyker to have.

1 Mass Hypnosis

Mass Hypnosis has a warp charge value of 7. If manifested, select a visible enemy unit within 18" of the psyker. Until the start of your next Psychic phase, the target cannot fire Overwatch, fights last in the Fight phase even if it charged, and must subtract 1 from its hit rolls.

2 Mind Control

Mind Control has a warp charge value of 6. If manifested, pick an enemy model within 12" of the psyker and roll 3D6. If the score is less than that model's Leadership nothing happens, but if it is equal to or greater, that model can immediately shoot another enemy unit of your choice, or make a single close combat attack against it, as if it were part of your army. Models cannot attack themselves, but they can attack other members of their unit.

3 Might From Beyond

Might From Beyond has a warp charge value of 7. If manifested, select a friendly **GENESTEALER CULTS INFANTRY** unit within 18" of the psyker. Add 1 to the Strength and Attacks characteristics of all models in that unit until the start of your next Psychic phase.

WARGEAR

Many of the units you will find on the following pages reference one or more of the following wargear lists (e.g. Special Weapons). When this is the case, the unit may take any item from the appropriate list below. The profiles for the weapons in these lists can be found in the appendix (pg 143-144).

SPECIAL WEAPONS
- Flamer
- Grenade launcher
- Webber

PISTOLS
- Bolt pistol
- Laspistol
- Web pistol

MELEE WEAPONS
- Chainsword
- Power maul
- Power pick
- Cultist knife

HEAVY MINING WEAPONS
- Heavy stubber
- Mining laser
- Seismic cannon

HEAVY WEAPONS
- Autocannon
- Heavy bolter
- Lascannon
- Mortar
- Missile launcher

PATRIARCH

7 POWER

NAME	M	WS	BS	S	T	W	A	Ld	Sv
Patriarch	8"	2+	5+	6	5	6	6	10	4+
Familiar	6"	3+	-	4	3	1	2	8	6+

A Patriarch is a single model armed with monstrous rending claws. It may be accompanied by up to 2 Familiars (**Power Rating +1**).

WEAPON	RANGE	TYPE	S	AP	D	ABILITIES
Monstrous rending claws	Melee	Melee	User	-3	D3	You may re-roll failed wound rolls for this weapon. In addition, each time you make a wound roll of 6+, that hit is resolved with an AP of -6 and Damage of 3.

ABILITIES	
	Cult Ambush, Unquestioning Loyalty (pg 112)	**Swift and Deadly:** A Patriarch can charge even if it Advanced during its turn.
	Brood Telepathy: You can add 1 to hit rolls in the Fight phase for friendly Purestrain Genestealer units that are within 6" of this model.	**Familiars:** If a Patriarch is accompanied by any Familiars, then once per game, after the Patriarch has manifested a psychic power, its Familiars can lend it additional power. If they do so, the Patriarch can immediately attempt to manifest an additional psychic power.
	Living Idol: GENESTEALER CULTS units within 6" of any friendly Patriarchs automatically pass Morale tests.	
	Lightning Reflexes: A Patriarch has a 5+ invulnerable save.	When rolling to wound this unit, always use the Patriarch's Toughness (while it is on the battlefield). The death of a Familiar is ignored for the purposes of morale.

PSYKER	A Patriarch can attempt to manifest one psychic power in each friendly Psychic phase, and attempt to deny one psychic power in each enemy Psychic phase. It knows the *Smite* power and one psychic power from the Broodmind discipline (pg 113).
FACTION KEYWORDS	**TYRANIDS, GENESTEALER CULTS**
KEYWORDS (PATRIARCH)	**INFANTRY, GENESTEALER, CHARACTER, PSYKER, PATRIARCH**
KEYWORDS (FAMILIARS)	**INFANTRY, GENESTEALER, FAMILIAR**

MAGUS

4 POWER

NAME	M	WS	BS	S	T	W	A	Ld	Sv
Magus	6"	3+	3+	3	3	4	3	8	5+
Familiar	6"	3+	-	4	3	1	2	8	6+

A Magus is a single model armed with an autopistol and force stave. It may be accompanied by up to 2 Familiars (**Power Rating +1**).

WEAPON	RANGE	TYPE	S	AP	D	ABILITIES
Autopistol	12"	Pistol 1	3	0	1	-
Force stave	Melee	Melee	+2	-1	D3	-

ABILITIES	
	Cult Ambush, Unquestioning Loyalty (pg 112).
	Spiritual Leader: Each friendly **GENESTEALER CULTS** unit within 6" of this model at the start of your opponent's Psychic phase can attempt to deny one psychic power that targets them during that phase as if they were themselves a **PSYKER** (measure range to any model in the unit).
	Familiars: If a Magus is accompanied by any Familiars, then once per game, after the Magus has manifested a psychic power, its Familiars can lend it additional power. If they do so, the Patriarch can immediately attempt to manifest an additional psychic power.
	The death of a Familiar is ignored for the purposes of morale.

PSYKER	A Magus can attempt to manifest one psychic power in each friendly Psychic phase, and attempt to deny one psychic power in each enemy Psychic phase. It knows the *Smite* power and one psychic power from the Broodmind discipline (pg 113).
FACTION KEYWORDS	**TYRANIDS, GENESTEALER CULTS**
KEYWORDS (MAGUS)	**INFANTRY, CHARACTER, PSYKER, MAGUS**
KEYWORDS (FAMILIARS)	**INFANTRY, GENESTEALER, FAMILIAR**

PRIMUS

4 POWER

NAME	M	WS	BS	S	T	W	A	Ld	Sv
Primus	6"	2+	3+	4	3	5	4	9	5+
Familiar	6"	3+	4+	4	3	1	2	8	6+

A Primus is a single model armed with a needle pistol, bonesword, toxin injector claw and blasting charges.

WEAPON	RANGE	TYPE	S	AP	D	ABILITIES
Needle pistol	12"	Pistol 1	1	0	1	This weapon always wounds targets (other than **VEHICLES**) on a roll of 2+.
Bonesword	Melee	Melee	User	-2	1	-
Toxin injector claw	Melee	Melee	User	-1	1	This weapon always wounds targets (other than **VEHICLES**) on a roll of 2+. Furthermore, each time you make a wound roll of 6+ with this weapon, that hit is resolved with an AP of -4 .
Blasting charge	6"	Grenade D6	3	0	1	-

ABILITIES	Cult Ambush, Unquestioning Loyalty (pg 112)
	Cult Demagogue: You can add 1 to all hit rolls in the Fight phase for **GENESTEALER CULTS** units that are within 6" of any friendly Primus models.
	Meticulous Planner: When a Primus arrives on the battlefield using the Cult Ambush ability, you can re-roll the result on the Cult Ambush table. If you chose for a unit to arrive with them, the new result applies to that unit as well.

FACTION KEYWORDS	TYRANIDS, GENESTEALER CULTS
KEYWORDS	INFANTRY, CHARACTER, PRIMUS

ACOLYTE ICONWARD

3 POWER

NAME	M	WS	BS	S	T	W	A	Ld	Sv
Acolyte Iconward	6"	3+	3+	4	3	4	4	8	5+

An Acolyte Iconward is a single model armed with an autopistol, rending claw and blasting charges.

WEAPON	RANGE	TYPE	S	AP	D	ABILITIES
Autopistol	12"	Pistol 1	3	0	1	-
Rending claw	Melee	Melee	User	-1	1	Each time you make a wound roll of 6+ for this weapon, that hit is resolved with an AP of -4.
Blasting charge	6"	Grenade D6	3	0	1	-

ABILITIES	Cult Ambush, Unquestioning Loyalty (pg 112).
	Nexus of Devotion: Roll a D6 each time a friendly **GENESTEALER CULTS INFANTRY** model within 6" of this model loses a wound; on a 6 the wound is ignored.
	Sacred Cult Banner: You can re-roll failed Morale tests for friendly **GENESTEALER CULTS** units that are within 6" of this model.

FACTION KEYWORDS	TYRANIDS, GENESTEALER CULTS
KEYWORDS	INFANTRY, CHARACTER, ACOLYTE ICONWARD

ACOLYTE HYBRIDS

NAME	M	WS	BS	S	T	W	A	Ld	Sv
Acolyte Hybrid	6"	3+	4+	4	3	1	2	7	5+
Acolyte Leader	6"	3+	4+	4	3	1	3	8	5+

This unit contains 4 Acolyte Hybrids and 1 Acolyte Leader. It may include up to 5 additional Acolyte Hybrids (**Power Rating +5**), up to 10 additional Acolyte Hybrids (**Power Rating +10**) or up to 15 additional Acolyte Hybrids (**Power Rating +15**). Each model is armed with an autopistol, cultist knife, rending claw and blasting charges.

WEAPON	RANGE	TYPE	S	AP	D	ABILITIES
Autopistol	12"	Pistol 1	3	0	1	-
Demolition charges	6"	Assault D6	8	-3	D3	The bearer can only use this weapon once per battle.
Hand flamer	6"	Pistol D3	3	0	1	This weapon automatically hits its target.
Bonesword	Melee	Melee	User	-2	1	-
Cultist knife	Melee	Melee	User	0	1	Each time the bearer fights, it can make 1 additional attack with this weapon.
Heavy rock cutter	Melee	Melee	x2	-4	2	Roll a D6 each time a model (other than a VEHICLE) suffers damage from this weapon; if you roll higher than the model's remaining number of Wounds, it is instantly slain.
Heavy rock drill	Melee	Melee	x2	-3	1	Roll a D6 each time a model suffers damage from this weapon; on a 2+ the model suffers a mortal wound, and you can roll another D6. This time, the model suffers a mortal wound on a 3+. Keep rolling a D6, increasing the score required to cause a mortal wound by 1 each time, until the model is slain or the roll is failed.
Heavy rock saw	Melee	Melee	x2	-4	2	
Lash whip and bonesword	Melee	Melee	User	-2	1	If the bearer is slain in the Fight phase before it has made its attacks, leave it where it is. When its unit is chosen to fight in that phase, the bearer can do so as normal before being removed from the battlefield.
Rending claw	Melee	Melee	User	-1	1	Each time you make a wound roll of 6+ for this weapon, that hit is resolved with an AP of -4.
Blasting charge	6"	Grenade D6	3	0	1	-

WARGEAR OPTIONS	• Any model may replace its autopistol with a hand flamer. • One Acolyte Hybrid may carry a cult icon. • For every five models in the unit, up to two Acolyte Hybrids can replace their cultist knife and rending claw with a heavy rock drill, heavy rock cutter, heavy rock saw or demolition charges. • The Acolyte Leader may replace its cultist knife with a bonesword. • The Acolyte Leader may replace its cultist knife and autopistol with a lash whip and bonesword.
ABILITIES	**Cult Ambush, Unquestioning Loyalty** (pg 112) **Cult Icon:** Whilst the bearer of a cult icon is alive, you can re-roll hit rolls of 1 for its unit in the Fight phase.
FACTION KEYWORDS	**TYRANIDS, GENESTEALER CULTS**
KEYWORDS	**INFANTRY, ACOLYTE HYBRIDS**

NEOPHYTE HYBRIDS

NAME	M	WS	BS	S	T	W	A	Ld	Sv
Neophyte Hybrid	6"	4+	4+	3	3	1	1	7	5+
Neophyte Leader	6"	4+	4+	3	3	1	2	8	5+
Neophyte Weapons Team	6"	4+	4+	3	3	2	2	7	5+

This unit contains 9 Neophyte Hybrids and 1 Neophyte Leader. It can include up to 10 additional Neophyte Hybrids (**Power Rating +5**). Each model is armed with an autogun, autopistol and blasting charges.

WEAPON	RANGE	TYPE	S	AP	D	ABILITIES
Autogun	24"	Rapid Fire 1	3	0	1	-
Autopistol	12"	Pistol 1	3	0	1	-
Lasgun	24"	Rapid Fire 1	3	0	1	-
Shotgun	12"	Assault 2	3	0	1	If the target is within half range, add 1 to this weapon's Strength.
Blasting charge	6"	Grenade D6	3	0	1	-

WARGEAR OPTIONS	• Any Neophyte Hybrid may replace its autogun with a shotgun or a lasgun. • One Neophyte Hybrid may carry a cult icon. • Up to two Neophyte Hybrids may replace their autogun with one item from the *Special Weapons* list. • A Neophyte Leader may replace its autogun and autopistol with one item from the *Pistols* list and one item from the *Melee Weapons* list. • Up to two Neophyte Hybrids may replace their autogun with one item from the *Heavy Mining Weapons* list. Instead, two Neophyte Hybrids may form a single Neophyte Weapons Team; this team does not have autoguns but instead has one item from the *Heavy Weapons* list.
ABILITIES	**Cult Ambush**, **Unquestioning Loyalty** (pg 112) **Cult Icon:** Whilst the bearer of a cult icon is alive, you can re-roll hit rolls of 1 for its unit in the Fight phase.
FACTION KEYWORDS	**TYRANIDS, GENESTEALER CULTS**
KEYWORDS	**INFANTRY, NEOPHYTE HYBRIDS**

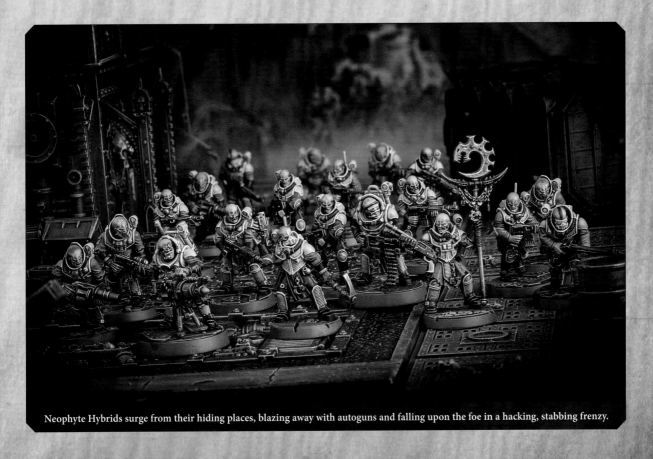

Neophyte Hybrids surge from their hiding places, blazing away with autoguns and falling upon the foe in a hacking, stabbing frenzy.

HYBRID METAMORPHS

POWER 6

NAME	M	WS	BS	S	T	W	A	Ld	Sv
Hybrid Metamorph	6"	3+	4+	4	3	1	3	7	5+
Metamorph Leader	6"	3+	4+	4	3	1	4	8	5+

This unit contains 4 Hybrid Metamorphs and 1 Metamorph Leader. It can include up to 5 additional Hybrid Metamorphs (**Power Rating +6**). Each model is armed with an autopistol, rending claw, Metamorph talon and blasting charges.

WEAPON	RANGE	TYPE	S	AP	D	ABILITIES
Autopistol	12"	Pistol 1	3	0	1	-
Hand flamer	6"	Pistol D3	3	0	1	This weapon automatically hits its target.
Bonesword	Melee	Melee	User	-2	1	-
Metamorph claw	Melee	Melee	+2	0	1	-
Metamorph talon	Melee	Melee	User	0	1	Add 1 to all hit rolls for this weapon.
Metamorph whip	Melee	Melee	User	0	1	If the bearer is slain in the Fight phase before it has made its attacks, leave it where it is. When its unit is chosen to fight in that phase, the bearer can do so as normal before being removed from the battlefield.
Rending claw	Melee	Melee	User	-1	1	Each time you make a wound roll of 6+ for this weapon, that hit is resolved with an AP of -4.
Blasting charge	6"	Grenade D6	3	0	1	-

WARGEAR OPTIONS	• Any model may replace its rending claw with a Metamorph talon. • Any model may replace its Metamorph talon with a Metamorph whip. • Any model may replace its Metamorph talon and rending claw with a Metamorph claw. • Any model may replace its autopistol with a hand flamer. • A Metamorph Leader may take a bonesword. • One Hybrid Metamorph may carry a cult icon.
ABILITIES	**Cult Ambush, Unquestioning Loyalty** (pg 112) **Cult Icon:** Whilst the bearer of a cult icon is alive, you can re-roll hit rolls of 1 for its unit in the Fight phase.
FACTION KEYWORDS	**TYRANIDS, GENESTEALER CULTS**
KEYWORDS	**INFANTRY, HYBRID METAMORPHS**

ABERRANTS

POWER 7

NAME	M	WS	BS	S	T	W	A	Ld	Sv
Aberrant	6"	3+	6+	5	4	2	2	7	5+

This unit contains 4 Aberrants. It can include up to 4 additional Aberrants (**Power Rating +7**). Each model is armed with a power pick and rending claw.

WEAPON	RANGE	TYPE	S	AP	D	ABILITIES
Power hammer	Melee	Melee	x2	-3	3	When attacking with this weapon, you must subtract 1 from the hit roll.
Power pick	Melee	Melee	User	-2	D3	-
Rending claw	Melee	Melee	User	-1	1	Each time you make a wound roll of 6+ for this weapon, that hit is resolved with an AP of -4.

WARGEAR OPTIONS	• Any model may replace its power pick with a power hammer.
ABILITIES	**Cult Ambush, Unquestioning Loyalty** (pg 112) **Bestial Vigour:** When inflicting damage upon an Aberrant, reduce the damage of the attack by 1 to a minimum of 1.
FACTION KEYWORDS	**TYRANIDS, GENESTEALER CULTS**
KEYWORDS	**INFANTRY, ABERRANTS**

4 POWER

PURESTRAIN GENESTEALERS

NAME	M	WS	BS	S	T	W	A	Ld	Sv
Purestrain Genestealer	8"	3+	-	4	4	1	3	9	5+

This unit contains 5 Purestrain Genestealers. It may include up to 5 additional Purestrain Genestealers (**Power Rating +4**), up to 10 additional Purestrain Genestealers (**Power Rating +8**) or up to 15 additional Purestrain Genestealers (**Power Rating +12**). Each Purestrain Genestealer is armed with rending claws.

WEAPON	RANGE	TYPE	S	AP	D	ABILITIES
Purestrain talons	Melee	Melee	User	0	1	When attacking with this weapon you can re-roll hit rolls of 1.
Rending claws	Melee	Melee	User	-1	1	Each time you make a wound roll of 6+ for this weapon, that hit is resolved with an AP of -4.

WARGEAR OPTIONS	• Any model may also take purestrain talons.	
ABILITIES	**Cult Ambush**, **Unquestioning Loyalty** (pg 112) **Flurry of Claws:** Purestrain Genestealers have 4 Attacks instead of 3 whilst their unit has 10 or more models.	**Lightning Reflexes:** Models in this unit have a 5+ invulnerable save. **Swift and Deadly:** Purestrain Genestealers can charge even if they Advanced during their turn.
FACTION KEYWORDS	**TYRANIDS, GENESTEALER CULTS**	
KEYWORDS	**INFANTRY, GENESTEALER, PURESTRAIN GENESTEALERS**	

Purestrain Genestealers are terrifyingly swift and agile predators, with claws sharp enough to shear through power armour.

GOLIATH TRUCK

NAME	M	WS	BS	S	T	W	A	Ld	Sv
Goliath Truck	*	6+	*	6	6	10	*	7	4+

DAMAGE

Some of this model's characteristics change as it suffers damage, as shown below:

REMAINING W	M	BS	A
6-10+	12"	4+	3
3-5	8"	5+	D3
1-2	4"	6+	1

A Goliath Truck is a single model equipped with a heavy stubber and twin autocannon.

WEAPON	RANGE	TYPE	S	AP	D	ABILITIES
Cache of demolition charges	6"	Assault D6	8	-3	D3	This weapon can only be fired if a unit is embarked upon the vehicle equipped with it.
Heavy stubber	36"	Heavy 3	4	0	1	-
Twin autocannon	48"	Heavy 4	7	-1	2	-

WARGEAR OPTIONS	• This model may take a cache of demolition charges.
ABILITIES	**Explodes:** If this model is reduced to 0 wounds, roll a D6 before removing it from the battlefield and before any embarked models disembark. On a 6 it explodes, and each unit within 6" suffers D3 mortal wounds. **Open-topped:** Models embarked on this model can attack in their Shooting phase. Measure the range and draw line of sight from any point on this model. When they do so, any restrictions or modifiers that apply to this model also apply to its passengers; for example, the passengers cannot shoot if this model has Fallen Back in the same turn, cannot shoot (except with Pistols) if this model is within 1" of an enemy unit, and so on. **Rugged Construction:** Roll a D6 each time this model loses a wound; on a 6 the wound is ignored.
TRANSPORT	A Goliath truck can transport up to 10 **Genestealer Cults Infantry** models.
FACTION KEYWORDS	**Tyranids, Genestealer Cults**
KEYWORDS	**Vehicle, Transport, Goliath Truck**

CULT CHIMERA

NAME	M	WS	BS	S	T	W	A	Ld	Sv
Cult Chimera	*	6+	*	6	7	10	*	7	3+

DAMAGE

Some of this model's characteristics change as it suffers damage, as shown below:

REMAINING W	M	BS	A
6-10+	12"	4+	3
3-5	8"	5+	D3
1-2	4"	6+	1

A Cult Chimera is a single model equipped with a multi-laser, heavy bolter and two lasgun arrays.

WEAPON	RANGE	TYPE	S	AP	D	ABILITIES
Heavy bolter	36"	Heavy 3	5	-1	1	-
Heavy flamer	8"	Heavy D6	5	-1	1	This weapon automatically hits its target.
Heavy stubber	36"	Heavy 3	4	0	1	-
Hunter-killer missile	48"	Heavy 1	8	-2	D6	Each hunter-killer missile can only be used once per battle.
Lasgun array	24"	Rapid Fire 3	3	0	1	This weapon can only be fired if a unit is embarked upon the vehicle equipped with it.
Multi-laser	36"	Heavy 3	6	0	1	-
Storm bolter	24"	Rapid Fire 2	4	0	1	-

WARGEAR OPTIONS	• This model may replace its heavy bolter with a heavy flamer. • This model may replace its multi-laser with a heavy flamer or heavy bolter. • This model may take a hunter-killer missile. • This model may take a storm bolter or a heavy stubber.
ABILITIES	**Explodes:** If this model is reduced to 0 wounds, roll a D6 before removing it from the battlefield and before any embarked models disembark. On a 6 it explodes, and each unit within 6" suffers D3 mortal wounds. **Smoke Launchers:** Once per game, instead of shooting any weapons in the Shooting phase, this model can use its smoke launchers; if it does so, until your next Shooting phase your opponent must subtract 1 from any hit rolls that target it.
TRANSPORT	A Cult Chimera can transport up to 12 **Genestealer Cults Infantry** models.
FACTION KEYWORDS	**Tyranids, Genestealer Cults**
KEYWORDS	**Vehicle, Transport, Chimera**

CULT SCOUT SENTINELS

2 POWER

NAME	M	WS	BS	S	T	W	A	Ld	Sv
Cult Scout Sentinel	9"	4+	4+	5	5	6	1	7	4+

This unit contains 1 Cult Scout Sentinel. It can include 1 additional Cult Scout Sentinel (**Power Rating +2**) or 2 additional Cult Scout Sentinels (**Power Rating +4**). Each model is equipped with a multi-laser.

WEAPON	RANGE	TYPE	S	AP	D	ABILITIES
Autocannon	48"	Heavy 2	7	-1	2	-
Heavy flamer	8"	Heavy D6	5	-1	1	This weapon automatically hits its target.
Hunter-killer missile	48"	Heavy 1	8	-2	D6	Each hunter-killer missile can only be used once per battle.
Lascannon	48"	Heavy 1	9	-3	D6	-
Missile launcher	When attacking with this weapon, choose one of the profiles below.					
- Frag missile	48"	Heavy D6	4	0	1	-
- Krak missile	48"	Heavy 1	8	-2	D6	-
Multi-laser	36"	Heavy 3	6	0	1	-
Sentinel chainsaw	Melee	Melee	User	-1	1	-

WARGEAR OPTIONS	• Any model may replace its multi-laser with a heavy flamer, autocannon, missile launcher or lascannon. • Any model make take a hunter-killer missile. • Any model may take a Sentinel chainsaw.
ABILITIES	**Explodes:** If a model in this unit is reduced to 0 wounds, roll a D6 before removing the model from the battlefield. On a 6 it explodes, and each unit within 3" suffers 1 mortal wound. **Scout Vehicle:** At the start of the first battle round but before the first turn begins, you can move this unit up to 9". It cannot end this move within 9" of any enemy models. If both players have units that can do this, the player who is taking the first turn moves their units first. **Smoke Launchers:** Once per game, instead of shooting its weapons in the Shooting phase, this unit can use its smoke launchers. If it does so, until your next Shooting phase your opponent must subtract 1 from any hit rolls that target it.
FACTION KEYWORDS	**TYRANIDS, GENESTEALER CULTS**
KEYWORDS	**VEHICLE, SCOUT SENTINELS**

Scout Sentinels are agile combat walkers, perfect for the lightning ambush tactics of the Genestealer Cults.

CULT ARMOURED SENTINELS

NAME	M	WS	BS	S	T	W	A	Ld	Sv
Cult Armoured Sentinel	8"	4+	4+	5	5	6	1	7	3+

This unit contains 1 Cult Armoured Sentinel. It can include 1 additional Cult Armoured Sentinel (**Power Rating +3**) or 2 additional Cult Armoured Sentinels (**Power Rating +6**). Each model is equipped with a multi-laser.

WEAPON	RANGE	TYPE	S	AP	D	ABILITIES
Autocannon	48"	Heavy 2	7	-1	2	-
Heavy flamer	8"	Heavy D6	5	-1	1	This weapon automatically hits its target.
Hunter-killer missile	48"	Heavy 1	8	-2	D6	Each hunter-killer missile can only be used once per battle.
Lascannon	48"	Heavy 1	9	-3	D6	-
Missile launcher	When attacking with this weapon, choose one of the profiles below.					
- Frag missile	48"	Heavy D6	4	0	1	-
- Krak missile	48"	Heavy 1	8	-2	D6	-
Multi-laser	36"	Heavy 3	6	0	1	-
Plasma cannon	When attacking with this weapon, choose one of the profiles below.					
- Standard	36"	Heavy D3	7	-3	1	-
- Supercharge	36"	Heavy D3	8	-3	2	On a hit roll of 1, the bearer is slain after all of this weapon's shots have been resolved.
Sentinel chainsaw	Melee	Melee	User	-1	1	-

WARGEAR OPTIONS	• Any model may replace its multi-laser with a heavy flamer, autocannon, missile launcher, lascannon or plasma cannon. • Any model may take a hunter-killer missile. • Any model may take a Sentinel chainsaw.
ABILITIES	**Explodes:** If a model in this unit is reduced to 0 wounds, roll a D6 before removing the model from the battlefield. On a 6 it explodes, and each unit within 3" suffers 1 mortal wound. **Smoke Launchers:** Once per game, instead of shooting its weapons in the Shooting phase, this unit can use its smoke launchers. If it does so, until your next Shooting phase your opponent must subtract 1 from any hit rolls that target it.
FACTION KEYWORDS	**TYRANIDS, GENESTEALER CULTS**
KEYWORDS	**VEHICLE, ARMOURED SENTINELS**

The Genestealer Cults use stolen Leman Russ tanks to add firepower and durability to their assaults.

CULT LEMAN RUSS

DAMAGE

Some of this model's characteristics change as it suffers damage, as shown below:

REMAINING W	M	BS	A
7-12+	10"	4+	3
4-6	7"	5+	D3
1-3	4"	6+	1

NAME	M	WS	BS	S	T	W	A	Ld	Sv
Cult Leman Russ	*	6+	*	7	8	12	*	7	3+

A Cult Leman Russ is a single model equipped with a battle cannon and a heavy bolter.

WEAPON	RANGE	TYPE	S	AP	D	ABILITIES
Battle cannon	72"	Heavy D6	8	-2	D3	-
Eradicator nova cannon	36"	Heavy D6	6	-2	D3	Units in cover do not receive any bonus to their saving throws against wounds caused by this weapon.
Exterminator autocannon	48"	Heavy 4	7	-1	2	-
Heavy bolter	36"	Heavy 3	5	-1	1	-
Heavy flamer	8"	Heavy D6	5	-1	1	This weapon automatically hits its target.
Heavy stubber	36"	Heavy 3	4	0	1	-
Hunter-killer missile	48"	Heavy 1	8	-2	D6	Each hunter-killer missile can only be used once per battle.
Lascannon	48"	Heavy 1	9	-3	D6	-
Multi-melta	24"	Heavy 1	8	-4	D6	If the target is within half range of this weapon, roll two dice when inflicting damage with it and discard the lowest result.
Plasma cannon	When attacking with this weapon, choose one of the profiles below.					
- Standard	36"	Heavy D3	7	-3	1	-
- Supercharge	36"	Heavy D3	8	-3	2	On a hit roll of 1, the bearer is slain after all of this weapon's shots have been resolved.
Storm bolter	24"	Rapid Fire 2	4	0	1	-
Vanquisher battle cannon	72"	Heavy 1	9	-3	D6	Roll two dice when inflicting damage with this weapon and discard the lowest result.

WARGEAR OPTIONS	• This model may replace its battle cannon with an eradicator nova cannon, exterminator autocannon or vanquisher battle cannon. • This model may replace its heavy bolter with a heavy flamer or lascannon. • This model may take two heavy flamers, two heavy bolters, two multi-meltas or two plasma cannons. • This model may take a heavy stubber or storm bolter. • This model may take a hunter-killer missile.

ABILITIES	**Explodes:** If this model is reduced to 0 wounds, roll a D6 before removing the model from the battlefield. On a 6 it explodes, and each unit within 6" suffers D3 mortal wounds. **Smoke Launchers:** Once per game, instead of shooting its weapons in the Shooting phase, this unit can use its smoke launchers. If it does so, until your next Shooting phase your opponent must subtract 1 from any hit rolls that target it.	**Grinding Advance:** This model does not suffer the penalty to turret weapon hit rolls for shooting a Heavy weapon on a turn in which it has moved. The following weapons are turret weapons: battle cannon, eradicator nova cannon, exterminator autocannon and vanquisher battle cannon. **Emergency Plasma Vents:** If this model fires a supercharged plasma cannon, and you roll one or more hit rolls of 1, it is not automatically destroyed. Instead, it suffers 6 mortal wounds and cannot fire any plasma cannons for the rest of the battle.

FACTION KEYWORDS	TYRANIDS, GENESTEALER CULTS

KEYWORDS	VEHICLE, LEMAN RUSS

GOLIATH ROCKGRINDER

6 POWER

NAME	M	WS	BS	S	T	W	A	Ld	Sv
Goliath Truck	*	5+	*	5	7	10	*	7	4+

A Goliath Rockgrinder is a single model equipped with a heavy stubber, heavy mining laser and drilldozer blade.

DAMAGE
Some of this model's characteristics change as it suffers damage, as shown below:

REMAINING W	M	BS	A
6-10+	10"	4+	6
3-5	6"	5+	D6
1-2	4"	6+	D3

WEAPON	RANGE	TYPE	S	AP	D	ABILITIES
Cache of demolition charges	6"	Assault D6	8	-3	D3	This weapon can only be fired if a unit is embarked upon the vehicle equipped with it.
Clearance incinerator	12"	Assault D6	5	-1	1	This weapon automatically hits its target.
Heavy mining laser	36"	Heavy 1	9	-3	D6	-
Heavy seismic cannon	When attacking with this weapon, choose one of the profiles below. All wound rolls of 6+ have an AP of -4.					
- Long-wave	24"	Heavy 4	4	-1	2	-
- Short-wave	12"	Heavy 2	8	-2	3	-
Heavy stubber	36"	Heavy 3	4	0	1	-
Drilldozer blade	Melee	Melee	+3	-2	D3	A model equipped with a drilldozer blade can make D3 additional attacks on a turn in which it charged.

WARGEAR OPTIONS	• This model may take a cache of demolition charges. • This model may replace its heavy mining laser with a clearance incinerator or heavy seismic cannon.
ABILITIES	**Explodes:** If this model is reduced to 0 wounds, roll a D6 before removing it from the battlefield and before any embarked models disembark. On a 6 it explodes, and each unit within 6" suffers D3 mortal wounds. **Rugged Construction:** Roll a D6 each time this model loses a wound; on a 6 the wound is ignored.
TRANSPORT	A Goliath Rockgrinder can transport up to 6 GENESTEALER CULTS INFANTRY models.
FACTION KEYWORDS	**TYRANIDS, GENESTEALER CULTS**
KEYWORDS	**VEHICLE, TRANSPORT, GOLIATH ROCKGRINDER**

Goliath Rockgrinders smash into fortified positions with astonishing force, pulverising defences and defenders alike.

A Genestealer Cult force emerges from the depths of its host city, falling upon a band of Skitarii intruders with murderous zeal.

BATTLE-FORGED ARMIES

When picking a Battle-forged army for matched play, you will need to record the details of your army on a piece of paper (your Army Roster). Here we show one example of how you can do this; using several Detachment Rosters, at least one for each Detachment in your army, and the summarising main Army Roster itself. Over the page are blank rosters you can photocopy.

DETACHMENT ROSTERS

Each Detachment Roster details all the units it includes. Each unit has a small entry of its own where you can write down the name and type of unit, its Battlefield Role, the number of models it contains, and the weapons each model in the unit is equipped with. Details of how many models make up each unit and what weapons, options and upgrades each can take can be found on that unit's datasheet.

The points value of each unit's models and each individual weapon is then noted down by referencing the points lists in the appendix (pg 130-144), and added together to give a points cost for the unit. The points cost of the entire Detachment is simply then the sum of the points costs of its units. This can be noted down alongside other useful information, such as the number of Command Points (if any) the Detachment gives you (see the *Warhammer 40,000* rulebook for more on Command Points).

Unit Champions

Many units are led by a champion of some kind such as a Sergeant. Unit champions often have better characteristics and weapon options than the models they command. All the champions in this book have the same points cost as the other models in their unit.

Under-strength Units

Sometimes you may find that you do not have enough models to field a minimum-sized unit; if this is the case, you can still include one unit of that type in your army with as many models as you have available. In matched play games, you only pay the points for the models you actually have in an under-strength unit (and any weapons they are equipped with). An under-strength unit still takes up the appropriate slot in a Detachment.

ARMY ROSTER

Once you have filled in all of your Detachment Rosters, you can then fill out the main Army Roster. The name and points value of each Detachment is noted down here for reference. The total points cost of your army is the sum of all the Detachment points costs in your army plus any reinforcement points you have chosen to put aside (see below). The points cost of your army should not exceed the points limit you are using for the battle.

There are lots of other useful things to write down on your main Army Roster, such as who the army's Warlord is (this should be done at the start of the battle) and the number of Command Points available to your army. Remember that all Battle-forged armies start with 3 Command Points, but certain Detachments, and occasionally certain models, can change this total.

Reinforcement Points

Sometimes an ability will allow you to add units to your army, or replace units that have been destroyed. One example is the Tervigon's 'Spawn Termagants' ability (pg 89), which can either replenish depleted Termagant units or create entirely new ones. In the latter case, and in any other case when new units are added to your army, you must set aside some of your points in order to use these units. The points you set aside are called your reinforcement points, and need to be recorded on your army roster. Each time a unit is added to an army during battle, subtract the number of points the unit would cost from your pool of reinforcement points.

ARMY ROSTER

PLAYER NAME:	Alex Smith	ARMY FACTION:	Orks
ARMY NAME:	Waaagh! Gritgob	WARLORD:	Warboss Gritgob

DETACHMENT NAME	TYPE	CPS	POINTS
Gritgob's Gitz	Battalion	3	642
Da Mek-mob	Patrol	0	500
Mork's Boyz	Patrol	0	358

WARLORD TRAIT		
FILL IN AT SET-UP:		

Total Command Points:	6
Reinforcement Points:	0
TOTAL POINTS:	1500

DETACHMENT ROSTER

NAME:	Da Mek Mob	TYPE:	Patrol

UNIT

UNIT TITLE:	BATTLEFIELD ROLE:	No. OF MODELS:	POINTS (MODELS):
Big Mek	HQ	1	55

WARGEAR:	POINTS (WARGEAR):
Shokk attack gun (45), choppa (0), stikkbombs (0)	45

	TOTAL POINTS (UNIT):	100

UNIT

UNIT TITLE:	BATTLEFIELD ROLE:	No. OF MODELS:	POINTS (MODELS):
Boyz	Troops	11	66

WARGEAR:	POINTS (WARGEAR):
Power klaw (25), kustom shoota (4), big shoota (6), 9 x sluggas (0), 9 x choppas (0), 11 x stikkbombs (0)	35

	TOTAL POINTS (UNIT):	101

UNIT

UNIT TITLE:	BATTLEFIELD ROLE:	No. OF MODELS:	POINTS (MODELS):
Nobz	Elites	5	85

WARGEAR:	POINTS (WARGEAR):
2 x power klaw (50), kombi-weapon with skorcha (19), 4x sluggas (0), 3 x choppas, ammo runt (4)	73

	TOTAL POINTS (UNIT):	158

UNIT

UNIT TITLE:	BATTLEFIELD ROLE:	No. OF MODELS:	POINTS (MODELS):
Deff Dread	Heavy Support	1	74

WARGEAR:	POINTS (WARGEAR):
3 dread klaws (60), skorcha (17)	77

	TOTAL POINTS (UNIT):	141

Total Points (Detachment):	500	Command Points:	0

NOTES:	All units in Da Mek Mob Detachment are Goffs.

ARMY ROSTER

PLAYER NAME:		ARMY FACTION:	
ARMY NAME:		WARLORD:	

DETACHMENT NAME	TYPE	CPS	POINTS

WARLORD TRAIT	
FILL IN AT SET-UP:	Total Command Points:
	Reinforcement Points:
	TOTAL POINTS:

DETACHMENT ROSTER

NAME: | **TYPE:**

UNIT

UNIT TITLE:	BATTLEFIELD ROLE:	NO. OF MODELS:	POINTS (MODELS):
WARGEAR:			POINTS (WARGEAR):
		TOTAL POINTS (UNIT):	

UNIT

UNIT TITLE:	BATTLEFIELD ROLE:	NO. OF MODELS:	POINTS (MODELS):
WARGEAR:			POINTS (WARGEAR):
		TOTAL POINTS (UNIT):	

UNIT

UNIT TITLE:	BATTLEFIELD ROLE:	NO. OF MODELS:	POINTS (MODELS):
WARGEAR:			POINTS (WARGEAR):
		TOTAL POINTS (UNIT):	

UNIT

UNIT TITLE:	BATTLEFIELD ROLE:	NO. OF MODELS:	POINTS (MODELS):
WARGEAR:			POINTS (WARGEAR):
		TOTAL POINTS (UNIT):	

Total Points (Detachment): | **Command Points:**

NOTES:

ORKS POINTS VALUES

If you are playing a matched play game, or a game that uses a points limit, you can use the following lists to determine the total points cost of your army. Simply add together the points values of all your models, as well as the wargear they are equipped with, to determine your army's total points value.

UNITS

UNIT	MODELS PER UNIT	POINTS PER MODEL (Does not include wargear)
Ammo Runt	N/A	4
Battlewagon	1	161
Big Gunz	1-6	8
Big Mek	1	55
Big Mek in Mega Armour	1	77
Big Mek on Warbike	1	81
Blitza-bommer	1	108
Bomb Squig	N/A	10
Boyz	10-30	6
Burna Boyz	5-15	14
Burna-bommer	1	102
Dakkajet	1	88
Deff Dreads	1-3	74
Deffkoptas	1-3	55
Flash Gitz	5-10	27
Gorkanaut	1	295
Gretchin	10-30	3
Grot Gunners	N/A	2
Grot Oiler	N/A	4
Grot Orderly	N/A	4
Killa Kans	1-6	51
Kommandos	5-15	9
Lootas	5-15	17
Meganobz	3-10	25
Mek	1	22
Mek Gunz	1-6	15
Morkanaut	1	270
Nob with Waaagh! Banner	1	75
Nobz	3-10	17
Nobz on Warbikes	3-10	42
Painboy	1	40
Painboy on Warbike	1	90
Runtherd	1-3	26
Skorchas	1-5	49
Stompa	1	900
Stormboyz	5-30	8
Tankbustas	5-15	5
Trukk	1	76
Warbikers	3-12	27
Warboss	1	55
Warboss in Mega Armour	1	107
Warboss on Warbike	1	86
Warbuggies	1-5	44
Wartrakks	1-5	49
Wazbom Blastajet	1	99
Weirdboy	1	62

RANGED WEAPONS

WEAPON	POINTS PER WEAPON
Big shoota	6
Bigbomm	0
Boom bomb	0
Bubblechukka	32
Burna	0
Burna bomb	0
Dakkagun	0
Deffgun	0
Deffkannon	0
Deffstorm mega-shoota	0
Grot blasta	0
Grotzooka	10
Kannon	15
Killkannon	27
Kombi-weapon with rokkit launcha	20
Kombi-weapon with skorcha	19
Kopta rokkits	28
Kustom mega-blasta	9
Kustom mega-kannon	23
Kustom mega-slugga	7
Kustom shoota	4
Lobba	18
Rack of rokkits	28
Rokkit launcha	12
Pair of rokkit pistols	12
Shokk attack gun	45
Shoota	0
Skorcha	17
Skorcha missile	20
Slugga	0
Smasha gun	16
Snazzgun	0
Squig bomb	0
Stikkbomb flinga	4
Stikkbombs	0
Supa shoota	10
Supa-gatler	28
Supa-rokkit	0
Tankbusta bombs	0
Tellyport blasta	11
Tellyport mega-blasta	18
Traktor kannon	15
Twin big shoota	14
Wazbom mega-kannon	12
Zzap gun	18

MELEE WEAPONS

WEAPON	POINTS PER WEAPON
Attack squig	0
Big choppa	9
Choppa	0
Deff rolla	19
Dread klaw/each subsequent dread klaw	30/15
Grabba stikk	0
Grabbin' klaw	5
Grot-prod	0
Kan klaw	0
Killsaw/two killsaws	28/38
Klaw of Gork (or possibly Mork)	0
Mega-choppa	0
Power klaw	25
Power stabba	3
Spinnin' blades	0
Tankhammer	10
'Urty syringe	0
Waaagh! banner	0
Weirdboy staff	0
Wreckin' ball	3

OTHER WARGEAR

WARGEAR	POINTS PER ITEM
Cybork body	5
Grot lash	0
Kustom force field	20
Squig hound	0

UNITS

UNIT	MODELS PER UNIT	POINTS PER MODEL (Includes wargear)
Boss Snikrot	1	69
Boss Zagstruk	1	88
Ghazghkull Thraka	1	215
Kaptin Badrukk	1	84
Mad Dok Grotsnik	1	74

ORKS WARGEAR

ORKS RANGED WEAPONS

WEAPON	RANGE	TYPE	S	AP	D	ABILITIES
Bigbomm		*See Bigbomm, page 28*				Each bigbomm can only be used once per battle.
Big shoota	36"	Assault 3	5	0	1	-
Boom bomb		*See Boom Bomb, page 30*				Each boom bomb can only be used once per battle.
Bubblechukka	36"	Heavy *	*	*	*	Roll 4 dice each time you fire this weapon, then take it in turns with your opponent (starting with you) to allocate one value at a time to its Strength, AP, Damage and number of attacks. Note that the dice assigned to AP is a negative number (e.g. a 3 is assigned to AP, so the shot is resolved at AP -3).
Burna (shooting)	8"	Assault D3	4	0	1	Before a unit fires its burnas, roll once for the number of attacks and use this for all burnas fired by the unit in this phase. When firing a burna, it automatically hits its target.
Burna bomb		*See Burna Bombs, page 29*				Each burna bomb can only be used once per battle.
Dakkagun	18"	Assault 3	5	0	1	-
Deffgun	48"	Heavy D3	7	-1	2	When a unit fires its deffguns, roll once for the number of attacks and use this for all deffguns fired by the unit in this phase.
Deffkannon	72"	Heavy D6	10	-4	D6	When attacking a unit with 10 or more models, this weapon's Type changes to Heavy 2D6.
Deffstorm mega-shoota	36"	Heavy 3D6	6	-1	1	-
Grot blasta	12"	Pistol 1	3	0	1	-
Grotzooka	18"	Heavy 2D3	6	0	1	-
Kannon		*When attacking with this weapon, choose one of the profiles below.*				
- Frag	36"	Heavy D6	4	0	1	
- Shell	36"	Heavy 1	8	-2	D6	
Killkannon	24"	Heavy D6	7	-2	D6	
Kombi-weapon with rokkit launcha		*When attacking with this weapon, choose one or both of the profiles below. If you choose both, subtract 1 from all hit rolls.*				
- Rokkit launcha	24"	Assault 1	8	-2	3	-
- Shoota	18"	Assault 2	4	0	1	-
Kombi-weapon with skorcha		*When attacking with this weapon, choose one or both of the profiles below. If you choose both, subtract 1 from all hit rolls.*				
- Shoota	18"	Assault 2	4	0	1	-
- Skorcha	8"	Assault D6	5	-1	1	This weapon automatically hits its target.
Kopta rokkits	24"	Assault 2	8	-2	3	-
Kustom mega-blasta	24"	Assault 1	8	-3	D3	If you roll one or more hit rolls of 1, the bearer suffers a mortal wound after all of the weapon's shots have been resolved.
Kustom mega-kannon	36"	Heavy D6	8	-3	D3	
Kustom mega-slugga	12"	Pistol 1	8	-3	D3	
Kustom shoota	18"	Assault 4	4	0	1	-
Lobba	48"	Heavy D6	5	0	1	This weapon can target units that are not visible to the bearer.
Pair of rokkit pistols	12"	Pistol 2	7	-2	D3	-
Rack of rokkits	24"	Assault 2	8	-2	3	-
Da Rippa		*When attacking with this weapon, choose one of the profiles below.*				
- Standard	24"	Heavy 3	7	-3	2	-
- Supercharge	24"	Heavy 3	8	-3	3	If you roll one or more hit rolls of 1, the bearer suffers D3 mortal wounds after all of this weapon's shots have been resolved.
Rokkit launcha	24"	Assault 1	8	-2	3	-
Shokk attack gun	60"	Heavy D6	2D6	-5	D3	Before firing this weapon, roll once to determine the Strength of all its shots. If the result is 11+, do not make wound rolls – instead, each attack that hits causes D3 mortal wounds.
Shoota	18"	Assault 2	4	0	1	-
Skorcha	8"	Assault D6	5	-1	1	This weapon automatically hits its target.
Skorcha missile	24"	Assault D6	5	-1	1	Units attacked by this weapon do not gain any bonus to their saving throws for being in cover.
Slugga	12"	Pistol 1	4	0	1	-
Smasha gun	36"	Heavy 1	*	-4	D6	Instead of making a wound roll for this weapon, roll 2D6. If the result is equal to or greater than the target's Toughness, the attack successfully wounds.
Snazzgun	24"	Heavy 3	5	-2	1	-

WEAPON	RANGE	TYPE	S	AP	D	ABILITIES
Squig bomb	18"	Assault 1	8	-2	D6	This weapon cannot target units that can FLY. Remove the bearer after making this attack.
Stikkbomb	6"	Grenade D6	3	0	1	-
Stikkbomb flinga	12"	Assault 2D6	3	0	1	-
Supa shoota	36"	Assault 3	6	-1	1	-
Supa-gatler	48"	Heavy 2D6	7	-2	1	*See Stompa datasheet*
Supa-rokkit	100"	Heavy D3	8	-2	D6	Only one supa-rokkit can be fired by the bearer a turn, and each can only be fired once per battle.
Tankbusta bomb	6"	Grenade D3	8	-2	D6	-
Tellyport blasta	12"	Assault D3	8	-2	1	If a model suffers any unsaved wounds from this weapon and is not slain, roll a D6 at the end of the phase. If the result is greater than that model's Wounds characteristic, it is slain.
Tellyport mega-blasta	24"	Assault D3	8	-2	1	
Traktor kannon	36"	Heavy 1	8	-2	D3	This weapon's Damage increases to D6 against units that can FLY. If a traktor kannon destroys a VEHICLE that can FLY, the model automatically explodes.
Twin big shoota	36"	Assault 6	5	0	1	-
Wazbom mega-kannon	36"	Heavy D3	8	-3	D3	If you roll one or more hit rolls of 1, the bearer suffers a mortal wound after all of this weapon's shots have been resolved.
Zzap gun	36"	Heavy 1	2D6	-3	3	Before firing this weapon, roll to determine the Strength of the shot. If the result is 11+, do not make a wound roll – instead, if the attack hits it causes 3 mortal wounds. The bearer then suffers a mortal wound.

WEAPON	RANGE	TYPE	S	AP	D	ABILITIES
Big choppa	Melee	Melee	+2	-1	2	-
Burna (melee)	Melee	Melee	User	-2	1	-
Choppa	Melee	Melee	User	0	1	Each time the bearer fights, it can make 1 additional attack with this weapon.
Deff rolla	Melee	Melee	User	-2	1	Add 3 to hit rolls made for this weapon.
Dread klaw	Melee	Melee	x2	-3	3	Each time the bearer fights, it can make 1 additional attack with each dread klaw it is equipped with.
Grabba stikk	Melee	Melee	+1	0	1	Each time the bearer fights, it can make 1 additional attack with this weapon.
Grabbin' klaw	Melee	Melee	User	-3	D3	The bearer can only make a single attack with this weapon each time it fights.
Grot-prod	Melee	Melee	+2	-1	1	-
Kan klaw	Melee	Melee	+3	-3	3	-
Killsaw	Melee	Melee	x2	-4	2	When attacking with this weapon, you must subtract 1 from the hit roll. If a model is equipped with two killsaws, add 1 to its Attacks characteristic.
Klaw of Gork (or possibly Mork)		When attacking with this weapon, choose one of the profiles below.				
- Crush	Melee	Melee	x2	-4	D6	-
- Smash	Melee	Melee	User	-2	2	Make 3 hit rolls for each attack made with this weapon, instead of 1.
Kustom klaw	Melee	Melee	x2	-3	3	-
Mega-choppa		When attacking with this weapon, choose one of the profiles below.				
- Smash	Melee	Melee	x2	-5	6	-
- Slash	Melee	Melee	User	-2	D3	Make 3 hit rolls for each attack made with this weapon, instead of 1.
Mork's Teeth	Melee	Melee	User	-1	2	-
Power klaw	Melee	Melee	x2	-3	D3	When attacking with this weapon, you must subtract 1 from the hit roll.
Power stabba	Melee	Melee	User	-2	1	-
Spinnin' blades	Melee	Melee	+1	0	1	Roll D3 dice for each attack made with this weapon.
Tankhammer	Melee	Melee	-	-	-	Make a single hit roll when attacking with this weapon. If it hits, inflict D3 mortal wounds on the target, then remove the bearer.
'Urty syringe	Melee	Melee	User	0	1	This weapon always wounds targets (other than VEHICLES) on a roll of 2+.
Da Vulcha's Klaws	Melee	Melee	+2	-3	D3	Each time the bearer fights, only 2 attacks can be made with this weapon.
Waaagh! banner	Melee	Melee	+2	0	2	-
Weirdboy staff	Melee	Melee	+2	-1	D3	-
Wreckin' ball	Melee	Melee	+1	-1	1	The bearer can only make 3 attacks with this weapon each time it fights.

T'AU EMPIRE POINTS VALUES

If you are playing a matched play game, or a game that uses a points limit, you can use the following lists to determine the total points cost of your army. Simply add together the points values of all your models, as well as the wargear they are equipped with, to determine your army's total points value.

UNITS

UNIT	MODELS PER UNIT	POINTS PER MODEL (Does not include wargear or Drones)
Breacher Team	5-10	8
XV88 Broadside Battlesuits	1-3	80
Cadre Fireblade	1	39
Commander	1	76
Commander in XV86 Coldstar Battlesuit	1	90
XV8 Crisis Battlesuits	3-9	42
XV8 Crisis Bodyguards	3-9	45
TY7 Devilfish	1	101
Ethereal	1	45
Ethereal on Hover Drone	1	50
Firesight Marksman	1	21
XV95 Ghostkeel Battlesuit	1	82
Kroot Carnivores	10-20	6
Kroot Hounds	4-12	4
Kroot Shaper	1	31
Krootox Riders	1-3	34
Longstrike	1	137
Pathfinder Team	5-10	5
TX4 Piranhas	1-5	45
AX3 Razorshark Strike Fighter	1	82
XV104 Riptide Battlesuit	1	209
XV25 Stealth Battlesuits	3-6	20
KV128 Stormsurge	1	180
Strike Team	5-12	8
AX39 Sun Shark Bomber	1	100
Tidewall Droneport	1	70
Tidewall Gunrig	1	70
Tidewall Shieldline	1	70
- Tidewall Defence Platform	0-1	70
TX7 Hammerhead Gunship	1	117
TX78 Sky Ray Gunship	1	119
Vespid Stingwings	4-12	15

DRONES AND SUPPORT TURRETS

MODEL	POINTS PER MODEL (Includes wargear)
DS8 Tactical Support Turret	20
MV1 Gun Drone	8
MV4 Shield Drone	8
MV5 Stealth Drone	10
MV7 Marker Drone	10
MV8 Missile Drone	20
MV17 Interceptor Drone	15
MV31 Pulse Accelerator Drone	8
MV33 Grav-inhibitor Drone	8
MV36 Guardian Drone	8
MV52 Shield Drone	11
MV62 Command-link Drone	6
MV71 Sniper Drone	18
MV84 Shielded Missile Drone	25
MB3 Recon Drone	12

UNITS

UNIT	MODELS PER UNIT	POINTS PER MODEL (Includes wargear but not Drones)
Aun'Shi	1	68
Aun'Va	1	65
- Ethereal Guard	2	5
Commander Farsight	1	151
Commander Shadowsun	1	167
Darkstrider	1	45

RANGED WEAPONS

WEAPON	POINTS PER WEAPON
Airbursting fragmentation projector	10
Burst cannon	10
Cluster rocket system	61
Cyclic ion blaster	18
Cyclic ion raker	39
Destroyer missile	10
Flamer	9
Fusion blaster	21
Fusion collider	44
Heavy burst cannon	55
Heavy rail rifle	63
High-output burst cannon	20
High-yield missile pod	41
Ion accelerator	107
Ion cannon	55
Ion rifle	7
Kroot gun	0
Kroot rifle	0
Longshot pulse rifle	0
Markerlight	3
Missile pod	24
Neutron blaster	0
Photon grenades	0
Plasma rifle	11
Pulse blastcannon	43
Pulse blaster	0
Pulse bomb	0
Pulse carbine	0
Pulse driver cannon	97
Pulse pistol	0
Pulse rifle	0
Quad ion turret	45
Rail rifle	22
Railgun	38
Seeker missile	5
Smart missile system	20
Supremacy railgun	69

MELEE WEAPONS

WEAPON	POINTS PER WEAPON
Equalizers	1
Honour blade	0
Kroot rifle	0
Krootox fists	0
Ripping fangs	0
Ritual blade	0

OTHER WARGEAR

SUPPORT SYSTEM	POINTS PER SYSTEM
Advanced targeting system	8
Counterfire defence system	5
Drone controller	5
Early warning override	8
Homing beacon	20
Multi-tracker (Ghostkeel and Stormsurge)	10
Multi-tracker (all other units)	2
Riptide shield generator	0
Shield generator (Ghostkeel and Stormsurge)	40
Shield generator (all other units)	8
Stimulant injector	5
Target lock (Ghostkeel, Riptide and Stormsurge)	12
Target lock (all other units)	6
Velocity tracker (Ghostkeel, Riptide and Stormsurge)	10
Velocity tracker (all other units)	2

T'AU EMPIRE WARGEAR

T'AU EMPIRE RANGED WEAPONS

WEAPON	RANGE	TYPE	S	AP	D	ABILITIES
Airbursting fragmentation projector	18"	Assault D6	4	0	1	This weapon can target units that are not visible to the bearer.
Burst cannon	18"	Assault 4	5	0	1	-
Cluster rocket system	48"	Heavy 4D6	5	0	1	-
Cyclic ion blaster	When attacking with this weapon, choose one of the profiles below.					
- Standard	18"	Assault 3	7	-1	1	-
- Overcharge	18"	Assault D3	8	-1	D3	If you make one or more hit rolls of 1, the bearer suffers a mortal wound after all of this weapon's shots have been resolved.
Cyclic ion raker	When attacking with this weapon, choose one of the profiles below.					
- Standard	24"	Heavy 6	7	-1	1	-
- Overcharge	24"	Heavy D6	8	-1	D3	If you make one or more hit rolls of 1, the bearer suffers a mortal wound after all of this weapon's shots have been resolved.
Destroyer missile	60"	Heavy 1	-	-	-	A unit hit by this weapon suffers D3 mortal wounds. Each destroyer missile can only be used once per battle. This weapon only hits on a roll of 6, regardless of the firing model's Ballistic Skill or any modifiers.
Flamer	8"	Assault D6	4	0	1	This weapon automatically hits its target.
Fusion blaster	18"	Assault 1	8	-4	D6	If the target is within half range of this weapon, roll two dice when inflicting damage with it and discard the lowest result.
Fusion collider	18"	Heavy D3	8	-4	D6	If the target is within half range of this weapon, roll two dice when inflicting damage with it and discard the lowest result.
Heavy burst cannon	When attacking with this weapon, choose one of the profiles below. You may only use the nova-charge setting in accordance with the Riptide Shas'vre's Nova Reactor ability (pg 63).					
- Standard	36"	Heavy 8	6	-1	1	-
- Nova-charge	36"	Heavy 12	6	-2	1	-
Heavy rail rifle	60"	Heavy 2	8	-4	D6	For each wound roll of 6+, the target unit suffers a mortal wound in addition to the normal damage.
High-output burst cannon	18"	Assault 8	5	0	1	-
High-yield missile pod	36"	Heavy 4	7	-1	D3	-
Ion accelerator	When attacking with this weapon, choose one of the profiles below. You may only use the nova-charge setting in accordance with the Riptide Shas'vre's Nova Reactor ability (pg 63).					
- Standard	72"	Heavy 3	7	-3	1	-
- Overcharge	72"	Heavy D6	8	-3	D3	If you roll one or more hit rolls of 1, the bearer suffers a mortal wound after all of this weapon's shots have been resolved.
- Nova-charge	72"	Heavy D6	9	-3	3	-
Ion cannon	When attacking with this weapon, choose one of the profiles below.					
- Standard	60"	Heavy 3	7	-2	2	-
- Overcharge	60"	Heavy D3	8	-2	3	Change the type to Heavy D6 against units containing 10 or more models. If you roll one or more hit rolls of 1, the bearer suffers a mortal wound after all of this weapon's shots have been resolved.
Ion rifle	When attacking with this weapon, choose one of the profiles below.					
- Standard	30"	Rapid Fire 1	7	-1	1	-
- Overcharge	30"	Heavy D3	8	-1	1	If you make one or more hit rolls of 1, the bearer suffers a mortal wound after all of this weapon's shots have been resolved.
Kroot gun	48"	Rapid Fire 1	7	-1	D3	-
Kroot rifle (shooting)	24"	Rapid Fire 1	4	0	1	-
Longshot pulse rifle	48"	Rapid Fire 1	5	0	1	This weapon may target a **CHARACTER** even if they are not the closest enemy unit.
Markerlight	36"	Heavy 1	-	-	-	*See Markerlights (pg 48)*
Missile pod	36"	Assault 2	7	-1	D3	-
Neutron blaster	18"	Assault 2	5	-2	1	-
Photon grenade	12"	Grenade D6	-	-	-	This weapon does not inflict any damage. Your opponent must subtract 1 from any hit rolls made for **INFANTRY** units that have suffered any hits from photon grenades until the end of the turn.
Plasma rifle	24"	Rapid Fire 1	6	-3	1	-
Pulse blastcannon	When attacking with this weapon, choose one of the profiles below.					
- Close range	10"	Heavy 2	14	-4	6	-
- Medium range	20"	Heavy 4	12	-2	3	-
- Long range	30"	Heavy 6	10	0	1	-

T'AU EMPIRE RANGED WEAPONS CONT.

WEAPON	RANGE	TYPE	S	AP	D	ABILITIES
Pulse blaster	When attacking with this weapon, choose one of the profiles below.					
- Close range	5"	Assault 2	6	-2	1	-
- Medium range	10"	Assault 2	5	-1	1	-
- Long range	15"	Assault 2	4	0	1	-
Pulse bomb						See Pulse Bombs (pg 68)
Pulse carbine	18"	Assault 2	5	0	1	-
Pulse driver cannon	72"	Heavy D3	10	-3	D6	When attacking a unit with 10 or more models, this weapon's Type changes to Heavy D6.
Pulse pistol	12"	Pistol 1	5	0	1	-
Pulse rifle	30"	Rapid Fire 1	5	0	1	-
Quad ion turret	When attacking with this weapon, choose one of the profiles below. Add 1 to hit rolls for this weapon against targets that can't **FLY**.					
- Standard	30"	Heavy 4	7	-1	1	-
- Overcharge	30"	Heavy D6	8	-1	D3	If you make one or more hit rolls of 1, the bearer suffers a mortal wound after all of this weapon's shots have been resolved.
Rail rifle	30"	Rapid Fire 1	6	-4	D3	For each wound roll of 6+ made for this weapon, the target unit suffers a mortal wound in addition to the normal damage.
Railgun	When attacking with this weapon, choose one of the profiles below.					
- Solid shot	72"	Heavy 1	10	-4	D6	Each time you make a wound roll of 6+ for this weapon, the target unit suffers D3 mortal wounds in addition to the normal damage.
- Submunitions	72"	Heavy D6	6	-1	1	-
Seeker missile	72"	Heavy 1	-	-	-	A unit hit by this weapon suffers a mortal wound. Each seeker missile can only be used once per battle. This weapon only hits on a roll of 6, regardless of the firing model's Ballistic Skill or any modifiers.
Smart missile system	30"	Heavy 4	5	0	1	Smart missile systems can target units that are not visible to the bearer. In addition, units attacked by this weapon do not gain any bonus to their saving throws for being in cover.
Supremacy railgun	72"	Heavy 2	10	-4	D6	Each time you make a wound roll of 6+ for this weapon, the target unit suffers D3 mortal wounds in addition to the normal damage.

T'AU EMPIRE MELEE WEAPONS

WEAPON	RANGE	TYPE	S	AP	D	ABILITIES
Dawn Blade	Melee	Melee	User	-4	D3	-
Equalizers	Melee	Melee	User	-1	1	A model armed with equalizers increases its Attacks characteristic by 1.
Honour blade	Melee	Melee	+2	0	1	-
Kroot rifle (melee)	Melee	Melee	+1	0	1	-
Krootox fists	Melee	Melee	User	0	2	-
Ripping fangs	Melee	Melee	User	-1	1	-
Ritual blade	Melee	Melee	User	0	1	If any enemy models are destroyed by this weapon, friendly **KROOT** units within 6" of the bearer do not have to take Morale tests at the end of the turn.

SUPPORT SYSTEMS

A model cannot have more than one of the same Support System.

SUPPORT SYSTEM	EFFECT
Advanced targeting system	A model equipped with an advanced targeting system increases the AP characteristic of all of its weapons by 1 (e.g. an AP of 0 becomes -1, an AP of -1 becomes -2).
Counterfire defence system	A model equipped with a counterfire defence system re-rolls failed hit rolls when firing Overwatch.
Drone controller	Friendly **<SEPT> DRONE** units within 6" of a model equipped with a drone controller add one to any hit rolls.
Early warning override	If an enemy unit is set up within 12" of a model equipped with an early warning override as the result of an ability that allows them to arrive mid-battle (i.e. teleporting to the battlefield), the model may immediately shoot at that unit as if it were your Shooting phase.
Multi-tracker	A model equipped with a multi-tracker can re-roll hit rolls of 1 if it is firing all of its weapons at the same target.
Shield generator	A model with a shield generator has a 4+ invulnerable save. You cannot take this support system on a Riptide battlesuit.
Stimulant injector	Roll a dice each time a model with a stimulant injector suffers a wound or mortal wound. On a roll of 6, ignore it.
Target lock	A model with a target lock does not suffer the penalty for moving and firing Heavy weapons, or for Advancing and firing Assault weapons. The model can also Advance and fire Rapid Fire weapons, but must subtract 1 from its hit rolls when doing so.
Velocity tracker	Add 1 to hit rolls for this unit when it shoots at a unit that can **FLY**.

TYRANIDS POINTS VALUES

If you are playing a matched play game, or a game that uses a points limit, you can use the following lists to determine the total points cost of your army. Simply add together the points values of all your models, as well as the wargear they are equipped with, to determine your army's total points value.

UNITS

UNIT	MODELS PER UNIT	POINTS PER MODEL (Does not include wargear)
Biovores	1-3	24
Broodlord	1	162
Carnifexes	1-3	67
Exocrine	1	150
Gargoyles	10-30	6
Genestealers	5-20	10
Harpy	1	78
Haruspex	1	267
Hive Crone	1	92
Hive Guard	1-3	18
Hive Tyrant	1	143
Hive Tyrant with Wings	1	170
Hormagaunts	10-30	5
Lictor	1	41
Maleceptor	1	162
Mawloc	1	104
Mucolid Spores	1-3	20
Pyrovores	1-3	23
Raveners	3-9	23
Ripper Swarms	3-9	11
Sky-slasher Swarms	3-9	11
Spore Mines	3-6	10
Sporocyst	1	79
Termagants	10-30	4
Tervigon	1	217
Toxicrene	1	135
Trygon	1	103
Trygon Prime	1	128
Tyranid Prime	1	100
Tyranid Shrikes	3-9	26
Tyranid Warriors	3-9	20
Tyrannocyte	1	98
Tyrannofex	1	174
Tyrant Guard	1-3	35
Venomthropes	3-6	25
Zoanthropes	3-6	40

UNITS

UNIT	MODELS PER UNIT	POINTS PER MODEL (Includes wargear)
Deathleaper	1	90
Old One Eye	1	140
The Red Terror	1	75
The Swarmlord	1	300

RANGED WEAPONS

WEAPON	POINTS PER WEAPON
Acid spray	31
Barbed strangler	15
Bio-electric pulse	11
Bio-electric pulse with containment spines	21
Bio-plasma	9
Bio-plasmic cannon	66
Choking spores	13
Deathspitter	8
Deathspitter with slimer maggots	10
Devourer	4
Devourer with brainleech worms	7
Drool cannon	16
Flamespurt	15
Flesh hooks	2
Fleshborer	0
Fleshborer hive	28
Grasping tongue	11
Heavy venom cannon	30
Impaler cannon	30
Massive toxic lashes	17
Rupture cannon	46
Shockcannon	21
Spike rifle	0
Spinefists (Ravener)	3
Spinefists (Termagant)	0
Spinemaws	2
Spore mine launcher	12
Stinger salvo	11
Stranglethorn cannon	38
Strangleweb	0
Tentaclids	24
Toxic lashes	6
Venom cannon	9

MELEE WEAPONS

WEAPON	POINTS PER WEAPON
Acid maw	4
Biostatic rattle	5
Blinding venom	0
Bone mace	2
Boneswords	4
Claws and teeth	0
Crushing claws	24
Distensible jaws	0
Grasping talons	0
Lash whip and bonesword	2
Lash whip and monstrous bonesword	25
Massive crushing claws	25
Massive scything talons (Tervigon and Maleceptor)	22
Massive scything talons (two or more pairs) (Trygon and Trygon Prime)	60
Massive toxic lashes	0
Monstrous boneswords	35
Monstrous crushing claws	15
Monstrous rending claws	0
Monstrous scything talons (Carnifex)	14
Monstrous scything talons (Hive Tyrant)	31
Monstrous scything talons (two pairs) (Carnifex)	20
Monstrous scything talons (two pairs) (Hive Tyrant)	41
Powerful limbs	12
Prehensile pincer tail	1
Ravenous maw	0
Rending claws	2
Shovelling claws	0
Scything talons	0
Scything wings	13
Thresher scythe	7
Toxic lashes	0
Toxinspike	1
Wicked spur	0

OTHER WARGEAR

BIOMORPH	POINTS PER BIOMORPH
Adrenal glands (**Monsters**)	5
Adrenal glands (other units)	1
Toxin sacs (Hormagaunt)	2
Toxin sacs (Hive Guard, Gargoyle, Mawloc, Termagant, Tervigon and Tyrant Guard)	1
Toxin sacs (Trygon and Trygon Prime)	8
Toxin sacs (Carnifex, Genestealer, Hive Tyrant, Tyranid Prime, Tyranid Shrike and Tyranid Warrior)	4

TYRANIDS WARGEAR

TYRANIDS RANGED WEAPONS

WEAPON	RANGE	TYPE	S	AP	D	ABILITIES
Acid spray	18"	Heavy D6	User	-1	D3	This weapon automatically hits its target.
Barbed strangler	36"	Assault D6	5	-1	1	You can add 1 to hit rolls for this weapon when attacking a unit with 10 or more models.
Bio-electric pulse	12"	Assault 6	5	0	1	-
Bio-electric pulse with containment spines	12"	Assault 12	5	0	1	-
Bio-plasma	12"	Assault D3	7	-3	1	-
Bio-plasmic cannon	36"	Heavy 6	7	-3	2	-
Choking spores	12"	Assault D6	3	0	D3	You can re-roll failed wound rolls for this weapon. In addition, units attacked by this weapon do not gain any bonus to their saving throws for being in cover.
Deathspitter	18"	Assault 3	5	-1	1	-
Deathspitter with slimer maggots	18"	Assault 3	7	-1	1	-
Devourer	18"	Assault 3	4	0	1	-
Devourer with brainleech worms	18"	Assault 3	6	0	1	-
Drool cannon	8"	Assault D6	6	-1	1	This weapon automatically hits its target.
Flamespurt	10"	Assault D6	5	-1	1	This weapon automatically hits its target.
Flesh hooks	6"	Assault 2	User	0	1	This weapon can be fired within 1" of an enemy unit, and can target enemy units within 1" of friendly units.
Fleshborer	12"	Assault 1	4	0	1	-
Fleshborer hive	18"	Heavy 20	5	0	1	-
Grasping tongue	12"	Assault 1	6	-3	D3	This weapon can be fired within 1" of an enemy unit, and can target enemy units within 1" of friendly units. In addition, when a model is slain by this weapon, the bearer regains 1 lost wound.
Heavy venom cannon	36"	Assault D3	9	-1	D3	-
Impaler cannon	36"	Heavy 2	8	-2	D3	This weapon can target units that are not visible to the bearer. In addition, units attacked by this weapon do not gain any bonus to their saving throws for being in cover.
Massive toxic lashes (shooting)	8"	Assault D6	User	-1	D3	This weapon can be fired within 1" of an enemy unit, and can target enemy units within 1" of friendly units. You can re-roll all failed wound rolls when attacking with this weapon.
Rupture cannon	48"	Heavy 2	10	-1	2	If both of this weapon's shots hit, the AP of the attacks is -4 and the Damage is D6.
Shockcannon	24"	Assault D3	7	-1	D3	If the target is a **VEHICLE** and you make a wound roll of 4+, the target suffers 1 mortal wound in addition to any other damage. If you make a wound roll of 6+, inflict D3 mortal wounds instead.
Spike rifle	18"	Assault 1	3	0	1	-
Spinefists	12"	Pistol *	3	0	1	When a model fires this weapon, it makes a number of shots equal to its Attacks characteristic.
Spinemaws	6"	Pistol 4	2	0	1	-
Spore mine launcher	48"	Heavy 1				*See Biovore datasheet (pg 104)*
Stinger salvo	18"	Assault 4	5	-1	1	-
Stranglethorn cannon	36"	Assault D6	7	-1	2	You can add 1 to hit rolls for this weapon when attacking a unit with 10 or more models.
Strangleweb	8"	Assault D3	2	0	1	-
Tentaclids	36"	Assault 2	5	0	1	You may re-roll failed hit rolls for this weapon against units that can **FLY**. In addition, if the target is a **VEHICLE** and you make a wound roll of 4+, it suffers 1 mortal wound in addition to any other damage. If you make a wound roll of 6+, inflict D3 mortal wounds instead.
Toxic lashes (shooting)	6"	Assault 2	User	0	1	This weapon can be fired within 1" of an enemy unit, and can target enemy units within 1" of friendly units. In addition, you can re-roll failed wound rolls when attacking with this weapon.
Venom cannon	36"	Assault D3	8	-1	1	-